Canoeing a Continent:
On the Trail of Alexander Mackenzie

MAX FINKELSTEIN

NATURAL HERITAGE BOOKS

Canoeing a Continent: On the Trail of Alexander Mackenzie
Max W. Finkelstein

Published by Natural Heritage / Natural History Inc.
P.O. Box 95, Station O, Toronto, Ontario M4A 2M8

www.naturalheritagebooks.com

National Library of Canada Cataloguing in Publication Data

Finkelstein, Max
    Canoeing a continent : on the trail of Alexander Mackenzie

Includes bibliographical references and index.
ISBN 1-896219-00-4

1. Finkelstein, Max – Journeys – Canada. 2. Mackenzie, Alexander, Sir, 1764-1820. 3. Alexander Mackenzie Voyageur Route. 4. Northwest, Canadian – Discovery and exploration. 5. Canada – Description and travel.
6. Canoes and canoeing – Canada. I. Title.

FC3212.1.M46F56 2002   917.104   C2002-901033-0
F1060.7.M1783F56 2002

Cover and text design by Sari Naworynski
Edited by John Parry and Jane Gibson
Printed and bound in Canada by Hignell Printing Limited, Winnipeg, Manitoba

Natural Heritage / Natural History Inc. acknowledges the financial support of the Canada Council for the Arts and the Ontario Arts Council for our publishing program. We also acknowledge the financial support of the Government of Canada through the Book Publishing Industry Development Program (BPIDP) and the Association for the Export of Canadian Books.

To my father and mother – my navigators and the shapers of my life – who taught me to look for happiness only where it might be found and to Connie – my One True Love and my guiding beacon from near and afar.

"From there to here.
From here to there,
Funny things are everywhere."
– Dr. Seuss

"This is one fantastic tale ... about two incredible journeys ... written by one extraordinary paddler."
– *Kevin Callan, Canoeist and Author, Peterborough, Ontario*

"A 'must-read' for everyone who loves wild places and the magic of canoes."
– *Cliff Jacobson, Outdoor Writer & Consultant, River Falls, Wisconsin*

Contents

Part III: Fort McMurray to Cumberland House, August-September 1999

Foreword

Max Finkelstein has provided us with a unique gift of Canadiana. His inspired record of Alexander Mackenzie's voyages has been gracefully interwoven with the story of his own journeys along the same route two hundred years later. Although some aspects have not changed, Max is able to identify many details that are quite different. Weather conditions, equipment, purposes of the voyages and more recent human interventions such as dams and hydro installations are all important alterations, and he is able to point to these in a fascinating and revealing way.

In his absorbing and thoughtful work, Max reveals the inspiration he has gained from his voyages. The descriptions he has so ably recorded are of an artist expressing himself in carefully selected word pictures. At the same time, he makes us vividly aware of the sheer torture that was endured by voyageurs who toiled in the fur trade. The life of a trader was most often traumatic and indeed marked by incredible hardship. Unpredictable weather, insects, poor food, inadequate equipment and other factors were the daily lot of those intrepid paddlers. Max Finkelstein shared many of these same discomforts and speaks with some authority on the trauma of their experience in the arms of great canoes. The one obvious advantage, if any, was that in Mackenzie's time the long trail was experienced by groups of paddlers, but Max accomplished much of the journey on his own. This fact adds a significant dimension to his adventure.

The route that Mackenzie navigated is no longer as obvious as it was at one time, and Max was forced at times to engage in a process of logic and deduction to determine his way. His reference to Cedar Lake, with the search for the mouth of the Saskatchewan River, is a good example.

Throughout his remarkable record of "their story" and "my story," it becomes increasingly obvious that the magnitude of Mackenzie's explorations is not generally understood or appreciated. By the same token, the voyages of Max Finkelstein and the consequent revelation of Mackenzie's exploits tend to help readers grasp the outstanding effort put forward in traversing this vast and varied land en route to the Pacific Ocean.

For recreational paddlers or for those who aspire to undertake more extended canoe journeys, or indeed for those who dream about the great treasure of Canadian waterways, Max's work must be a source of inspiration, especially for Canadians. It is not only a tribute to Alexander Mackenzie, but also a stirring reference to the lives of those who travelled the same waterways for untold centuries before – that is, the people of the First Nations. They knew so well those aquatic highways for such a long time. Because of their knowledge and experience, the challenges of the wilderness faced by explorers, although still tough, became much less rigorous.

By his own declaration, Max observed that he had witnessed first-hand much more of Canada as it used to be seen. By innuendo he also suggested that it can be seen again by paddlers who wish to feel what it is to be Canadian. This privilege, of course, is partially dependent on our willingness to ensure the health and welfare of our waterways. These arteries of life now need our protection and support if they are to survive the onslaughts of the New World. Abuse and overuse coupled with indifference has profoundly affected our water. Although in some regions, the deteriorating condition of our water resources is obvious, it is not too late to restore our great national treasure to better health now and for the future.

Kirk Wipper CM
Professor Emeritus, University of Toronto

Acknowledgements

I received a lot of help from many people both before I started and along the way. I would like to thank my friend Michael Greco, president of the Canadian River Management Society, for his unwavering enthusiasm and support; Bob Hellman of Hellman Canoes, for providing the tanden canoe that I used on the journey; Beth and Michael Peterson (sadly, Michael died of cancer during my trip, a great loss to the canoeing community) of Ottawa Valley Canoe, for helping me to acquire *Loon* many years ago and encouraging me to pursue my paddling endeavours: Wally Schaber and the staff at Trailhead in Ottawa, who have worked hard to promote canoeing in Canada and encouraged me in all my canoeing endeavours; Don Gibson, National Manager, Canadian Heritage Rivers Systems (CHRS), for his understanding and patience during my absences from my position with the CHRS and for doing the work of two people while I gallivanted across the country; and Wayne Roach, also of the CHRS, who gave me unwavering support and helped fill in while I was absent.

I would like to thank every person who helped me along the way. A dry place to sleep at night, a hot cup of coffee on a cold, rainy day, an encouraging wave, a friendly "hello" ... it all helped enormously. I also thank Alexander Mackenzie and all the other fur traders, explorers, dreamers and adventurers who blazed a trail for me to follow.

Most of all, I want to thank the rivers and lakes that made this journey possible.

The author wishes to acknowledge the assistance of the Canada Council during the writing of this book.

Preface

Alexander Mackenzie was the first European to cross North America, reaching the Pacific Ocean on 22 July 1793. This was thirteen years before the famous overland expedition in the United States, led by Meriwether Lewis and William Clark, reached the Pacific. In fact, it was Mackenzie's explorations that spurred President Thomas Jefferson of the newly formed nation of the United States to sponsor the Lewis and Clark expedition. Yet Mackenzie remains relatively unknown, while Lewis and Clark have become household names.

I spent three summers, in 1997, 1998, and 1999 – a total of almost two hundred days and nights – retracing the route of Alexander Mackenzie across Canada, from my home in Ottawa to the Pacific Coast at Bella Coola. The book that these trips gave birth to is not just a travelogue of a 200-day canoe trip across a continent, but an account that also crosses more than two hundred years. During the trips, I looked into the heart and mind of Mackenzie, the explorer, and of Max, the "voyageur-in-training." In this book I draw extensively from Mackenzie's journals, as well as from my own journal writings, to bring to the reader a view of North America from the seat of a canoe in the latter years of both the eighteenth and the twentieth centuries.

Through this book, I hope to accomplish three ambitious goals: first, to depict a view of the land along the first transcontinental route as seen through Mackenzie's eyes as well as my own; second, to pass on my insights into Mackenzie the explorer and fur trader and into Mackenzie the man; and third, to highlight changes that have occurred in the two centuries since Mackenzie travelled this route.

Get ready to take a journey across Canada and through history, to glimpse the tapestry of land and waterscapes, cultures and communities, that makes up the fabric of Canada. Get ready for the vivid details that any long journey entails – from the depths of exhaustion and frustration, to the heights of elation reached at the end of a long portage or of a windy lake crossing, and also to the peace brought on by watching a sunset paint the sky with the colours found only in opals, clamshells and the embers of a dying campfire.

For me, this was the canoe trip of a lifetime and a life-changing experience. As the journey progressed I felt ever more deeply connected with the land, the water, and Mackenzie himself. As I paddled along the route, the book he wrote about his adventures, *Voyages From Montreal*, was my constant companion. When water and wind allowed, I would read Mackenzie's words about the rivers, lakes, lands and the people he encountered as I drifted or paddled past the exact locations he described. The gap of centuries between us closed and sometimes I felt that we were paddling together. The farther I/we paddled, the more my relationship with him deepened. At the end, I felt that I had the right to exclaim (as in the beer commercial seen on television): "I am Canadian." For I had seen so much of our nation – its land, its peoples, its communities and its history – first-hand. My clothes are stained with the dirt of this land; my mind is filled with its images and stories. I have drunk its waters from sea to sea.

As a long-distance, cross-continental paddler, I pale before many others – those who have paddled farther, faster, coast to coast in one season, totally solo with a policy of not accepting any help from others. I do not feel a need to apologize for this. I chose to undertake this journey on my terms. Although I received much support and encouragement from friends, strangers and colleagues, unlike Mackenzie, I was not paid in any way. My renumeration was paid in terms far more valuable than money.

This book is not intended to be a historical treatise. I did not take on this project because of my fascination for history, but rather because of my love of travelling by canoe. But as my travels progressed, so did my curiousity about those who came before me. And just as I have learned more about canoeing, I have also had to learn more about the history of the canoe trails I followed. Every effort has been made to ensure historical accuracy, but people more historically astute than myself may find misconceptions or other concerns. Any such findings brought to the attention of the publisher or myself will be corrected in subsequent editions.

When Mackenzie's book, *Voyages from Montreal*, was published in 1801, it became an instant bestseller in England, Europe and the United States. Meriwether Lewis, co-leader, along with William Clark, of the first American Expedition to the Pacific, is said to have carried a copy! Less than two months after its release, Mackenzie was knighted.

Inspired by his success, I humbly present this account of my adventures, following the trail Mackenzie blazed for me. This book is my attempt to make the story of Mackenzie and his heroic exploration of Canada more accessible and, by doing so, I hope to give a gentle nudge that may make a difference to the future of this route. Officially proclaimed in 1997, by Canada's federal, provincial and territorial governments, the Alexander Mackenzie Voyageur Route (AMVR) is the most significant water trail in North America, and perhaps in the entire world. To a large extent, it defines this country and what being "Canadian" means. Yet to most of my fellow citizens, and to people elsewhere, Mackenzie the explorer, and his route, remain unknown. This is a story that needs to be told.

– Max Finkelstein, Ottawa, Ontario

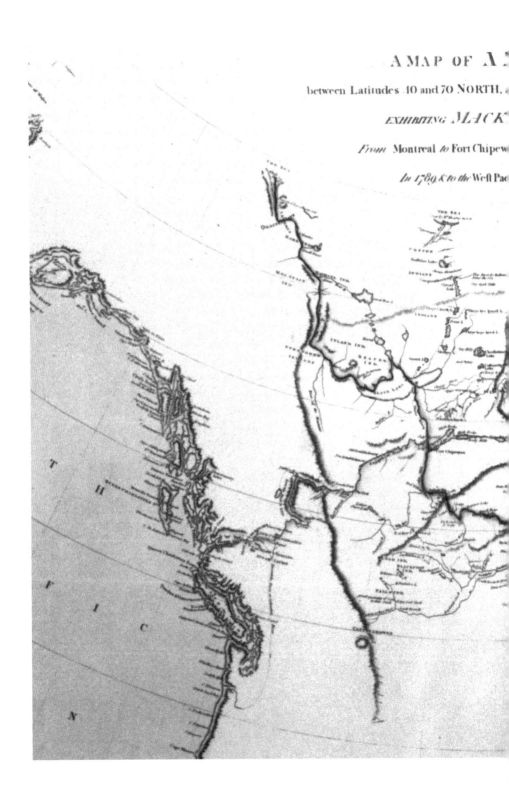

A MAP OF A...

between Latitudes 40 and 70 NORTH, ...

EXHIBITING MACK...

From Montreal to Fort Chipew...

In 1789, & to the West Pac...

C.A.
les 45 and 180 WEST.

TRACK

mer to the North Sea

1793.

Introduction to the Journeys

*I now mixed up some vermilion in melted grease and described
in large characters on the Southeast face of the rock on which
we had slept last night this brief memorial*

— ALEXANDER MACKENZIE
FROM CANADA BY LAND
22 JULY 1793

"LET'S EAT THESE DAMNED CANTALOUPES," Chris said, swinging his backpack to the ground. We had packed carefully, eliminating all but the most necessary items – except for the cantaloupes. We toted two beauties almost 1,800 m (6,000 feet) up the Mackenzie Trail to Hump Lake, a lovely alpine body of water rimmed by spruce trees and overlooking the Bella Coola Valley. As we slurped down the sweet, refreshing, tropical taste of the cantaloupes under the watchful gaze of snow-covered Mount Stupendous, we agreed that it was worth the effort of carrying them. The mountain was putting on a great show for us, framed by a double rainbow, with shafts of sunlight highlighting the snow and the bold black rock. The showers and thunder squalls that had followed us here were dissipating, and our first night on the trail promised to be memorable. Could anyone imagine a more beautiful home for the night? – the dining-room wallpapered with the setting sun and silhouetted mountains, the bedroom ceiling studded with stars, the bathroom with a view, well, as big as all outdoors. Ahead lay a host of uncertainties. But tonight, with the stars blazing, Mount Stupendous shining in the evening glow, and our muscles aching, we are at peace.

More than 200 years earlier, Alexander Mackenzie had stood on this very same spot, gazed into the cloud-shrouded valley of the Bella Coola River, and faced the unknown. But his uncertainties were exponentially bigger than ours – great blank spaces on maps, starvation, hostile Natives, unknown mountain ranges to cross.

Alexander Mackenzie was the first European to reach the Pacific Ocean by travelling overland across North America – thirteen years before the famous U.S. expedition by Meriwether Lewis and William Clark. The routes of both expeditions are now commemorated, as the Alexander Mackenzie Voyageur Route (AMVR) and the Lewis and Clark Trail, respectively.

More than two centuries after Mackenzie's birchbark canoe had passed by the site of my home on the banks of the Ottawa River, heading for the unknown country of the Northwest, I found myself staring up the river, feeling the river pulling me, and wondering how much had changed since Mackenzie's days. I could not resist, any more than a salmon can fend off the urge to return upriver to its birthplace to spawn. Ottawa, Mattawa, Nipissing, French, St. Marys, Superior, Pigeon, Rainy, Winnipeg, Saskatchewan, Sturgeon-Weir, Churchill, Missinipi, Clearwater, Blackwater, Bella Coola, Peace ... their names ring like the songs of the voyageurs. Come-hither rivers, they call out, they lead you into a continent, into the unknown spaces of geography and mind.

In total my trips took more than six months and covered more than 7,000 km (4,425 miles), 135 portages, some 5 million paddle strokes and 200,000 steps. It was a most amazing adventure. The AMVR has a story to tell along every turn and bend of its length. Most are still waiting to be told; many are still waiting to happen. Perhaps if you travel the route yourself, you will discover some of these stories or, better yet, become part of them.

Now I am about to embark on another big undertaking – to recount the journey in words. I'm filled with doubts. Why would anyone be interested in what I have to write? Am I so egocentric to think that you, gentle reader, would take the time in your busy life to read what I write?

This is going to be a long journey for me: perhaps 250 pages, maybe 200,000 words. That is not so long – if I write 500 words a day. I will start with the most important word: Water.

I

Mackenzie and Canada

THIS IS A STORY OF WATER. It is a story held together by birchbark and spruce root, by Kevlar and epoxy. It was a vast, interconnected web of lakes and rivers that carried the fragile birchbark canoes of Mackenzie – and the not-so-fragile canoes that I paddled – across the watersheds of North America. I had simple, though somewhat vague, reasons for traversing the continent – mostly curiosity and a quest for beauty and simply because it was something that I wanted to do. Mackenzie clearly had these motivations in common with me, but they were hidden under a more obvious impetus – the quest for wealth and power.

For four centuries, the insatiable appetite of Europeans for furs was the incentive for penetrating ever deeper into the maze of forests, rivers and lakes that covers much of what is now Canada. The beaver was the mainstay of the fur trade. Everyone was after this gentle rodent. Beaver fur made the best felt for fashionable hats for trendy gentlemen. And so the fur rush was on, and the innocent, hard-working beaver became the symbol of Canada. It was only during the waning decades of the nineteenth century that the reasons for exploration shifted towards the search for timber, minerals, new farmlands, and potential railway routes, and towards biological and anthropological research.

When the first Europeans arrived in what is now Canada, there were plenty of furs for everyone. There seemed to be an endless supply of beavers. But in what is now a familiar pattern (think of Atlantic salmon, bison, cod, passenger pigeons, sturgeon, whales, white pine, and so on), as beavers were trapped out, fur traders had to go farther west and north to find new, untapped sources of furs. After two centuries, the competition for furs became very intense. By the end of the eighteenth century, two rivals – the Hudson's Bay Company and the North West Company – were in an intense competition for control of the trade. The former was the longest continually operating fur-trading company, formed in 1670; the latter, created in 1783 from an amalgamation of several private firms operating out of Montreal, was the newest.

Into this world – where furs were the currency, rivers the highways, canoes the transport trucks, pemmican and hominy grits the fuel, and voyageurs the engines – stepped a young Scotsman, Alexander Mackenzie. And what a world it was. (If I had a wish, it would be for a time machine.)

Alexander Mackenzie was born in 1764 in Scotland and immigrated with his father to New York after his mother died. As his father served in the British army, it was aunts who raised young Alexander. They sent him to school in Montreal. Had they sent him to school in, say, Philadelphia, this story would be very different.

At the tender age of fifteen, young Alex got his first job, working for John Gregory, a pioneer of the inland fur trade. Gregory's brigades were among the first to reach what is now Saskatchewan, following in the footsteps of the early French explorers. Imagine what a day in the youth's life would have been like as he watched the start of the season and perhaps dreamed of joining the expeditions when he was older. He might be tallying trade goods as they were bundled into 41-kg (90-pound) *pièces* and loaded onto the *canots de maître* ("Maître" is the family name of the biggest and oldest manufacturer of birchbark canoes). These craft had a length that ranged from 9.5 to 12 m (35 to 40 feet). The most highly skilled voyageurs would be strutting around like roosters in their finest, most colourful clothes, while the less experienced *milieux* loaded the big canoes. In that era, more than 100 canoes left Lachine[1] each spring. As they sped upriver, no doubt Alex watched them wistfully, thinking about the tales that he had heard about the camaraderie of life on the river, the excitement of running rapids, the awesome beauty of the *pays d'en haut*, the fabled sexuality of the Native women, and the fortunes that could be made in the fur country.

Mackenzie spent five years in the counting houses of Mr. Gregory, learning the fur trade business. When Gregory, McLeod and Company joined the North West Company in 1787, Mackenzie was given the opportunity to travel to the farthest reaches of the fur empire, to the newly opened-up post on the shores of Lake Athabasca, more than 4,800 km (3,000 miles) from Montreal.

Here's how the fur trade worked in Mackenzie's time. Brigades of *canots de maître* left Lachine each spring, loaded with three tons of trade goods, plus another ton of gear and food. With a full load, they would float low in the water, with only six inches (15 cm) of freeboard left – truly loaded to the gunwales. They were paddled by a crew of twelve and could make 8 knots when under sail. Normal cruising pace was about five knots, or 50 strokes per minute, but this could be increased to 60 or even 70 at times. (Going full out, I might be able to keep up for a little while with a fur trade canoe loaded with four tons of gear. I definitely could not keep up with an express canoe.) Express canoes were specially designed to travel fast to carry messages and important people between posts, with elite paddlers and a light load. Each hour, crews would stop for a five-minute break to smoke their pipes. Distances were measured in "pipes," rather than in miles. This makes sense, as a mile of upstream travel could take five times as long as, and be ten times harder than, a mile of canoeing downstream.

The brigades pushed up the Ottawa, stopping briefly at a small stone chapel at Sainte-Anne-de-Bellevue to pray. Thirty-six portages lifted them 197 m (659 feet) to the height of land between the Mattawa River and Lake Nippissing. It was a one-day run down the French to Georgian Bay. Then the route carried on up the North Channel to the rapids at Sault Ste. Marie. It was 720 km (450 miles) more along the rugged north shore of Lake Superior to the inland headquarters of the North West Company at Grand Portage. The trip from Lachine to the western end of Lake Superior took seven to eight weeks, at an average of 40 km (25 miles) per day.

At the lakehead, the trade goods were transferred to smaller *canots du nord*, 26 feet long, designed for the smaller waterways to the west. Fully loaded with 1,400 kg (3,000 pounds) of cargo and gear, they had a draft of about 55 cm (18 inches) and were paddled with a crew of five or six. The route followed lakes, portages, and rivers to Rainy Lake, through Lake of the Woods, and down the Winnipeg River (considered by many the most beautiful river on the route) to Lake Winnipeg. From there, trade goods were paddled up the North Saskatchewan, north up the Sturgeon-Weir to the Churchill, and over the 19 km (12 mile) Methye Portage into the Arctic-flowing waters. Fort Chipewyan was the farthest trading post from

Montreal in Mackenzie's time – more than 2,560 km (1,600 miles) from their inland headquarters on Lake Superior.

Mackenzie's new job was to be the assistant to Peter Pond. It would be a gross understatement to say that Pond is a very colourful personality in the history of the fur trade. Pond was not a nice man. If you were his business partner, the odds on your being around very long would not be good. In fact, Peter Pond had shot and killed two associates in the fur trade. But still he was Mackenzie's inspiration.

Peter Pond was born in Milford, Connecticut, in 1740. He made his way to Detroit, where he got his start in the fur trade. A restless soul, he moved north and west, paddling rivers yet unnamed and unmapped by Europeans. It was Pond who "discovered" the Methye Portage, linking the Churchill River to the Arctic-flowing waters and the rich beaver country of the Athabasca region. Lake Athabasca soon became a hub of the fur trade, much like Grand Portage and Lake Winnipeg, with trade routes leading in all directions.

Peter Pond had a dream, and a theory, which he shared with a young and ambitious Mackenzie. His dream was to reach the Pacific. He had even approached the fledgling U.S. Congress for funds for an expedition to find a route to the ocean, but was turned down. But had it been supported, I might be following the American "PPVR," Lewis and Clark might not be famous, and British Columbia might belong to the United States.

The mystery that Pond wanted to solve was the location of the source of a big river that the famous navigator Captain James Cook of the Royal Navy, had mapped as a big inlet when he landed along the Alaska coast in 1778. We can imagine the grizzled veteran Pond and the young Mackenzie hunkered down over a table in the flickering candlelight in the chill of winter, their breath crystallizing in a silver cloud above them. They blow into their cupped hands to warm them, as they peer over the maps with huge blank areas spread out before them. Could "Cook's river" be one flowing out of Lake Athabasca to the Pacific?

In the summer of 1788, Mackenzie travelled with Pond back to Grand Portage to present his ideas of finding a route to the Pacific to the senior officers of the North West Company. These men endorsed the scheme, and an excited Mackenzie returned to Lake Athabasca in a record fifty-two days. His crew for the new expedition sounds like the starting lineup for the Montreal Canadiens in the 1960s, before the National Hockey League expanded: François Barrieu, Charles Ducette, Joseph Landry, Pierre de Lorme and John Steinbruch (where did this fellow come from?). The expedition was accompanied by a small group of Natives, led by the Chipewyan known as "English Chief," who had accompanied Samuel Hearne eighteen years earlier on his historic trek from York Factory on Hudson Bay to the Coppermine River. Included were his two wives and two other men.

On 3 June 1789, Mackenzie and his group headed off, heading down the river into the unknown. Their progress was slow and arduous. Rapids, ice, and headwinds slowed them down (hmmm, sounds familiar). Eventually, they found the mouth of the river flowing out of Great Slave Lake that now bears Mackenzie's name. The young Scot's hopes no doubt rose as the river headed west. But then it turned north, and after a few days Mackenzie realized that *"these waters empty into the Hyperborean Sea"* (Arctic Ocean). However, despite the pleas of his expedition members to turn back, he was determined to paddle all the way to the river's end. On 14 July, rising water flooded the camp, and Mackenzie saw that it was tidal. The next day, he and his party paddled out into the Beaufort Sea, among ice floes. This was clearly not the Pacific Ocean described by Cook, and they hightailed it home. By 12 September, they were back in Fort Chipewyan on Lake Athabasca, after a round trip of over 4,800 km (3,000 miles). They had been away 102 days.

Take it from me, travelling "up" the Mackenzie River is no cakewalk. Mackenzie noted that the Indian wives were kept busy repairing moccasins, which were constantly being worn out by the rough work of tracking the canoes upstream.

Mackenzie had a rough winter. He considered his expedition a failure. The next summer, he travelled again to Grand Portage on Lake Superior to report his disappointing findings. On the way there, at Peter Pond Lake, he met an English surveyor, Philip Turnor, who convinced him to go back to England to study surveying and navigation.[2] Two years later, in the summer of 1792, he was back in Fort Chipewyan, ready to try again. That autumn, he travelled 600 km (375 miles) up the Peace River, the big river flowing into Lake Athabasca, and established an advance post, which he named Fort Fork. This is just upstream from the present-day town of Peace River. Mackenzie spent the winter there, in order to get an early start the next spring for a daring attempt to *"crack the mountain ramparts"* – to go up and over the continental divide and find a route to the Pacific Ocean.

On 9 May 1793, Alexander Mackenzie set out on his BIG TRIP. With him were François Beaulieux, Baptiste Bisson, François Courtois and Jacques Beauchamp, along with two from his expedition of 1789 to the Beaufort Sea – Charles Ducette and Joseph Landry – a testament to his leadership. Alexander Mackay, a clerk of the North West Company, two Indians and a

This is the only known portrait of Alexander Mackenzie, painted by British artist Sir Thomas Lawrence when Mackenzie was in his late thirties. The painting is in the National Art Gallery of Canada in Ottawa. Courtesy of Old Fort William, copy of NAC 1348.

big dog, which Mackenzie refers to simply as "Our Dog," rounded out his party. He had a 25-foot birchbark canoe with a reinforced hull built for the expedition.

The men poled and paddled against the relentless current of the Peace. They hauled up the gorges that are now flooded by the Peace Canyon Dam and hacked a nine-mile (14.4-km) portage through the Rocky Mountains to bypass a long series of tumbling rapids – where, Mackenzie notes, *"On the river above us, as far as we could see, was one white sheet of foaming water."* These rapids now lie under 180 m (600 feet) of water backed up by the W.A.C.

Bennett Dam. On they journeyed, up the Parsnip River, making their way painstakingly towards the continental divide. They had no idea where they were going. On the Parsnip, they ran into a band of Sekanni, *"brandishing their spears, displaying their bows and arrows...."* Mackenzie, who seemed to know no fear, boldly strode up to the nearest warriors and shook their hands. One of them drew his knife in such a way that Mackenzie knew it was not a threat, and presented it to Mackenzie as a gesture of goodwill. The Sekanni showed Mackenzie a route over the continental divide across three little lakes that led to the *"Great River"* and on to the *"Stinking Lake."* Mackenzie and his crew must have rejoiced when they finally crossed the ridge between waters flowing to the Arctic and waters flowing to the Pacific, between what are now known as Arctic Lake and Portage Lake.

Now it would be downhill all the way to the Pacific, and Mackenzie was certain that the Great River would be the Columbia. Downhill – but not smooth going. The very next day they wrecked their canoe, running rapids on what is now called James Creek. But Mackenzie referred to it as *"the Bad River"* in his diaries. Ever resourceful, and with endless, boundless energy, his men built a new canoe and carried on. Finally, they reached the *"Big River."* They saw a band of Carrier across the river, and Mackenzie once again showed his bravado by going alone to the opposite shore and spreading beads on the ground – but not before instructing his best shot to hide in the bushes and cover him. The Carrier drew a map in the mud along the river showing that many rapids and canyons blocked the route to the *"Stinking Lake"* and that the quickest route to the Pacific was by a trail to the west.

Mackenzie was still determined to follow the river. But somewhere between where the towns of Quesnel and Williams Lake are now located, the violent rapids made him reconsider the advice of the Carrier. The *"Stinking Lake"* was just too far away by means of this wild and rollicking river, and the route was too dangerous. He abandoned his dream of following Pond's great river to its end. That must have been a tremendously difficult choice for Mackenzie. I'm sure that he lay awake at night weighing the two options over and over and over again. The expedition returned UP the Fraser, back to the junction of the Blackwater River, cached a load of pemmican there, and headed west on a trail. A series of Native guides led Mackenzie and his party through the endless forests of the Interior Plateau, over the Rainbow Range, and finally over the Coast Ranges down to the humid rainforest of the Pacific.

There, the Bella Coola nation welcomed them and lent them a dugout canoe for the final dash to the ocean. A few days later, on a rock in Dean

Channel, Mackenzie made his famous, terse inscription: *"Alexander Mackenzie, from Canada by land, July 22, 1793."* An amazingly short thirty-three days later, the expedition was safely back at Fort Chipewyan. These guys really knew how to get around – travellers like that are not around today.

V O Y A G E S

FROM

M O N T R E A L,

ON THE RIVER ST. LAURENCE,

THROUGH THE

CONTINENT OF NORTH AMERICA,

TO THE

FROZEN AND PACIFIC OCEANS;

In the Years, 1789 *and* 1793.

WITH A PRELIMINARY ACCOUNT

OF THE RISE, PROGRESS, AND PRESENT STATE OF

THE FUR TRADE

OF THAT COUNTRY.

ILLUSTRATED WITH MAPS.

BY ALEXANDER MACKENZIE, ESQ.

L O N D O N:
PRINTED FOR T. CADELL, JUN. AND W. DAVIES, STRAND; COBBETT AND MORGAN, PALL-MALL; AND W. CREECH, AT EDINBURGH.
BY R. NOBLE, OLD-BAILEY.

M.DCCC.I.

From The Journals and Letters of Sir Alexander Mackenzie, *edited by* W.K. Lamb, 1970. Courtesy of the author.

During the long winter, Mackenzie – just as I do – set himself the task of writing up his journals. Alas – the same as I – he procrastinated for years. He returned to Grand Portage, where the results of his expedition were coolly received. His route was clearly not a feasible trade route. Depressed, despondent, disappointed, Mackenzie went to England, where he became a celebrity, hob-knobbed with the rich and famous, and finally, with the help of a ghost writer named William Coombe,[3] published a 550-page account of his exploits with a title much longer than his inscription (and I quote):

> *VOYAGES*
> *FROM*
> *MONTREAL*
> *ON THE RIVER ST. LAURENCE*
> *THROUGH THE*
> *CONTINENT OF NORTH AMERICA*
> *TO THE*
> *FROZEN AND PACIFIC OCEANS*
> *IN THE YEARS, 1789 AND 1793*
> *WITH A PRELIMINARY ACCOUNT*
> *OF THE RISE, PROGRESS AND PRESENT STATE OF*
> *THE FUR TRADE*
> *OF THE COUNTRY*

It became an instant bestseller (I hope to emulate Mackenzie's success as a writer, but I haven't quit my day job yet). When Mackenzie was forty-eight (I turned forty-eight just two weeks before typing this line), he married a fourteen-year-old Scottish lassie (hmmm!). Mackenzie was knighted in 1802. He died quite suddenly at the age of fifty-six. I hope that God has lent me more time.

2

Crossing Canada by Canoe: A Brief History

W HY DO SOME PEOPLE UNDERTAKE long canoe journeys? Everyone who goes on a long voyage, no matter what the means of transportation, shares similar challenges and rewards. There is the mixture of thrill, fear and excitement at entering the unknown. This is as true for the modern canoeist equipped with maps and a geographic positioning system (GPS) as it was for Mackenzie, although the uncertainties that Mackenzie faced would seem overwhelmingly daunting to us mollycoddled modern explorers. All explorers and adventurers also share, I believe, a selfish, egotistical desire to experience places and feelings that most other people do not, either through choice or circumstance. They (and I'm chagrined to say that I include myself in this group) see themselves as apart from most others. Not superior, but different, and a little bit privileged.

Speaking for myself, I feel that I have experienced through my canoe trips beauty and feelings of well-being that have been so complete, so satisfying, that I have felt close to God. This gives me a strong sense of self, of accomplishment, meaning, purpose and identity, and, yes, it makes me feel just a little bit above the crowd. But I also know that others achieve these same feelings through others activities and passions. Canoeing is just my route to the same place. It was also the route of Mackenzie, and many others, though not by choice.

There's more. The biggest part of any adventure is, as the famous epithet says, not the destination, but the journey. To be a truly satisfying journey, it MUST involve physical discomfort, deprivation, extreme exertion, and elements of DANGER (real or imagined). That is why driving to the top of a mountain does not pack the same sense of satisfaction as climbing there. A road takes away all the key elements of adventure – danger (although it could be argued that driving is the most dangerous human activity, we all share this danger, so that negates its value), physical exertion, deprivation and hardship. Although the same beautiful view is there at the mountain-top, the value of the view is diminished if we drive there. The thrill is gone, at least for me, for Mackenzie, and for many others like us.

Big journeys are exclamation points in our mundane little lives. Completing them, or just surviving them, gives us memories that we use to define, or redefine, ourselves. I am a canoe tripper, a voyageur-in-training. I look back on my canoe journeys, and look forward to more, with happiness and not just a little bit of pride. The value of any canoe trip grows in proportion to the effort expended, the danger involved, the challenges overcome and the depri-vation endured. I'm not sure which of these is most important. The beauty of the northern sky at night? The terror of listening to a grizzly bear snuffle around your tent? The bone-wrenching weariness during a day of repeated portages? Or the thrill and satisfaction of eating French fries, followed by apple pie (made with canned pie filling) and ice cream, at a greasy spoon restaurant at the end of the trip – which can become a Zen-like experience. It depends on the individual circumstances and the state of mind of the paddler.

But I know that all canoe trippers thrive on deprivation. I am not a masochist. I do not actually enjoy being wet and cold and weary. I do not like putting on frozen shoes and gloves in the morning. I do not like rationing my Mars bars, eating one-quarter of a bar when my body craves a twelve-pack. But a little deprivation makes the value of things that we take for granted increase exponentially, which makes life a very thrilling, rich experience indeed. A hot cup of coffee, an entire Mars bar, a dry sleeping bag – ecstasy. Kings and queens could know no greater happiness!

I can't resist telling you about an experience, one of those epiphanies of life, that happened to me many years ago, on my way home from a seventy-five-day canoe trip in the western Arctic. I was on a flight from Inuvik to Yellowknife, back in the days when passengers were treated really well. The flight attendant (they called them "stewardesses" in those bygone days) offered all the passengers complimentary coffee with liqueur, which she called "fancy coffee," and a Mars bar. I was revelling in my good fortune, dipping the Mars bar in the coffee, and licking the melted chocolate, then taking a sip of coffee. Each sip and lick bordered on orgasmic. Then, fingers firmly tapping on my shoulder broke into my reverie.

"Sir," said the flight attendant impatiently, "you'll have to put up your tray and finish your coffee."

"Why?" I asked, blinking as if someone had hit me in the nose.

"Because we're landing in Yellowknife."

I looked around at the other passengers. Not a sign of coffee or Mars bars. Trays up. Seat belts fastened. I had been enjoying this treat for over an hour. If only we would relish in that way all that life has to offer us, how rich it would be. Perhaps that is the goal and the motivation of Eastern mystics. To experience the joy in small, everyday things is a darned good reason to keep on going out into the wilderness. Not the only reason, but a darned good one.

Perhaps Sir William Logan, founder of the Geological Survey of Canada in 1842 and one of Canada's most renowned scientists, best stated why people go on long canoe trips: "I have dined with lords and ladies, chatted with Queen Victoria, and have been formally received by the Emperor Napoleon III. Yet my most cherished memories come from a leaky tent, a bark canoe and the vast and mysterious wilderness of Canada."[1] Right on, Sir William, except for the bit about the leaky tent.

But back to those crazy mad fools – in the era of the fur trade and in the very different conditions of the twentieth and twenty-first centuries – who paddle across the continent, for whatever reason.

Mackenzie was the first European to reach the Pacific travelling overland by canoe and foot. He and his party in 1793 hiked the last 347 km (215 miles) following a traditional Native trading path over the Coast Ranges from the Fraser River. The path was established for eulachon or oolichan trade. Eulachon or candlefish is an oily species belonging to the smelt family that lives in the Pacific. The oil was a valuable trading item for oil-poor inland tribes. Today, we'd build a pipeline and pump the fish inland, but in those days they were carried in baskets by foot over the mountains.

Mackenzie's route to the Pacific over the continental divide was difficult, but we are a species driven to explore. It was not long before others – most notably, Simon Fraser, David Thompson, George Simpson, and Alexander Henry, the younger, as well as the Americans Lewis and Clark – were pushing their way to the Pacific. Their obvious motivation, like Mackenzie's, was wealth, control and empire building. But in their hearts, they were explorers.

South of the border, the government of the fledgling United States sent Meriwether Lewis and William Clark. They reached the Pacific in 1804 at the mouth of the Columbia River. Unlike Mackenzie's expedition, theirs was a big venture. A party of forty soldiers, known as the Corps of Discovery, headed by Captain Meriwether Lewis, set out, on the personal instructions of President Jefferson, to find an overland route to the Pacific. In the upper Missouri, several French-Canadian voyageurs joined the group. They also travelled with a map prepared by David Thompson in 1798. Although the expedition achieved its goal, and its members were well rewarded with cushy jobs in the U.S. government, Lewis committed suicide shortly afterwards. He apparently was always susceptible to fits of "melancholy," as depression was then called, but his moods were upbeat when he was facing the vast unknown, constant danger, starvation, and imminent death. Perhaps, as W.B. Yeats wrote: "Who hears the rippling of waters cannot utterly despair of anything."[2]

Once on a long road trip to the southwest United States, shortly after having completed the Mackenzie odyssey, I stopped where the highway crossed the Missouri River near its confluence with the Mississippi. I watched its brown, muddy water swirl past and threw a stick into the current for my dog, Mica, who swam out to fetch it. While poor Mica, who has only three legs, was being swept downstream, my mind was moving upstream, feeling the pull of the river to follow it to its source. "Another time," I mused, as an exhausted Mica waded ashore, bedraggled, his tawny yellow coat stained brown by the dust of mountains thousands of kilometres to the west.

After Lewis and Clark's expedition, the North West Company was in a hurry to find its own route to the Pacific. Everything west of the Rockies could become U.S. territory if the Montreal paddlers were not to move fast. Simon Fraser was given the job of establishing new trading posts on the headwaters of the Peace River. In the spring of 1808, he led an expedition down Mackenzie's Great River in what turned out to be one of the most daring whitewater adventures ever attempted. If he were recounting his tale today, he might well begin with the words: "No shit, I was there!" In the high water of summer, the rapids of the glacier-fed Fraser were too much for birchbark, even for a determined Scotsman. After several harrowing and heroic adventures, where entire canoes were sucked into whirlpools and smashed on rocks, the men abandoned their canoes and continued on foot. Friendly Natives lent them dugouts to continue on their way, which they did until they reached tidewater.

Then Fraser took out his sextant and determined that the latitude of the river was 49 degrees. The reading that American sea captain Robert Gray had given for the mouth of the river, named the Columbia after his ship, the *Columbia Reidiva*, in 1792, was 46 degrees North Latitude. Fraser concluded that this river was not the Columbia, and it was not a feasible trade route to the west coast. Wearily, the expedition retraced its route upstream, not realizing that it had completed a trip of historical proportions. If Fraser could have looked into the future and seen the cities of Vancouver and Richmond sprawled across the estuary of the river that now bears his name, he might have thought differently.

A few years later, in 1811, David Thompson, in a canoe made of cedar planks, finally journeyed down the river flowing out of the Rocky Mountains that actually was the Columbia and reached its mouth. This journey realized the dream of a feasible coast-to-coast trade route. David Thompson, explorer, scientist, astronomer, and map-maker extraordinaire, probably logged more distance by canoe in his life than anyone else in the history of Canada – over 80,000 km (50,000 miles), according to his biographer J.B. Tyrell, himself a noted Canadian explorer and map-maker. Thompson's journals – 4,000 handwritten pages – are preserved in the Archives of Ontario in Toronto. They have never been published. When I finish this book and finally have some time on my hands, I may just go there and read them for fun.

When Thompson reached the mouth of the Columbia on 15 July 1811, he found fur trader John Jacob Astor firmly ensconced in a well-defended and well-provisioned fort, named Astoria. The American party had arrived by sailing ship just four months earlier. But Astor gave the Canadians the most glowing praise that any paddler could receive, saying that "one Canadian voyageur was worth three American canoemen."[3]

War broke out in 1812 between the United States and British North America, and one of the issues that they were arguing over was control of the Pacific coast. The North West Company sent an expedition of 100 men across Canada. The group arrived in Astoria on 5 October 1813 and told the men of the Pacific Fur Trade Company that they were at war and that the Royal Navy would soon be coming to blast them out of existence. Interestingly, the Americans chose to sell the fort, its furs, its supplies, and its trade deals to the North West Company. On 15 November, a North West party arrived on the coast, led by Alexander Henry, the younger. Unfortunately, Henry died the following spring in a boating accident while crossing the mouth of the Columbia to pick up the first white woman to arrive on the Pacific coast, Jane Barnes, a very well-travelled English barmaid. And in the end, Fort Astoria was given back to the Americans, who have it still.

Henry kept meticulous journals of his travels from Lake Superior to the Pacific. They are a treasure of details of fur trade life. Reading his journals is like stepping through one of those magic portals leading to other worlds that you find in fantasy novels, except that Henry takes you into a world that once was real. But that is another story.

It is not possible to write about continent-crossers without including Governor George Simpson, the feisty tyrant of the Hudson's Bay Company for more than four decades, starting in 1821, when the Hudson's Bay Company and the North West Company amalgamated. Simpson liked to do what he called "inspection trips," and he would purposely arrive unexpectedly at remote inland posts. He holds many records of canoe travel, some of which have never been surpassed. In one season, he travelled over 10,000 km (7,000 miles). Once, he descended the Fraser River, continuing to paddle past where the dauntless Fraser had abandoned his canoes. It was October 1838, and the water was low, but never since have bark canoes run the mighty Fraser. He set the speed record for cross-continent travel on that trip, travelling from York Factory on Hudson Bay to the Pacific in an amazing sixty-five days, for an average pace of 75 km (47 miles) per day! He and his men also did the dreaded 19-km (12-mile) Methye Portage in a single day, albeit with the help of ten Natives who met them there.

Simpson travelled in specially designed express canoes, 33 feet long and 4 feet wide, manned by an elite crew of twelve Iroquois paddlers from Caughnawaga (near Montreal). They kept up an average pace of sixty strokes per minute and would regularly cover over 160 km (100 miles) in a single day. Not only did he set speed records, but no one has ever done canoe trips with more panache and style. Simpson would stop just out of sight of a trading post, where he would don his beaver felt top hat, and his crew members would dress up in their brightest shirts and feathered caps. Then they would sprint to the post, with the men singing at full voice, a bugler blaring, and a bagpiper wailing, as if the king of England himself had arrived. One can well imagine the spectacle, as the "royal procession" approached a remote post in the wilderness.

On his daring run down the Fraser, Governor Simpson didn't follow Mackenzie's route over the continental divide. It was just too difficult, and a much better route existed. Perhaps Mackenzie misunderstood the instructions given to him by a band of Sekanni that he met. Perhaps he just made a mistake and took a wrong left turn. (I've taken more than one wrong turn in my travels. Who hasn't?) Perhaps the Sekanni were playing a little joke on Mackenzie. I can imagine them laughing as the bedraggled group headed up the Parsnip River, saying: "Hey, those dumb white guys actually believed us." Or maybe the Sekanni made a mistake or didn't want to admit that they didn't know a route to the ocean for fear of looking stupid in front of strangers.

Whatever the reason, Simpson and the other fur traders who followed Mackenzie took a much easier route, following the Pack River instead of the Parsnip and going up the little Crooked River to lovely Summit Lake. Here, they followed the relatively flat Giscombe Portage to the Fraser, meeting that mighty river just above the present-day city of Prince George (once known as Fort George). This route follows the Rocky Mountain Trench and stays far away from lofty summits.

Towards the end of the nineteenth century, railways, steamships, and roads put an end to the transcontinental fur trade routes and to transcontinental canoe travel. It just was not economical to paddle any more. If you wanted to see the country, it was easier to take the train.

That is, until a new bunch of paddlers began to turn up. These canoeists were not sponsored by businessmen for the purpose of increasing the size of their empires and profits. No, these guys were in it for the fun and adventure (and discomfort, deprivation and exhaustion). This is the kind of paddler that I can really relate to. The stories of modern cross-continental canoe expeditions form their history. As we see below, 1936 and, especially, 1967 were "watermark" years. Canada's Centennial seemed to launch a thousand canoes (I exaggerate slightly), and the saga continues into the twenty-first century.

The year was 1936 – the depths of the Great Depression. Two young city slickers, Sheldon Taylor and Geoffrey Pope, left New York City for Nome, Alaska, in an old cedar-canvas canoe bought through the want ads. They named their canoe *Muriel* after Shel's older sister and major trip sponsor. Their plan was to spend the winter at Fort Chipewyan in northern Alberta and continue to Nome the next summer. True to American hyperbole, they touted their trip to be the first-ever crossing of North America by canoe. They also claimed that it would be the longest canoe trip ever taken. Their second claim was arguably correct.

They swamped before the first day was over. However, they persisted.

One month later, in Ottawa, they met Mr. Woods, owner of the then-famous Woods Manufacturing Company. Woods completely re-outfitted them with the best camping gear. They sold *Muriel* for $35 and on his advice purchased a 17-foot Peterborough Prospector. They were thrilled with their new canoe – according to Taylor "a beautiful ballerina skipping from wave top to wave top, dancing, receptive, sensitive, alert and enthusiastic."[4] What better testimony to a canoe could there be? I agree 100 percent. No better canoe for tripping has ever been designed.

Almost as important as their new canoe were two eiderdown sleeping bags to replace their wet woollen blankets. The only drawback? The sleeping bags were so cosy that Taylor and Pope, particularly Pope, didn't want to get up in the mornings.

On the Ottawa, they met their first Native, Joe Whiteduck, who taught them how to bake bannock, use a tumpline and portage with paddles serving as a yoke. They also met their first hordes of mosquitoes, no-see-ums, deer flies and black flies. Welcome to Ontario! On Lake Superior, they were invited aboard a 161-foot yacht, the *Seaforth*, filled with beautiful, young, single women, every continent-crosser's fantasy.

At Grand Portage, there was nothing. Not a building or even a sign or stone marker to indicate that this was once one of the most important historic sites on the continent. They pushed on down the Winnipeg River and up Lake Winnipeg (after a side trip by bus to the city for a night in a hotel) to Grand Rapids. At that time, a 5.6 km (3.5 mile) tramway led around the rapids, where a huge hydro dam now plugs the river. The two men hired a Native with a pony to haul their gear for $2. Most of the Natives whom they met now spoke only Cree. It was 1936 and the fur trade era had not yet quite passed.

Taylor and Pope wintered in Fort Smith on the Slave River in the Northwest Territories. The next spring, they followed the Mackenzie River downstream almost to the Arctic Ocean. They took a left turn up the Peel and followed the Rat River over the continental divide. This was one of the routes followed to the Klondike in the Gold Rush of 1898. Once over the divide, they followed the Little Bell River, then the Bell, and finally the Porcupine, which dumps into the mighty Yukon. After a memorable fist fight erupted on the banks of the Yukon River, the result of two years of two conflicting personalities crammed into one canoe and one tent, they made it to salt water on 11 August 1937.[5]

Canada's Centennial, 1967, was a banner year for cross-continental paddling, highlighted by a race in voyageur canoes from Rocky Mountain

House to Montreal. Teams from all provinces and the Northwest Territories participated. Other groups of modern voyageurs travelled in brigades on the old fur trade routes. The races and re-enactments did much to instil a sense of our history into young minds, as Wayne Roach, an avid paddler today and a young, impressionable boy in 1967, explains:

"During the rainy afternoon of August 27, 1967, eleven *canots du nord* came around a bend in the Calumet Channel of the Ottawa River, on the eastern side of Grand Calumet Island, Quebec. Once a common sight, these were likely the first big canoes to paddle this way in almost a century.

"The village of Campbell's Bay is located on the opposite shore of the channel. As part of the Centennial celebrations, the 26-foot canoes were scheduled to stop for the night. Having come almost 3,125 miles from the Rocky Mountains, these voyageurs were going to put up their tents in the schoolyard. There were six or seven paddlers per craft. Since Campbell's Bay was the first Quebec stop on their journey to Montreal's Expo 67, the honour of landing first was given to the Quebec boat.

"My grandparents lived in a house just a few hundred feet down the shore from the landing area. My family was visiting for the weekend, and I was part of the crowd at the water. The sight of those canoes coming around the bend up the river has remained indelibly etched in my mind. Not being the brightest ten-year-old in town that day, I knew very well that just beyond that bend lived the wild dogs, trappers and polar bears of the far north. To me, the canoes had just made their way out of the wilderness and into civilization. A few hundred other people who were also in Campbell's Bay on that Sunday afternoon may have the same intense memories of the armada's arrival as I do. And what is heritage if not 'shared memories'?"[6]

Don Starkell was one of many famous paddlers in that race from Rocky Mountain House to Montreal and a member of the winning Manitoba team in the 1967 Centennial Cross-Canada Canoe Race, finishing the course in a breathtaking forty days – a pace that would rival Governor Simpson's express canoes. Starkell went on to paddle the Northwest Passage and set a Guinness record for the longest canoe trip ever taken when he paddled with his son Dana, twenty-one years old at the end of the trip, from their home in Winnipeg to the mouth of the Amazon in 1980-82. His record was short-lived, however, for Verlen Kruger and his wife, Valerie, broke it by paddling all the way from the Arctic Ocean to the tip of South America – a whopping 34,000 km (21,000 miles) – in two years. Wow!

Another Centennial trip of note was taken by Ralph Brine and his crew, who took a freighter canoe from the mouth of the Fraser to Lachine (Montreal). They used a 20-hp outboard and carried a cargo of 2,000 letters from the west coast. The trip took three and a half months and involved, in addition to canoe travel, a five-day ski trip over Howe Pass in the Rockies. When I was in Prince George, I stayed with Ralph Brine's son, Rick.

However, Taylor and Pope's two-year journey from New York to Nome remained the longest canoe trip on record until 1971. Then came Verlen Kruger. Then forty-nine, he and Clint Waddell paddled a 21-foot fibreglass canoe from Montreal to the Bering Sea – more than 14,400 km (9,000 miles) – in a single season. This eclipsed all previous recorded expeditions for speed and endurance and rivalled even those of Simpson and his express canoes. Clint and Verlen were fuelled mainly by pancakes (I prefer oatmeal for breakfast), and they calculated that they averaged 6.4 km (4 miles) per pancake. I would sure like to know just what went into their pancake mix. Their energy, perseverance and enthusiasm are amazing. They even stopped in the middle of their trip to take a detour to Flin Flon, Manitoba, to participate in a five-day marathon canoe race. This little diversion was almost disastrous, as they raced winter to the Bering Sea. Did they make it? Read their account in their book, *One Incredible Journey*. I personally believe that the secret to Verlen's energy is the fact that he had already raised nine children. This was great training for long ordeals. I figure that, for him, this trip was, in comparison to his day-to-day family life, a vacation.

This was a short trip for Verlen. He went on to paddle 44,800 km (27,000 miles) criss-crossing North America in a 3 1/2-year canoe trip that still stands as the longest ever. He followed that by covering 33,600 km (21,000 miles) from the Arctic Ocean at Tuktoyaktuk to the tip of South America – the second longest ever, and probably the longest honeymoon on record.

All previous and subsequent cross-continent expeditions pale, however, when measured against the Shepardsons' trip. Carl and Margie Shepardson set off from their home in New Hampshire on 17 May 1980, en route to Alaska. They travelled with their two children, Tina and Randy, then eight and four years old, respectively. They used a 20-foot canoe, weighing in at 45 kg (100 pounds), and hauled three 34-kg (75-pound) packs. I will never feel justified whining about a portage ever again. Not only did they have a prodigious outfit to portage, a load to challenge even the toughest voyageur, but they also had the responsibility and work of caring for their young family.

Their burden was heavy, but Carl and Marjorie are not, weighing in at 60 kg (132 pounds) and 48 kg (105 pounds), respectively – small even for voyageurs. No voyageur or North West Company trader ever showed more perseverance than this family. The Shepardsons travelled in traditional style, baking bannock each day, cooking over fires (no stove for this family!) and using canvas Duluth packs. Hats off to the Shepardsons. They plan to do the route again, but next time they will use a 25-pound canoe, carry lightweight gear, and take lots of money so that they can stay in hotels and eat in restaurants more often.

In May 1983, Gary and Joannie McGuffin set their canoe into the St. Lawrence River at Baie Comeau, Quebec, and did not stop until they reached Tuktoyaktuk on the Beaufort Sea – 10 million paddle strokes and two years later. They followed the fur trade route to Fort Chipewyan and then Mackenzie's *"River of Disappointment"* to the sea. The McGuffins were awed by the diversity and beauty of the natural world through which they paddled. Arguably the best-looking couple ever to paddle across a continent, Gary and Joannie made their honeymoon trip an inspirational story. They brought Canada to Canadians through their book and slide presentations. They have continued their adventurous way of life, using the canoe as a communication tool to draw attention to many environmental and wilderness issues in Canada. Kudos for the McGuffins!

In 1987, Alec Ross launched his canoe at Lachine, where the voyageurs had set out 200 years earlier. Over three summers, he retraced the voyageur route across Canada, finally descending the Fraser River to the Pacific. Alec Ross was struck by the people whom he met and the lives that they led. I feel an empathy with him. Like me, he set off because of restlessness and a need to search for something – in so far as these things can be explained. Like me, Alec met his one true love during an interlude between legs of his trip. For both Alec and me, our trips were a coming of age, where we made the transition, or transformation, from teenagers to adults. Alec just did it when he was a decade or two younger than I was.

During the years from 1989 to 1993, four groups of students, led by Professor Jim Smithers, from Lakehead University's School of Outdoor Recreation, paddled and portaged 12,000 km (7,500 miles) from Montreal to both the Arctic and the Pacific oceans. These modern-day voyageurs paddled fibreglass replicas of fur trade canoes. But that is about all that was different from the voyageurs of old. They dressed as voyageurs and gave demonstrations of voyageur life in towns and schools all across Canada. They faced the same challenges – violent storms, extreme heat, freezing water, huge wind-swept lakes, rapids, endless upstream travel against the relentless current of prairie rivers, the Grand and Methye portages, and all the rest. For the first time since Mackenzie, as far as we know, people took a voyageur-style canoe on the exact route that he followed over the continental divide, instead of going by the easier Crooked River–Giscombe Portage route. But when they arrived in a town, like the voyageurs of old, they did so in grand style, with pipers, salutes and ready smiles. The modern-day Lakehead voyageurs agreed that the school and community programs were more difficult than the longest portage or the windiest day.

One of the most unusual cross-continent trips was taken by William Least Heat-Moon in 1995. He set out from New York City in the 22-foot *Nikawa* – "River Horse" in Osage, the language of his ancestral people – powered by twin 45-hp outboard motors. Very traditional. His route took him west via canals and rivers to Lake Erie, down the Ohio, and up the Mississippi and Missouri in the footsteps of Lewis and Clark. The *Nikawa* overcame dams, log jams, sweepers, barbed-wire fences and bridges with low clearance. (Don't we paddlers know all about these rural hazards? If the barbed-wire fence doesn't rip your head off, the bridge with no clearance will!) *Nikawa* saw it all. William and his companion, whom he called "Pilotus," also travelled in a 17-foot aluminum canoe with a small outboard when the waters were too shallow for *Nikawa*. Over the continental divide, they resorted to hiking, while the boats were hauled by road overland. Finally, they descended the Columbia to the Pacific in Oregon.

The Sea-to-Sea Paddle for Life Expedition in 1995 by Roman Rockcliffe and Frank Wolf, which took them from Saint John, New Brunswick, to Vancouver in a single season, added a new twist to transcontinental paddling. This was the first major fund-raising canoe trip, collecting money for, and raising awareness of, AIDS. The pair took a 17-foot Clipper Tripper along the fur trade route to the Rockies, crossed the continental divide by the route of David Thompson and Alexander Henry, the younger, and followed the Thompson River to the Fraser and on all the way to Vancouver.

Two years later, a lanky young man named Chris Taggart left Lachine on 17 April 1997 to paddle the Alexander Mackenzie Voyageur Route (AMVR) as far as he could in a single season. He had a 16-foot Old Town Penobscot and his trademark, big green Carlyle plastic paddle. Chris wore more than an inch off that paddle that year. Fuelled by instant oatmeal, tortillas and Kraft Dinner (Chris is threatening to write a book entitled "500 Easy Kraft Dinner Recipes"), he pushed across the continent. Paddling upstream on the relentless North Saskatchewan between Cedar Lake and The Pas, he paddled thirty-six hours without a break. It took him a biblical forty days to ascend the mighty Peace, 1,200 km (750 miles) against a current that never tires. He faced all the usual challenges, plus loneliness and Giardia (a nasty intestinal parasite). Finally, in mid-November, winter caught up with him just after he crossed the continental divide, in the canyons of the McGregor River. He camped for ten days in the snow, waiting for the ice to firm up. Chris crossed the continental divide via Mackenzie's route – the only solo cross-continental paddler to do this, as far as I know.

In 1998, Chris and I teamed up. We left from Bella Coola and travelled together to Prince George, thus completing Chris's journey. It is not a canoe romance, but Chris and I came to know each other through our mutual interest in paddling the AMVR. We met first through e-mail, then face to face when he passed through Ottawa. By the end of our journey to Prince George, we felt like brothers. And we still do.

I would not want to leave out my old friend, Bob Kelly. He left Ottawa the same year I did, but went east instead of west and ended up at the Confederation Bridge in Prince Edward Island. Over the following two years, he paddled from Banff to Ottawa and from the headwaters of the North Thompson west to Victoria. In 2000, he completed a 55-km (34 1/2-mile) gap in his continental traverse, the section of the Boundary Waters Route from North Fowl Lake to Lake Superior. This "day trip" turned out to be the toughest part of his entire journey. Tornadoes had ripped down the forest, making the 1.5 km (about one mile) portage from South Fowl Lake to the Pigeon River "a soul-shattering ordeal." The obstacles he overcame went beyond merely geographical – he was also faced with a crippling disease, the loss of his wife, and two hernia operations. His resolve and determination define the adjective "heroic."

A young Ilya Klvana, then twenty-one, left Prince Rupert on 11 May 1999, with a set of canoe wheels and a homemade wooden kayak. On 22 November, he arrived at l'Anse aux Meadows in Newfoundland, where the first Europeans to reach North America had settled 1,000 years earlier. Ilya gave a new meaning to "travelling light." When I met him in Ottawa, he had only a daypack. He explained that the farther he went, the less he needed, and lightness was a key to his rapid travel. He did all portages in one carry. He knocked off the mighty Methye in a short day. He even sent home his stove. He explained to me that cooking takes too much time. "It's more efficient to soak your oatmeal or dried supper goop in cold water for a few hours, and then just eat it." Thanks for the advice, Ilya, but I'll stick to cooking my oatmeal and sipping hot chocolate by the fire on cold northern nights before I turn in. Ilya is the youngest person to cross the continent by canoe or kayak. I wonder what he'll do next?

As I write this, there are several groups on their way across the continent. Erin McKnight, a determined young woman from Mississauga, Ontario,

Ilya Klvana, the "crazy kayaker," in 1999, on his epic trip from the Pacific coast to Newfoundland.

just completed a cross-Canada odyssey to raise awareness of mental health. She chose this cause because her mother was manic-depressive and took her own life when Erin was eight years old. She began her journey in Lachine in 1998 and reached her goal, Tuktoyaktuk, two years later. Erin paddled with different women partners each year. She is the first woman to paddle across the continent, to the best of my knowledge. Congratulations, Erin.

On Saturday 26 May 2001, Carrie Mortson and Martha McGown pushed off from Wawa, Ontario, and started the last leg of their three-summer, 9,000-km (5,625-mile) journey across the continent – the Many Waters Expedition. They paddled 1,627 km (2,600 miles) from Wawa to Killbear Provincial Park and then from Montreal to Saint John, New Brunswick. They reportedly had a great time and arrived in Saint John on 21 July. That left them with just 10 km (6 miles) to finish in their journey. On 28 July, they paddled with a flotilla of friends and well-wishers from Killbear to their hometown of Parry Sound, to become the first woman team to travel by canoe from the Atlantic to the Arctic.

There are many more such intrepid people, but to include everyone would entail writing a book devoted solely to this topic. My apologies to those not mentioned here.

Today, no one is paddling canoes laden with furs or trade goods, but many, like Erin, are carrying something equally important – messages about important issues and about threats to our nation's heritage. As Canadians, we have been given our boreal forests, our rivers, our prairies and our lakes. We have done nothing to deserve them. They have taken care of us and helped us create this nation that is our home. But now it is our turn to take care of our heritage. Are we up to it? What kind of country will our children paddle through?

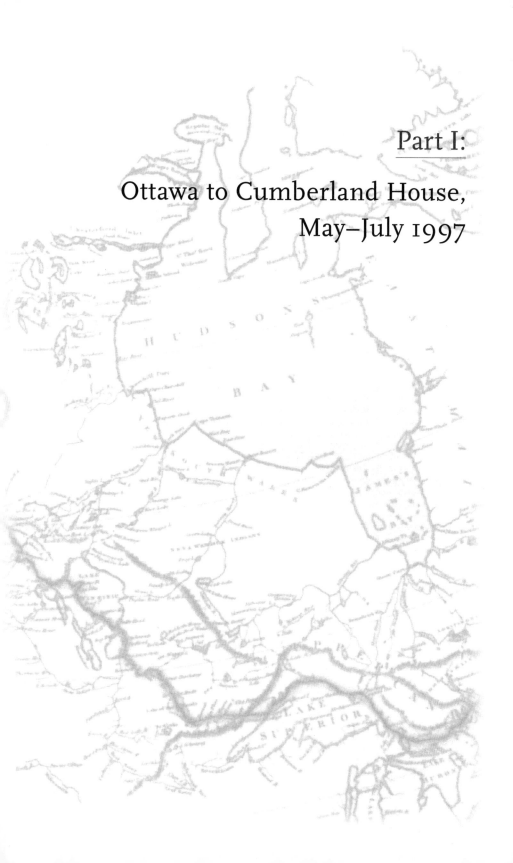

Part I:

Ottawa to Cumberland House,
May–July 1997

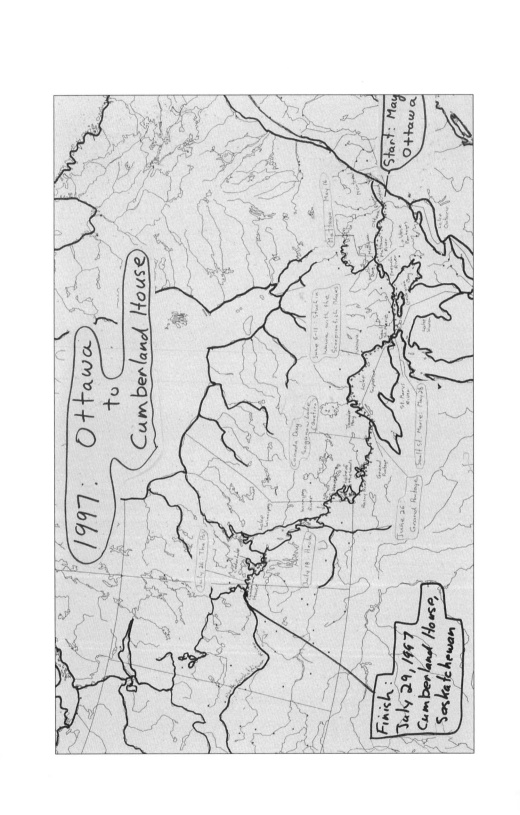

1997: Ottawa to Cumberland House

Start: May Ottawa

Finish: July 29, 1947 Cumberland House, Saskatchewan

Mattawa May 16

June 6–11 Stuck in Wawa with the Scorpionfish Blues

Canada Day

Saganaga Lake, Quetico

Thunder Bay

June 26 Grand Portage

Sault St. Marie May 28

July 18 Hole

July at The Pas

3

Getting Ready

Beginnings

B ACKPADDLE! BACK TO THE BEGINNING – but when is the beginning? A cold day in early May when it would have been better to have stayed in bed than to fight the wind and waves up the Ottawa River.

Or is the beginning on another cold, blustery day in May 1784, when Alexander Mackenzie left the offices of the fur trading company of Gregory, McLeod and Company in Lachine (Montreal) to use a 36-foot birchbark canoe to travel the known water routes west to Detroit, and then to Grand Portage, with instructions to proceed beyond, into Indian country?

Or is the start two centuries before then, when Europeans first ventured inland, the excuse being to trade for furs, but the real reason being to answer the call of the unknown, the allure of a land filled with mystery?

Or does the beginning go back still deeper, to the most basic drives of life – to explore, to expand what is known, to find out what is around the next bend, or over the next ridge, or beyond the end of the sidewalk?

I guess the latter is why I went on this journey. My home is steps from the Ottawa River. It is a tradition in our neighbourhood to go down to the river on warm summer evenings to watch the sun set. In midsummer, the sun floats down into a widening of the river called "Lac Deschênes." For

29

years, I had watched the sun and the water and imagined the flotillas of fur trade canoes that used to ply these waters, heading west into the wilderness. For years, I had thought about following their trail, beyond where the sun sets. Although it is not the wilderness that it was two centuries ago, for me it was still a journey into the unknown.

One spring day, for reasons that still remain a mystery to me, I decided to go, to paddle beyond where the sun sets, and to keep paddling until I reached the salt water of the Pacific. And that is why in early May 1997, on a cold, blustery spring day, I carried my canoe, named *Loon*, from my home to the banks of the Ottawa. There I began my journey, retracing the route of Mackenzie across the continent, with a stuffed bear named Sir Alex tied securely to the bow as my lookout. My plan was to paddle the 3,000 km (some 1,500 miles) to Cumberland House, at the centre of the continent, by the end of July. And here is how that plan came about.

I made the decision to go on this journey only about one month before I left. As usual, I did things backwards, or at least not in the usual order. This seems to be a pattern in my life. Often I have made a point of not planning things, because if I did, it would all turn out backwards. I am better off just letting the currents of life take me wherever they go. In this case, I had asked to take an eight-month unpaid sabbatical from my job with the Canadian Heritage Rivers Program. Unlike most people who take sabbaticals, I did not have any concrete plans for my time off. But I knew that retracing Mackenzie's route was one option, as this idea had been percolating through my brain for about five years. My friends were full of suggestions, including research on grizzly bears in the Rockies, a long road trip around North America and a variety of canoe trips in various parts of the world. I finally decided that this was the right time to paddle across a continent – North America.

My biggest consideration was my elderly mother and her little black-and-white dog, Peppy. Since my father passed away, I have spent a lot of time visiting them and taking Peppy for long walks. My mother lives alone. My sister lives far away, so I feel a heavy responsibility. While I enjoy being with and helping my mother, I also like to travel. I explained to Mom what I was about to undertake by bringing home a big map of Canada and drawing a heavy black line (Mom doesn't see very well any more) along the route. I told her that the trip would take six months. She (and I) thought that that was too long for me to be away. So I agreed to go for three months that year. I could always finish the route the following year.

My mother's name is Rose, and she is as sweet as the flower, and as

Rose Finkelstein, my mom, and her feisty little dog. We will miss each other very much.

thorny. She has a height of 147 cm (four foot ten) and might weigh 41 kg (90 pounds), with her rubber boots on. I stand 175 cm (five feet nine inches) tall and weigh 86 kg (190 pounds). At the time, a widow for five years, at the venerable age of 84, she was feisty and independent, just like her little dog. Mom had no conception of why anyone would want to go on a canoe trip. In fact, she has no idea what a canoe trip is like. "I'm just a city girl," she once said to a friend, when he asked if I had inherited my love of wilderness from her.

Mom asked me the same series of questions that she puts to me before I leave on any canoe trip, and I answer, almost by rote:

"Where are you going to sleep?"

"Well, in my tent," I stammer.

"Are there any motels?"

"Well, a few," I answer hesitantly.

"What are you going to eat?"

"You know, the same stuff I eat all the time – noodles and oatmeal and dried food and raisins and stuff," I sigh.

"Are there restaurants where you're going?"

"Well, there'll be some," I perk up.

"What about the wild animals?"

"Mom, there's really nothing dangerous out there."

"The wolves will eat you," she concludes. "Peppy and I will miss you." I don't know if she means while I am gone or after the wolves start licking my bones.

Once I had made the decision to go, I had a lot to do to get ready – food to prepare, equipment to buy or fix, boxes to pack and mail out for resupplying myself en route.

But this soon grew to be more than just another canoe trip. Brenda Beck and Eric Harris, canoeing friends who run a video company, urged me to document the trip on video, and we made tentative arrangements to meet at several points on the route. Other canoeing friends (Wade Hong and Don Haines) volunteered to set up a web site so that anyone who wanted to could follow my progress on-line.[1] The story created a small furor of media interest (I guess nothing interesting was going on in Ottawa at the time), and interviews on TV and radio were set up for the big departure day.

All this meant that I needed a (shudder!) schedule. A schedule is anathema to the freedom of a long, solo canoe trip. Seldom do we have an opportunity to exist with no schedule other than that dictated by the needs of our bodies to sleep and eat. Rarely can we do what we want to do all the time for an extended period. I could see the dream of complete freedom to do as I please fading.

I picked 6 May as my day to leave. I pulled out provincial road maps of all the provinces I would be crossing and, using my thumb and index finger held about an inch apart as a measure, I let my fingers do the walking across Canada. Each "step" was about 30 kilometres, or approximately 19 miles (the scales varied, of course, on each map) – or one day's travel, when you add in all the wiggles and portages. Using this incredibly accurate method, I figured that I should get to Cumberland House by 31 July, which works out to about 36 km per day, not including any days off. Real voyageurs paddle on weekends.

No stranger to canoe travel, I had been on a few long, solo trips, hence did not have to buy any special equipment. I already had the perfect canoe for the trip – my beautiful *Loon*! Designed by the dean of long-distance paddlers, Verlen Kruger, *Loon* is a solo travelling canoe. This is the best all-round solo travelling craft that I have ever paddled. She is as seaworthy as a sea kayak yet can run Class-3 rapids with ease. She can carry a big load (a whole summer's worth of supplies), and she is fast, stable, easy to portage and a joy to paddle.

Loon, as her name implies, has a low profile on the water, like her namesake bird. Her length is about 17 feet, and her width, about 2 feet, and she has a hard cover. She has a large cockpit – big enough for an over-stuffed canoe pack, or two – that can be sealed off with a fabric cover. *Loon* has a rudder, and most people think that she is a kayak. To be truthful, I do not know when a kayak becomes a covered canoe. *Loon* has qualities and characteristics of both.

Loon is graceful, with softly rounded lines. I once saw a fellow admiring her when she was pulled up on a beach. As he gently stroked her sides, I quietly walked up to him and said: "Like a woman's thigh, eh?" He looked a little embarrassed. "Well, I guess it gets lonely out there sometimes," he said, and walked off.

Loon is fast. I have been clocked at 9.6 km (6 miles) per hour on calm water and can sustain this speed even with a considerable load in her. *Loon* is very efficient paddling into a headwind or wind from the beam. With the rudder down, she tracks dead straight. She moves at 6.4 km (4 miles) per hour into a wind and chop. Into waves, she tends to cut through them, and so keeps a good rate of speed. Fifty-mile (80-km) days are easy in her, 60-mile days have occurred, and even one 70-mile day. I find her to be as fast as some solo boats built for speed, but, in addition, she can carry loads, run rapids and cross oceans. I have never felt in any danger in *Loon*, although there have been several times when my nerves were very frayed. But she never seemed worried.

The lines of *Loon*'s bow tend to shed water weeds, an important consideration for a solo boat. Fast solo boats often have sharp, squared-off bows that pick up weeds, and the only way to clear them is by stopping and backing up, or with a long stick or kayak paddle.

On flat water, I usually employ a bent-shaft racing paddle, but *Loon* also paddles well with a double-blade. I had my favourite 50-inch carbon-fibre "Barton,"[2] about ten years old and already a veteran of many long trips and races. For a double-blade, I took a laminated wooden Grey Owl,[3] 93 inches in length.

Loon is big. Space is not a problem and she can carry a lot. For this trip, my pile of gear looks impressive – one humongous canoe pack, a generous daypack with camera and video gear and an overflowing duffle bag. More than you would ever want to portage. *Loon* paddles well with a big load, I rationalize, and the weight just makes her more stable. *Loon* is easy to load. My big canoe pack drops in just behind the seat, the duffle in the stern. The daypack fits in front of me, between my knees.

Loon is responsive. For a long, sleek boat, she is very manoeuvrable in rapids, with her rudder up. I prefer to use a double-blade in heavy rapids for quick bracing. In shallow, rocky rapids, I use a straight single-blade paddle for quick manoeuvring. Obviously, with a length of 17 feet, *Loon* does not pivot and spin as quickly as a white-water kayak or canoe, but for her length, she is pretty good. And she crosses eddy lines with scarcely a wiggle.

Loon is seaworthy. I hoped that I would not have to test her limits on this trip. I have paddled her through some rough conditions – 1.7-m (6-foot) breaking waves from the front, side and quartering on the stern – and the open side always stayed up. Never have I felt at risk. But the thought of capsizing or swamping weighed on my mind. If I did, I would be in a lot of trouble, especially in freezing water. I just made up my mind not to tell my mother this little detail.

Portaging *Loon* is a snap. Really. I use a wooden yoke that I strap on with "fast-ex" straps and buckles around the belly of the boat. While not a perfect system, it is simple and works well enough. My *Loon*, made of Kevlar and Epoxy,[4] weighs less than 23 kg (50 pounds).

Don Haines, my computer-geek paddling friend who can fix anything, even without duct tape, is an expert canoe sailor. He offered to make a sailing rig for *Loon*. A few days before I left, he came to my house with a beautiful sail and mast. I was too chicken to use it, and too chicken to tell him so. It was too big for me, a neophyte canoe sailor, and I decided to make a smaller sail, with the help of another friend, Dot Bonnenfant. I rummaged in my basement and came up with a piece of red nylon tent fly material. She cut and stitched it into a friendly rectangular sail. We cut a 1.2-m piece of maple dowelling for a mast and a fibreglass footing for the mast on the floor of *Loon*. The entire rig could be rolled up and stowed in her stern. She was now a sailing canoe, and I just had to wait for tailwinds. Little did I know, but I would be waiting a very long time.

I needed maps, lots of them. Being cheap and lazy, I borrowed 1:250,000 topographic maps that covered the entire route. Then I made six piles in a big empty room in my basement, each containing food, maps, film and other gear to mail ahead to friends in North Bay, Sault Ste. Marie, Thunder Bay, Kenora and Hecla. And one pile to take with me.

Here's what my "to do" list looked like a few days before I left:

> pack boxes
> mail boxes
> reinforce seat posts in *Loon* with fibreglass and epoxy
> waterproof spray cover
> touch up paint on my car (why was I fixated on this?)
> buy a live trap and catch the mouse in my house
> rake Mom's lawn

plant Mom's garden
buy two pulleys and one friction lock for the sailing rig
buy D-rings (to glue on the floor of *Loon*)
buy 50 feet (15 m) of 1/2-inch rope for lining
buy fibreglass repair kit

For two weeks before I left, I was busy drying and packaging food for the trip. I used a food drier to prepare most of my trail food. This is an easy method, and I can dry a prodigious amount of food very quickly. The best way to dry food is to cook the meal, spread it out on the trays, and turn on the dehydrator. But since I am lazy and disorganized – or rather, since I get organized only at the last minute, I rarely have time to do things the best way. I just buy bottles of spaghetti sauce, salsa, canned beans, frozen vegetables and other prepared foods and spread them out on the drying racks.

Spaghetti sauce and salsa, when dried, resemble the sole of an old leather shoe. They rehydrate in hot water in a few minutes back into a remarkable resemblance to the original. Dried canned beans are amazing. They rehydrate exactly as they are from the can. Fruit leather can be made quickly from canned applesauce and frozen fruit, blended or squashed. It can be eaten dried, but I like it better rehydrated into a sauce for bannock or pancakes.

I had a few failures. My attempt to dry coleslaw resulted in a gooey glob of green mush. In an inspired moment, I thought of drying frozen orange juice to make a super-concentrate. Do not waste your time trying this. Sometimes the dried peas are a little chewy. But the only real limit is your imagination.

I may have had more diversity in my meals than Mackenzie, but no advantage in nutrition. Mackenzie and his crew, and the entire fur trade enterprise, were fuelled by pemmican, dried peas and cracked corn. Pemmican is a mixture of dried buffalo meat, pounded between two rocks and mixed with an equal amount of melted fat. Often, marrow and dried Saskatoon berries were added, which, according to Mackenzie, made pemmican "of superior quality." Pemmican keeps for months, even years. It was eaten raw in chunks or mixed with flour and water and cooked into a stew called "rubbaboo." One and a half pounds of pemmican would sustain a hard-working voyageur all day. It would take the place of eight to ten pounds of fresh meat! *"A little time reconciles it to the palate,"* wrote Mackenzie.

I have never tasted pemmican, but I imagine it to have the consistency of modern-day "power bars" and perhaps a similar taste. H.M. Robinson, in his book *The Great Fur Land*, describes pemmican: "Take the scrapings from the driest outside corner of a very stale piece of roast beef, add to it lumps of rancid fat, then garnish all with long human hairs and short hairs of dogs and oxen, and you have a fair imitation of common pemmican."[5] Add a few dried berries, and that sounds pretty good to me.

My favourite fuels are oatmeal, bannock, noodles, beans and grains, with liberal quantities of cheese, peanut butter and dried fruit. Verlen Kruger and Clint Waddell, on their epic cross-continent dash in 1971, subsisted mainly on pancakes and achieved record-breaking, never-to-be-achieved-again fuel efficiency ratings of four miles (about 6.4 km) per pancake. Let me tell you how I prepare oatmeal and bannock.

Oatmeal is one of my staples. I pity the people who travel with me if they do not like it, since that is what they get for breakfast every morning. I mix up the oatmeal at home, adding dried fruit and powdered milk to the mix. The key for creamy oatmeal is to add cold water to the mix and cook it slowly over a fire. It can be cooked over a camp stove, but constant vigilance is required, or it will burn. Don't worry about cooking too much. If there is any left over, you can always add some flour and fry it up for lunch. I figure that I get about eight kilometres or about five miles to a cup of oatmeal.

Bannock is my other main staple. It is trail bread, made with flour and baking soda. I am not sure who "invented" bannock, but it has been a staple trail food for almost two centuries; Mackenzie never mentions eating bannock, although in his time flour was added to pemmican to form glue-like lumps of stew known as rubbaboo, something like dumplings. Everyone has his or her own particular method and recipe for baking bannock. Inuit folks with whom I have travelled use lots of oil, so the bannock bakes quickly. It is deep fried like a giant doughnut, very satisfying on a cold, blustery Arctic day when the body cries out for grease.

Bannock is a great energy source. I figure that I get about 16 kilometres or about 10 miles per cup.

The calendar was sprinting towards D-Day (departure day). Two days before leaving, I played Laser Quest at my nephew's birthday party and got riddled with laser beams. Mackenzie was probably tallying the lading of every canoe in his brigade two days before he left Lachine for the *pays d'en haut*.

His equipment, in addition to trade goods and food, would have included:
mast and sail
60 yards of rope for hauling and lining

canoe repair kit that included a pail of pine pitch and spare rolls of birchbark – but *watap* (spruce root for sewing bark) instead of my duct tape and fibreglass

axe

bailing sponges

two oiled canvas tarps

10-foot (3-m) setting poles for upstream travel

4-foot (1.2-m) paddles for the *milieu*

six- and nine-foot (1.8- and 2.7-m) paddles for the *avant* and *gouvernail* (bow paddler and sternsman)

tent, bear skins, and guns (black powder muskets) for Mackenzie.

One day was left. My friends arranged a going-away game of ball hockey and supper. During the game, as I stickhandled my way through the opposition in my usual Bobby Orr–style, I felt a sharp pain in my ankle. Sure enough, I had pulled a ligament or tendon or muscle or something else that holds my foot on to my leg. Lucky for me, I planned to spend most of the next three months sitting. My ankle would hurt for more than two weeks, but that was a minor annoyance compared to some of the other difficulties that I was to face.

4

Up the Ottawa:
Road to the *Pays d'en haut*

[T]he river ends at the first Portage de Chaudière ... the water falls 25 feet over excavated rocks in a most wild, romantic manner.

— ALEXANDER MACKENZIE

IT POURS RAIN ALL MORNING that Tuesday, and then the wind picks up. It's an ocean, an angry ocean, out there in Lac Deschênes. White caps and rollers – no day to paddle.

"Well," I think, "one day behind schedule already. Behind what schedule? Not mine, but the schedule that has been imposed on me, or rather, that I had imposed on myself."

There is no particular reason that I picked 6 May as my day to depart, other than that I figure that I will be all packed and ready to go and I want still to be in Ottawa for my nephew Jesse's fourteenth birthday party on 4 May. My house is a beehive of activity, verging on chaos. The telephone is ringing, and everyone is expecting me to leave today. Friends are dropping by to say their farewells, and media people are knocking on the door. Brenda Beck and Eric Harris, friends and videographers, arrive with video equipment and tools to rig my canoe with a tripod and microphone for the video camera.

The activity starts early. Rita Celli, a reporter from the local CBC radio station comes at 8:30 a.m., and we do an interview for CBO's "Morning Show" parked by the river in her car, rather than in the canoe as had been planned. The wind and rain make it impossible to do an interview outside.

A crew from CBC-TV, Nancy Cooper and Simon Gardiner, come to the door and ask if I am really leaving today. They have just listened to the weather forecast and tell me I would be crazy to go. They do not want to do a story about recovering my drowned and beaten body, they tell me. As they leave, the telephone rings. It's my mom, worried as usual, and begging me not to go today. Another friend, Dot, phones, and advises the same.

More friends drop in. Wade and Don, who have created the web site for my trip, show up to get words and images for the first web pages. Eric is drilling holes in the canoe to mount the microphone and trying to figure out how the tripod can stay put with the camera on it. More CBC calls – this time from Halifax – CBC Newsworld. For my tired, emotionally overwrought brain, all this activity is overwhelming. Already I am exhausted, and I'm not even out of my living room yet. Mackenzie never had to put up with these kinds of pressures.

Or did he? Can you imagine the scene at Lachine as the big *canots de maître* were loaded? The crews, French and Iroquois, were loading each canoe with the bulky *pièces*, each wrapped in burlap and containing European-made trade goods and, for each craft, 99 gallons of rum in nine-gallon kegs plus all the provisions needed for the journey from Lachine to Grand Portage, at the western end of Lake Superior. Each canoe would be loaded until the gunwales were only 15 cm (6 inches) above the water. Each craft would carry: 277 kg (600 pounds) of hard biscuit (you can still buy hard biscuit, or hard tack, made by Purity Mills in Newfoundland and at Northern stores all across the north); 90 kg (200 pounds) of salt pork; 90 kg of dried peas, sugar, flour lard; personal gear for the crew; and all the equipment – paddles, setting poles, oiled canvas tarps, sail and mast, a pail of pine pitch and *watap* (spruce roots for thread).

A little past noon, my telephone stops ringing, and I realize that I have not even eaten yet. Wade and Don urge me to get away from the phone and join them for lunch. All my friends have been so supportive. All this concern and care overwhelms me. If I "succeed" – whatever that means – I am not paddling alone, and a lot of my strength will come from my friends and Mom. And Chris Holloway, a former Olympic kayaker, who has just phoned to wish me luck after he heard the interview on CBC radio. He doesn't even know me. Where would I be without a lot of help from my friends?

Leaving makes me realize the power and value of relationships. They are the most important element of being human – relationships with family, friends, lovers; with community; with the land and water; and with yourself. Leavings like this one make relationships stronger by making one feel just how important they are. But a long solo canoe trip is a very egotistical undertaking – very selfish. It feeds one's relationship with oneself, but it is hard, or can be hard, on others, especially family members. I hope that this trip strengthens my relationships on all levels.

All my past trips have, for the most part, been punctuation points in my life – highlights from which to measure time – a source of inspiration and wonderful, vivid memories. I hope the same for this trip.

The wind is lessening. Tomorrow should be a good day for paddling.

No city in Canada reverberates as strongly to the fur trade days as does Ottawa. To stand on the bridge, at the paper mill, just below the dam that now obliterates the Chaudière (French for "kettle") Falls that so enchanted Mackenzie, with the tips of the standing waves (over 3 1/2 m – about 12 feet – high in the spring) licking your feet, you can feel the power of the river. Above the dam, traces of the original portage trail can still be found – steps cut into limestone and worn smooth by the passage of thousands of moccassined feet.

For the voyageurs, and for me, the Ottawa River is the road to the interior – a difficult road – eighteen portages to the Mattawa. It is easier today. With many of its rapids flooded by hydro dams, it requires as few as seven portages, depending on the water level. But in the springtime flood, it is still a big, powerful river.

The seventh of May dawns bright and sunny and cold – winter cold. The wind is still whipping out of the west. But I'm anxious to be off. I have to leave twice. The first time is for the television interviews. The CBC Newsworld crew arrives at 6:30 a.m.! I have planned to portage *Loon* to the end of my street, a mere 150 m (500 feet) to the river. But the CBC technician explains that they cannot get a signal there, and I will have to launch her in Britannia Bay, about 1.6 km (a mile) away. I sigh. But Don Haines has arrived early to help. We load *Loon* onto his car and drive to the river, where the interview will take place.

I bob around in the waves with a wireless microphone, speaking to someone in Halifax, I think. Mackenzie never had to do that!

Then I paddle back to the end of my street for the real start. A small crowd of friends have gathered there, including, to my pleasant surprise, Dot's father, Louie, who is eighty-eight and still paddles. And, of course, Mom is there. Karen MacKay gives me a little teddy bear for the trip named Sir Alex (for Alexander Mackenzie, knighted in 1802).

It's a tough place to launch with waves crashing in, but I get under way reasonably dry. With the cameras rolling, I have to make this look good. But the rudder on *Loon* is stuck in the "up" position. I put the double-blade

*Heading up the
Ottawa River
with "Sir Alex"
as my lookout.*

together and use it as a pole to reach back and push the rudder down. But bobbing around in the waves, I cannot get it to fall into position. The waves are pushing me back into the shore, so I take my beloved Barton carbon-fibre bent-shaft paddle and head out, rudderless, through great big breaking waves to the nearest shelter that I can find, about a mile upriver. I am hoping that the launch won't look too embarrassing on the evening news.

I cross Britannia Bay and head inside the breakwater of the Nepean Sailing Club. Less than a mile, and already I am taking a break. Don Haines meets me there, with Mom, Dot and Karen. I had arranged this before, so I can say a proper goodbye without the news media looking on. We fix the rudder with tools borrowed from a member of the sailing club, I give Mom a goodbye kiss, and I head out once again. My friends reassure her that I will not capsize. But they may not be certain themselves.

This is not as easy as it could be. Even with the spray cover on, my butt is getting wet. Progress is painfully slow into the wind and waves as I cross the mouth of Shirley's Bay to Innis Point. I am already cold and soaked, a state that I would have to get used to during this particularly cold, windy and rainy spring. Innis Point is a bird banding station, and I have been there several times to observe the procedure with my ornithologist friend, Connie Downes – more on Connie to come. Most important, with the spring migration in full swing, this migrant paddler should be able to find some shelter for his first "mug-up" in one of the buildings there.

Sure enough, the bird-banders are there. They offer me a cup of coffee and some cookies. I have been out three hours, but it feels as though I have been paddling for days already. I am cold, wet and exhausted. After a short break, I walk back to where I have pulled *Loon* gently up on shore, among big slabs of limestone.

"You're sure you know what you're doing?" one of the banders asks me, as I prepare to cross the river to the Quebec shore, where I think that I can get some shelter from the wind and waves. The river here is about a mile across.

"Oh yes," I answer brightly. "I've been doing this for three hours now." And off I go.

I later heard from Connie, who met the banders the next morning, that they told her about this very strange man who arrived by canoe. That's ironic, I thought, calling me strange. What would you think if you stumbled on a bunch of people in the pre-dawn darkness wearing funny hats and carrying bags of squirming warblers? In comparison, I think that I look reasonably normal. However, Connie did not admit that she knew me. Who would have thought at that time that she would end up marrying this weird guy?

Six cold, wet, windy hours later, I arrive at my friend David Andrew's home, on the Quebec side of the Ottawa River. I had planned to stop here for lunch, but after fighting the wind, with gusts up to 80 km (50 miles) per hour, waves, and currents, I am pooped. And I have gone only about 19 km (not even 12 miles). What a way to "ease" myself into the trip!

One advantage to the nasty weather is that David invites me to stay the night. He also asks over some paddling buddies, and we have a small going-away party!

The next morning, the river is dead flat – a nice change from yesterday. I tie Sir Alex, the teddy bear, on the deck of *Loon*, facing forward, as my lookout. It is a pleasant paddle up to Chats Falls Dam. Although the dam has obliterated the rapids, the river here is still beautiful, broken into many small rocky channels. Mackenzie wrote:

> *"Portage des Chats, over which the canoe and lading are carried two hundred and seventy-four paces, and very difficult it is for the former. The river is here barred by a ridge of black rocks, rising in pinnacles and covered with wood. The river finds its way over and through these rocks, in numerous channels, falling fifteen feet and upwards."*

The rocky area below Chats Falls Dam is now one of my favourite places to paddle on a lazy sunny afternoon for a picnic. Today, however, there is no time for a picnic. I paddle towards a bay on the Ontario side of the river, just below the dam. The dam is not very tall, but it is miles wide – a very imposing structure. Two fellows are fishing, and I ask them the best way to portage.

"Up the ditch, and past the airplane at Fitzroy Creek," they say.

It is no surprise that I cannot find any of these landmarks, and I end up portaging about a mile along a road, about five times as far as Mackenzie had to portage.

Above the dam, the water level is down by about 1.2 m or about four feet. The dam is being left open to drop the levels of the reservoirs in anticipation of the spring runoff. This creates a lot of fast water and rapids. Under the railway bridge, I just manage, on my second try, to jump up a 30-cm (12-inch) drop. But I cannot make it up the next drop and have to portage. I cut through the backyards of cottages and homes to a road. As I am about to pass a house with the screen door open, I stop to ask to use the telephone to call my nephew Jesse Hastie, who lives in Carleton Place, a town about 32 km (20 miles) away. Jesse says that he and his grandparents will meet me in Arnprior, 9 km (6 miles) upriver, where the Madawaska River empties into the Ottawa.

Late in the afternoon, I paddle into the bay at the confluence of the two rivers, and there they are. Of course, they invite me to join them for supper and stay the night. Jesse's grandfather will drive me back to the river in the morning. Although I know that it will mean a late start, it is hard for me to refuse one of Hazel's home-cooked meals. We hide *Loon* among some bushes and pile into the car. I begin to wonder if I should have bothered to take camping gear. My food pack is expanding faster than I can eat it, as everyone I meet gives me treats for "the road."

The next day a strong east wind helps me paddle upriver. Just when I am thinking about lunch, a voice from shore shouts: "How about a coffee?" Pat and Sandy invite me for lunch, although I insist on eating some of my own provisions, as my pack is getting mighty heavy. My next obstacle is the dam at Portage du Fort, and they advise me to portage on the Quebec side of the river. As I paddle across, in the middle of the river there are big rolling standing waves, making me feel as if I am paddling on Ogopogo's back. The strong current piling into the east wind has created these waves, where no waves should be. But at least I don't have to dodge logs, as the McGuffins, the Shepardsons, and Verlen Kruger and Clint Waddell and other modern-day voyageurs all described in their accounts.

But the bottom of the river is smothered in logs. Pat and Sandy told me that crews were hired to salvage these old logs, which are perfectly preserved in the cold water. The logs are piled so thickly that the members of one crew anchored their boat in one place and continued to fish out log after log. I was told that the wood debris in the Ottawa below the Chaudière Dam is almost 6 m (around 18 feet) thick! Imagine all the spawning beds of sturgeon and pickerel smothered under an avalanche of logs. I can imagine how prolific this river was in Mackenzie's day, with sturgeon and pike reported to be up to two metres or six feet in length. Sturgeon are incredibly long-lived creatures, and sturgeon that were adults when Mackenzie came this way could still be alive. But they are very sensitive to pollution and slow to reproduce. They do not even begin to lay eggs until they are about twenty-five years old.

I paddle between islands against an increasingly strong current, choosing the smallest channels that I can find, working my way as close to the dam as I can. Stroke by stroke, I battle the current, as the voyageurs did. But before the dam is even in sight, I find myself stuck below a one-metre drop and wonder how the big canoes had gone up this, as no portage was noted in Mackenzie's diaries. I land in a little bay below the drop and see a trench, a ditch, overgrown now, but clearly the old high-water portage, still obvious after two centuries of disuse. I half-float, half-drag *Loon* along this ancient trail.

After this it is hard slow slogging, but I continue to work my way upriver. The current seems to fill every channel. Just when the dam and road across the river come into view, I see a disheartening sight – what appears to be bank-to-bank, big standing waves gushing out from the bottom of the dam. The fast water keeps pushing me towards the shore, where I can keep moving upstream paddling through the flooded shrubbery. I then find myself in a very powerful eddy where the standing waves are actually going upstream, forced that way by the main current slamming into the shore and splitting, with most of the water going downstream, but some heading up. I let out a big whoop, because I know now that I can paddle to the very foot of the dam in this giant eddy.

It is an easy portage over the dam. Above the dam, I paddle peacefully through a beautiful lake that now drowns three sets of rapids – Rapide du Sable, Mountain Chute, and Rapide d'Argis. Then I reach the Wilderness Tours Whitewater Rafting Outfitters, marked by a huge crane, where clients, for reasons unfathomable to me, bungee jump. I meet my friend Alistair Baird, who works here, and the owner, Joe Kowalski. We have supper, discuss heritage rivers and voyageurs, and relax in front of a fireplace. Joe is quite a visionary fellow and wants to see this section of the Ottawa preserved.

Once again, no camping is necessary, as Alistair invites me to stay over. I wonder just how far I can paddle without having to set up a tent?

I have to make a big decision. The river breaks into several channels here. The voyageurs usually took the easternmost channel, known as the Calumet. But the water there is very high, the current powerful, and I am just one paddler. Native travellers traditionally avoided this section of the

Ottawa and took a shortcut, following a series of lakes to the Muskrat River and descending the Muskrat to the Ottawa at the town of Pembroke, above all the fast water. This is the route that Samuel de Champlain took in 1603. Somewhere along it, he lost his astrolabe, a kind of sextant used for surveying. The missing instrument turned up over 250 years later, in 1867, and now resides in the Museum of Civilization in Hull, across the river from Ottawa.

But the old portage trails are gone. Fences, roads, farms have changed the landscape. Chris Taggart took this route, about a month before I got here. He also decided that the current in the Ottawa was too strong to fight alone. The portage is not marked, but Chris took out his canoe in a small bay on the Ontario side about 3 km (1 1/2 miles) below the Chenaux Dam and he followed a stream to Town Lake. From there, he tried to follow the creeks and trails through a series of lakes to the Muskrat River, as Champlain did almost 400 years ago. But barbed wire, fallen logs, rusty wrecked cars and other debris of modern civilization jammed the creeks. Fences and private lands blocked the trails. Chris said: "It was a mess!"

Having heard about Chris's adventures, I decide to take advantage of the roads. Alistair has brought my homemade canoe wheels up from Ottawa, and I decide to hoof it 21 km (13 miles) to the town of Cobden on Muskrat Lake, rather than portaging from lake to lake on Champlain's route or battling up against the current of the Ottawa in full flood. From Muskrat Lake, which is about 19 km (about 12 miles) long, I will follow the Little Muskrat River to where it empties into the Ottawa, at Pembroke, above all the rapids. Not only is the route easier, but it is a lot shorter.

But first, time for a little fun. I accept Alistair's invitation to go rafting on the Ottawa. The river is gushing, and the rapids are amazing to look at.

To avoid the major rapids of the Ottawa, I decided to take a 21-km (about 12 1/2 miles) portage along the road to Cobden at the eastern end of Muskrat Lake.

It feels strange to be going downstream, and I can't help planning how I would go up each rapid. I guess I must be a salmon at heart. Some of the standing waves are truly awe-inspiring, especially at a rapid named Coliseum. No one who did not harbour a deep-seated death wish would run this rapid at this water level. The standing waves are reputed to be among the biggest in the world!

After the raft trip, I am anxious to walk to Cobden with the canoe. Lynn Clark, a videographer who lives nearby, comes with me to document this somewhat-silly undertaking. She drives ahead and stops to photograph and videotape me as I jog by. Sadly, Lynn died in a kayaking accident a couple of years later.

It's about 21 km (13 miles) to Cobden. The weather is cool and blustery – strong west winds, but no rain. The roads run straight through endless fields of corn. At each crossroad, I look hopefully for a sign directing me to Cobden. Finally, as I jog over a small hill, I can see the lake. Then I pick up the pace, always trying to look as good as possible when approaching a town, just like the voyageurs. At the lake, I pass a house, and an elderly man comes out, shakes my hand, and says, "You must be Max." Les Tuttle has lived on the lake all his life. He talks of the changes in fish (walleye declined after lake trout were stocked; the lake trout are so fat that they are inedible). No camping again tonight!

Tomorrow, I have arranged for a treat. I will meet my friends David Kippen and Jill Jensen at noon at the bridge where the Trans-Canada Highway crosses over the Muskrat River. The Trans-Canada Highway meets the Trans-Canada Canoe Route! The three of us will then paddle down the Muskrat to Pembroke, where the river joins the Ottawa.

It is tough slogging on Muskrat Lake. The wind is whipping up whitecaps, but I am happy not to be fighting the current in the Ottawa. The lake lies in a fault line – one side is rimmed by banded pink-and-black granite and drops steeply from the hills; the other side is limestone and gently slopes away from the shore – one side has forest, and the other, farms. I feel as if I am paddling through the Barrens of the Northwest Territories, as the wind whips unimpeded across open fields.

I reach the agreed-upon meeting point precisely at noon. David and Jill have just arrived from Ottawa. We have a windy but leisurely paddle on the Muskrat, a pleasant, winding stream. Talk runs high about what it was like when Champlain came this way. Near Pembroke, where the river picks up speed, we meet Ken, the Kayaker, Timmins. He is the second paddler whom I have met since leaving Ottawa, not counting David and Jill. The

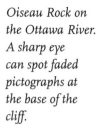

Oiseau Rock on the Ottawa River. A sharp eye can spot faded pictographs at the base of the cliff.

first was an elderly man paddling from Arnprior to Ottawa. He had a few days' growth of grizzled beard and was paddling slowly downstream. We chatted for only a minute before each of us paddled on, both probably wondering about the other, but too shy to ask.

David, Jill, Ken and I paddle together down the last leg of the Muskrat to the Ottawa River. It is almost a brigade now. Ken is most helpful and friendly, inviting all of us to his house for beer and asking me to stay over (no camping again!) His wife, Pauline, drives David and Jill back to his car.

Pembroke is on beautiful Allumette Lake, a widening of the Ottawa River. From here, it is a portage-free paddle all the way to the next dam, at Des Joachims (locally pronounced "duh Swisha"). This is one of the prettiest stretches of the Ottawa – *"bounded on the north by very high rocks, with low land on the south,"* wrote Mackenzie, who often speaks in understatements. Oiseau Rock near Deep River is a 141-m (475-foot) vertical cliff towering over the river. The river is very deep here – I wonder just how deep. A trail leads to the top of the cliff. Although it is cloudy, I get a bird's eye view of the river from the top. There is a small lake here, and a beautiful cliff-side campsite.

Back on the Ottawa, the rain intensifies as I pass Point au Baptême, a long sandy point extending into the river, an obvious campsite for voyageurs, who reputedly initiated novices in their crews at this site by drinking their personal supply of whisky. Today, Atomic Energy of Canada Ltd (AECL) owns this section of river.

A few miles farther on, I eddy out at the Eddy Inn, a hostel for paddlers in Deep River run by Don Smith and his wife, Ginty. Here I meet Don – a well-known outfitter and paddler who has done many long northern trips – giving a canoeing lesson in the sheltered harbour. Of course, he invites me to stay over. No camping again.

Travelling up the Ottawa, I see on my left the farms and fields and groves of hardwoods and pines; on my right, on the Quebec shore, the rocky Laurentian hills roll down to the river, still wild land. I walk up from the river and find ancient potholes, worn into the granite by rushing water, a reminder that the Ottawa was once a much larger river, larger than imaginable, gushing glacial meltwaters out to the Atlantic.

The water is dead calm. Flocks of brant like black strings stretched over the grey water, set out with me. I have barely started when the now-familiar cry of "Coffee!" comes across the calm waters of the Ottawa. I may never get far, but I won't starve, that's for sure. John and Irma were watching for me and make a habit of providing coffee for all cross-continent voyageurs. High on caffeine, I paddle hard to the dam at "Duh Swisha" and tie *Loon* up at an old wooden dock beside a rusted steel-hulled logging tugboat, known as a Russell boat, left over from the days when logs were floated down the Ottawa. These boats carried over a mile of steel cable and a huge winch. They were mostly a floating winch, used to move logs on the water.

I walk to the Esso station (sadly, the local hotel was closed, but it was too early for a beer) to buy a soft drink and find out about the easiest way to get around the dam. Ann Mykolyshyn runs the station and store with her husband.

"How 'bout I take you in the van," she says. "That's the easiest way."

I do not argue. I have thought about the "purity" of my trip and had decided early on that I would graciously accept the help of strangers if it was offered. This is a great way to meet people and learn about the country. Ann drives me to the river, where I unload *Loon*, and then she takes me to the top of the dam, where I am able to take some great video and photos. This dam is huge, over 24 m (80 feet) high, and plugs the river like a giant thumb. Three gates are open at the base of the dam, and the water is gushing in a huge white plume over 30 m (100 feet) high.

Ann tells me about the steamboats that used to come up from Pembroke. What a wonderful way to travel! In the heyday of steam, one could have

The dam at Des Joachims, the biggest on the Ottawa River. Rumour has it that bodies of several workers, accidentally killed on-site are entombed in concrete at its base.

gone all across the continent by steamboat, with a few portages in between. Ann speaks of the beauty of this site before the dam was built. I can only imagine what the river would have been like then. The dam at Des Joachims drowns out the sets of rapids that Mackenzie had to portage – the two Joachims, Roche Capitaine, Décharge de Trou, and Levellier. What were they like? Now almost 112 km (70 miles) long, Holden Lake (who was Holden anyway?) extends from the dam to the Mattawa River.

Sara and Ken Baird remember the drowned rapids. They are Alistair's parents and have a home on Holden Lake. I make a detour to stop for lunch at their home. It is worth it, every delicious morsel.

Holden Lake may have drowned out the rapids, but it is still a beautiful stretch of the Ottawa. The hills of the Canadian Shield crowd in from both sides. Streams swollen with spring meltwater plunge into the lake down the side of the steep hills. A bald eagle soars overhead. There is little trace of civilization. In places, the Trans-Canada Highway cuts close to the river, and I see railway trestles made of stone and thick wooden beams when I gaze up the streams flowing in from the Ontario side. The dam has raised water levels and submerged the old beaches, so there are few campsites. The rocky shore rises straight up from the water. It is very pretty, but a problem for me, especially as it is now pouring rain. I am anxious to stop for the night. A light can be seen ahead. A log cabin takes up the only campsite that I have seen for hours. Smoke is coming out of the chimney, and I need a coffee. An elderly man answers my knock at the door. Harvey Ballard is from Ottawa. He flew up here to do some fishing in the lakes back in the hills.

"Care for a coffee?" he asks.

"Um ... sure," as I stand there dripping water on the floor.

We sit down at an old wooden table, the kind that you stick a big hunting knife into when you are making a point.

"My dad," I say, "he told me about a lake he used to fly into near here called Broadcorb, 'way back in the early '50s, when he was in the Air Force. They'd fish from the floats of a Canso and catch all the trout they wanted."

"Oh, yeah, I know Broadcorb Lake, and others where you'll still catch 5-lb speckled trout," he says.

He lights a cigarette and offers me one.

"No thanks," I say. Most cross-continental paddlers seem to smoke, at least the ones whom I have met or read about. But not me.

"I should be pushing on," I say.

"Not before you try some of my venison meat loaf," Harvey offers.

Always a tough call for a vegetarian, but I have relaxed my vegetarian habits over the years, relenting to my mother's requests to eat chicken when I am visiting her.

"You look so thin," she says in that Jewish motherly way. "Eat some roast chicken."

How can a son say "No"?

My basic rule now is to eat animals that have two legs only. However, one has to be flexible, and I have always felt that it makes complete ethical sense to eat "country food." When travelling with Inuit, I have no compunction about caribou meat. In Zimbabwe, travelling with the Shona people, I consumed "meat." While they would not tell me what animal it was, I suspect that it was illegally taken from a national park, where hunting is prohibited.

Also, I am almost ashamed, as a somewhat-fallen vegetarian, to admit that there is nothing like a big hunk of meat when one is really tired, wet and cold. Munching bean sprouts and cheese, eating sunflower seeds, drinking carrot juice – these just do not satisfy a craving for calories in the same way that a huge slab of meat does.

This is a long, complicated way of explaining that I have seconds of his venison meat loaf, and it is fantastic. We have Jane Parker apple pie for dessert.

Harvey asks me to stay over and, as it is still pouring rain, I see no reason to break my string of "no camping." There's only one problem. Harvey is a chain smoker, and the cabin is filling up with cigarette smoke. I am hesitant to ask him to open a window.

The rain stops during the night, and first thing the next morning I get ready to leave. Harvey is up early, smoking, and cooks me an amazing breakfast of fried potatoes, speckled trout and bacon, followed by steaming cups of coffee. I think that Harvey smoked all night, so thick is the pall of cigarette smoke in the cabin.

"No socializing today," I say to myself, "or I'll never get to Mattawa."

After I pass the town of Deux Rivières, the current picks up. I remember that there were once rapids here, now submerged. I stay near shore to avoid the current and take advantage of big gentle eddies. But the eddies are filled with floating gunk: cedar sprigs, leaves, twigs, grass, sticks and other relics of the spring runoff. They catch on the bow of *Loon* and form a big wad of gunk that creates a noisy bow wave – very annoying. I use the double-blade to sweep off the mess of detritus. Handy things, these double-blades.

Holden Lake seems to go on forever. I pass point after point after point, each one just revealing the next. (I do not know at the time that this would be the pattern for much of the next few months.) I am anxious to reach the town of Mattawa. I have driven through Mattawa many times, returning from trips to Algonquin Park or Temagami. Every time, I stop at Valois' Restaurant and order their raspberry pie – the best raspberry pie that I have ever had (except for Connie's, of course). Voyageurs had their traditions, and I have mine. I am looking forward to stopping for my raspberry pie.

At last, I see the church spire in Mattawa, and soon I tie up at the dock below Valois' Restaurant and Motel. I swagger in, probably still smelling of cigarette smoke, and sit down at a vacant table. I like this restaurant. It is very homey, comfortable, reassuring in some way about the continuity of good family values. I have the feeling that its decor and menu have not changed for about half a century – or the uniforms of the waitresses. A waitress in a starched white dress briskly walks over to take my order.

"I've paddled all the way from Ottawa for a piece of your raspberry pie," I say.

She doesn't react.

"Is that all?" she asks.

"With ice cream and coffee," I add.

It's as good as I remember it.

Two men and a woman in their early twenties at the next table look at me, and one inquires:

"Are you the fellow who's paddling across the country?"

Gosh. I'm famous!

In celebration of my new status, and of the rain, which has settled in again, I decide to book a motel room. I may not have paddled, like Big Joe Montferrand in Stompin' Tom's song, "all the way from Ottawa to Mattawa in just one day." It has taken me seven days. But I did not camp once.

5

Over to Georgian Bay

The Petite Rivière is full of rapids and cataracts to its source.
— ALEXANDER MACKENZIE, 1793

THE NEXT SECTION OF THE ROUTE heads up the Mattawa River, over the La Vase Portages to Lake Nippissing, and then down the French River to Georgian Bay. Somewhere along the La Vase Portages I will cross over my first of many watersheds along Mackenzie's trail.

The Ottawa River does not want to let me go. Paddling under the railway bridge, just below the confluence with the Mattawa River, the current is strong, stronger than it looks. I can paddle *Loon* about 10 km (6 miles) an hour, and I am losing ground. I give up, exhausted, and drift back, eddying out below one of the huge concrete supports for the bridge. I take a few deep breaths and try again. This time, I find some slower water near shore and I am up. I turn *Loon* to the left, heading up the Mattawa. You would not guess that this was once the transcontinental route. Compared to the Ottawa, it is a minor stream, only 64 km (about 40 miles) long. In its short course, it drops over 46 m (150 feet) in fourteen portages. Mackenzie considered *"la petite rivière"* one of the most dangerous in Canada. He describes Talon Portage: *"275 paces for its length is the worst on the communication; Portage Mauvais de Musique, where many men have been crushed to death by canoes."*

To paddle up the Mattawa today is to see the river much as the voyageurs did. A dam near the town of Mattawa has drowned out the first two rapids, and there are two other smaller dams, but otherwise the rapids and, most important, the original portages are still there. The entire Mattawa River, including the La Vase Portages, is designated as a Canadian Heritage River. It is also a Provincial Waterway Park. All the portages are maintained and identified with interpretive signs. This river is a great little canoe trip, especially going downstream. Each summer, a marathon canoe race takes place on the Mattawa. The top racers paddle the entire route from the westerly end of Trout Lake (the headwaters of the river) to the dam above the town of Mattawa – almost 80 km (50 miles) – in less than six hours!

On this day, I can identify with Mackenzie's view of the Mattawa and with thousands of voyageurs who toiled up this little river. It is pouring rain, a cold slimy rain that slithers off the brim of my beat-up oiled-cotton hat, as I read the bronze plaque identifying this as one of Canada's most significant waterways.

I slip on the same rocks that they did, wade through equally cold icy water, just like they did, sweat and freeze at the same time on the portage around Talon Falls. I climb the steep ice and rock slope to a cave, the *Porte de l'Enfer*, loosely translated as the "Door to Hell," where Native peoples mined red ochre, a pigment rich in iron oxides, to draw pictographs that I will see much farther on in my journey. I stop for a hot lunch at Paresseux Falls, a spectacular curtain of white in the floodwaters of this spring, and reminisce about how it got its name.

Here's how the story goes, but is it to be believed? I do not know. A brigade of voyageurs had lost a canoe here early one spring. Two men were left here with the salvaged gear while the rest of the crew returned to Montreal to get a new canoe. They were instructed to portage all the salvaged gear to the top of the falls. When the crew returned two weeks later with a brand-new *canot de maître*, they found their companions and all the gear still at the bottom of the falls – hence the name *Paresseux*, which means "lazy ones" in French.

I feel lazy myself, sipping my hot chocolate, but it is too cold to sit around. I continue on, around rapids, falls and dark wet canyons where snow and icicles hang from the black rock walls. I notice a cedar tree on a steep bank just emerging from the ice, like some ice age relic. I carry *Loon* over the steep, slippery rocks around Talon Falls and the much easier carry called *Anse des Perches*, the last section of fast water on the trip to Grand Portage. Here, the voyageurs threw away the 4-m (13-foot) setting poles used to get the big canoes up the rapids. I finally pitch camp at the foot of Turtle Portage and watch the rain turn to snow.

Taking off my soggy clothes, I pile them in a corner of the tent. I am not pleased at the prospect of donning those clothes again tomorrow morning. I put together a hearty meal for four of rice, lentils, dried vegetables and cheese and soon have the pot boiling merrily in the vestibule of the tent. Four servings of hot chocolate pudding finally make me feel almost satisfied. With the glow of four candles lighting up the tent, and filled up with hot food, I am actually starting to feel quite cosy. Just as I am relaxing with my second cup of coffee mixed with hot chocolate (how did the voyageurs survive without chocolate?) both my hamstrings develop severe muscle cramps. I bounce around the tent, fighting to straighten my legs, trying not to knock over the candles, and shouting to the wind and snow: "Hey! This isn't fair! This is harder than it should be."

There is a small, inconspicuous divide that separates waters flowing into the Ottawa River watershed and waters flowing into the Great Lakes. The divide lies between Trout Lake, at the head of the Mattawa River, and Lake Nipissing. I am not sure exactly where, but I don't really care. Eleven kilometres (almost six miles) separates Trout Lake from Lake Nipissing. The route begins at the end of Dugas Bay at Trout Lake's southwestern corner. It is a real mess.

When Mackenzie came this way, it must have been a very well-trodden trail, as this was the main fur trade route. Mackenzie describes the portage in a dry matter-of-fact tone: *"one thousand, five hundred and thirteen paces to a small canal in a plain that is just sufficient to carry the loaded canoe to the next vase ... a narrow creek dammed in beaver fashion ... a swamp of two miles to the last vase ... care is necessary to avoid the rocks and stumps and trees."* Mackenzie seems to use the term *"vase"* as synonymous with "portage," but I think that he means a slimy, muddy trail. *Vase* in French translates as "muddy."

Halfway along the 11-kilometre (about 7-mile) La Vase Portages, the link to Lake Nipissing. These historic portages were added to the Mattawa Canadian Heritage River designation in 2001.

Today, the route is a muddy, confusing morass of beaver ponds and creeks. To make matters worse, the land between Trout Lake and Lake Nipissing is cut by the Trans-Canada Highway, a railway, a hydroelectric power transmission line, a gas pipeline and an industrial dump. It is unlikely to think that I would have found my way through, but a friend in North Bay, Paul Chivers, has duct-taped a detailed map of the portage to the back of the historic plaque where the Trans-Canada Highway crosses the trail, right beside Dugas Bay.

This route is one of the oldest known trade routes in Ontario, if not in all of Canada. But today, there is not a trace of the old portage left. It's hard to imagine that this was a trans-Canada highway for thousands of years. Paul is a member of the Friends of La Vase Portages. This community group is purchasing land along the old portage route and plans to re-establish the trail as it used to appear.

Paul meets me where the little La Vase River runs into Lake Nipissing, at a beautiful park appropriately named after Samuel de Champlain, and invites me to stay over. I decide to take a day off paddling. I have lots of little chores to do that Mackenzie did not have to worry about: fax my journal notes back to Ottawa for the web site, mail back my film and video, buy a few groceries, wash my clothes (phew!) and, most important, waterproof *Loon*'s spray cover. The rain is soaking through alarmingly fast, and I am tired of getting out of *Loon* each day with a wet bottom. A dry ass – what more could one ask for? Well, one more thing. The NHL playoffs are on. I hope that a game is on tonight, but I am out of luck. I haven't seen one game since I left; I wonder when I'll be close to a television set again.

I set off across Lake Nipissing with presents from Paul: nautical charts to guide me through the maze of the 30,000 islands and tobacco to offer the water witch. The tobacco works. Lake Nipissing is so calm that I set up the video camera on a tripod tied to the deck of *Loon* with bungee cords. I ramble on, talking and singing to the camera, as I course the big lake's southern shore. I try to imitate Robert Perkins,[1] creator of the video "Into the Great Unknown," and lick my lips a lot like he did. I now know why. Both of us have chapped lips. That night, as I camp by the Chaudière Rapids at the outlet of the lake, the sounds of nature, which are supposed to lull you to sleep, keep me awake. Loons are wailing, spring peepers are peeping and the rapids are roaring.

The French River was a one-day downstream run for the voyageurs. The river is gushing. There is so much water, the trail around the rapids is a flowing stream, and I float, rather than carry, *Loon* along the portage. Bonus. It is great to be going downstream after such a long uphill slog.

I have arranged to meet my friends Brenda Beck and Eric Harris, professional videographers, at Little Pine Rapids. They have rented a motorboat and are coming upriver to meet me and videotape me for the day. I wonder how they will get here, with the water so high. But there they are, sitting on a rock beside the rapids. Amazing what a 20-hp outboard can run up! The rapids in the French are deep and powerful – big, powerful eddies. Scary. I feel very small in *Loon*. But the rapids are all fun and easy to run. I put on a bit of a show for the video camera, running through the biggest standing waves. The sun comes out for about seven minutes this morning, and then the rain settles in for the day.

We stop at Schell's Camp, where Brenda and Eric had rented the boat and motor. There are some very cosy cabins here, and I am, as usual, cold, wet and tired. Shyly, I ask Christine, the woman who runs the camp, if any of the cabins are vacant.

"Well," she replies, "none of the cabins are ready yet for the season, so I wouldn't charge you."

"That's great," I say.

"But," she breaks in, "the beds aren't made."

"I don't care," I said, "I have a sleeping bag."

"And there's no clean towels," she continues.

"I have a towel," I answer quickly.

"And they're not neat."

"Look like Heaven to me," I say, maybe a little too quickly.

Christine shows me the cabin, and I notice a toaster.

"The only thing that would make this more like Heaven," I say hopefully, "would be a loaf of white bread. Can I buy one at the store?"

"I'm sorry," she replies sincerely. "We're out of bread."

But later she comes by with four slices of bread and a tub of margarine.

By now, you must think that I am a wimp, staying in cabins every chance that I get. But my philosophy of travel is to use the resources of the country. In this cold, wet, head-windy spring, I am trying to save all the energy that I can and put it into covering distance. Staying in a cabin saves me lots of energy, especially on cold rainy days.

"There is hardly a foot of soil to be seen from one end of the river to the other, its banks consisting of hills of entire rock," wrote Mackenzie about the French River. I surmise that the river today looks much the same as when he went down it. Glacier-smoothed granite and wind-sculpted pines characterize the route. The French's rich fur trade history and its unchanged appearance earned it the distinction of being the first designated Canadian

Heritage River. I wander in the rain on a small island where there are several rough wooden crosses, commemorating the martyrdom of Récollet missionaries four centuries ago and reminding me that I am walking among ghosts of Canada. The French is also one of Canada's most popular canoe routes in summer, but in this raw wet spring, with the water black and icy, I am the only paddler on the river.

Below the steel bridge at Highway 69 lies the most beautiful section of the French. This is a great bridge. Motorists can look up and down the river, framed here by vertical cliffs of smooth pink granite. I am very annoyed that most modern bridges, even the ones over little creeks, have solid concrete sides that obscure the view of the water below. What are the engineers thinking? Are drivers more likely to drive off the road on a bridge, perhaps distracted by the beautiful view? Is it more dangerous to drive off the road into the water than into a tree or cliff? Is it cheaper to build a solid concrete rail than a steel rail that you can look through? I do not know the answers. But I do know that beauty seems to be far down the list of priorities in our society. I believe that this is a very serious matter – a symptom of our society's deep spiritual crisis. You can save all the money in the world, but without beauty and love, you have nothing.

I drift beside the cliffs, mesmerized by the beautiful patterns formed by the grey, green and orange lichens growing on the rock. I fantasize about wallpapering my bedroom in granite and lichens.

Récollet Falls is the only portage for me on the French. There is a wooden ramp built around the falls along the route of the old portage, so motorboats can be taken up and down the river. The water coming over the falls flows smack-dab into a vertical rock wall just below the put-in, forming a huge eddy. Voyageurs in their heavily loaded craft had some anxious moments here.

Récollet Falls on the lower French River. Other than a short portage, where the river leaves Lake Nipissing, this is the only obstacle on the downstream run to Georgian Bay.

I have an anxious moment too, and as the eddy tries to sweep me under the falls, I understand why many canoes were lost here. I struggle to paddle *Loon* up the eddy along the rock wall, heading downriver, but dead against the direction of the current. The eddy is winning the race and slowly carrying me backwards towards the maw of the falls. I try a different strategy, angling the bow of *Loon* towards the middle of the river and ferrying upstream across the eddy. I can see the water, hemmed in by current and rock, mounded up in front of me, a pile of foaming water at least 45 cm (18 inches) high. I crest the height of water and zoom downriver. I cannot help but think about eddies as a metaphor for life. We all have eddies in our lives, dragging us down. If we are not strong enough to paddle against the current, we have to figure out another way to move on. But if you find yourself tiring, losing ground, stop doing what you're doing, and think of another way out. There is always a way downstream.

The mouth of the French River is like no other landscape on the planet. The river splits into four main channels, with cross-channels so that it looks like a city street map. It is a landscape reduced to simple elements – rock, water and pine trees. But there is a lot more here than the most beautiful scenery imaginable. Relics of the logging era can be found along the river: rusting hulks of "alligators" – amphibious, steam-driven mobile winches used to move logs; and the stone walls of the mill at the old town of French River, now long deserted.

Mackenzie followed the standard fur trade route, still identified on topographical maps as the "Old Voyageur Channel." In this maze of rock and water, the correct channel is hard to find, especially since the critical split falls almost exactly on the edge of the two topographical map sheets. I almost always get lost going from one map sheet to the next.

Paul has told me to watch for a white arrow painted on a rock where the channel splits off. No white arrow, but the channel that I am in sure seems like the one that Mackenzie followed: *"In several parts are guts where the water flows with great velocity, which are not more than twice the breadth of a canoe."* I slide over *"la Petite Faucille,"* the only portage noted by Mackenzie, and am flushed down *"La Dalles"* (loosely translated as "the eavestrough," an apt description) to Georgian Bay. It is an amazing ride, as the river is squeezed between smooth rock walls.

On the bay, the water is calm, and I am tempted to paddle out into the vast emptiness. For too long I have been hemmed in by rock and forest. At an old cottage on an island, I meet Lyon Newton, whose family lived here

Old Voyageur Channel on the French River near Georgian Bay. This was the pre-ferred route for voyageurs in the flood waters of spring.

when Mackenzie came by. He invites me to stay over, but the weather is clear and the water still, and I make excuses to push on.

I set up camp in a large meadow, an anomaly in this land of forest and rock. Clearly, I am not the first to camp here. Around an old fire pit are rusted cans and old Coke bottles made of green-tinted glass half-buried in the sandy soil. I fall asleep under the full moon, the first time I have seen the moon since leaving Ottawa. The spring peepers are active, and a white-throated sparrow whistles, "Oh, sweet Canada, Canada, Canada," in the gloaming. The ghosts of the fur trade are beside me. "I bet Mackenzie camped here," I think to myself.

6

Georgian Bay to Lake Superior: Coursing the Crystalline Hills

The course runs through numerous islands to the North of West to the river Tessalon and from thence crossing, from island to island, the arm of the lake that receives the water of Lake Superior.

— ALEXANDER MACKENZIE

I T'S 320 KM (OR 200 MILES) along the north shore of Lake Huron to Sault Ste. Marie. A frieze of tiny, rocky islands along the shore provides a handy hiding place if the wind blows. This is an incredible landscape or, rather, waterscape. The rocks are polished smooth by glaciers. Some barely rise above the waves, smoothly curved and glistening like a whale's back, or a woman's buttock, depending on how long you have been "at sea." West of the town of Killarney, once a fur trade post, the shore is backed by the 150-m (500-foot) La Cloche Mountains, made of gleaming white quartzite. The combination of crystal-clear water, gleaming white hills, wind-swept pines and thousands of islands and rocks of polished pink granite is breathtaking. And best of all, I have it all to myself!

Well, almost. I find that I am sharing this amazing place with someone else. How did I find this out? I am cutting through the maze of islands lying north of Point Grondine (French for grinding, or moaning). The point is exposed to the full brunt of the wind and waves of Georgian Bay and is no doubt named for the sound of the pounding waves and stones clattering in the backwash. My objective is the town of Killarney. Today's challenge is WIND – real wind, the kind that blows your paddle away –

The Georgian Bay coastline near Killarney, Ontario. The pink granite aisles, sculpted and smoothed by wind and waves and set like jewels into the clear waters of Georgian Bay, make for one of the most beautiful land/waterscapes on the planet.

wind that really hits the side of *Loon* and shakes her, as if a transport truck had just passed very close at high speed. You get the idea?

With the wind gusting to 50 or 60 km (say, 30 to 40 miles) per hour, I hide among the maze of islands, working my way northwest. Passing one particularly attractive island, with a nice stand of pine trees and sheltered cove, I see a tent. Curious, I pull into shore, and an elderly man waves me up to the tent. His name is Mike Ward. Seventy-four years old, he spends his summers here. He arrived just a few days ago. He offers me a cigar from his fine stock.

"You can't buy good cigars in Killarney," he says, "so I bring enough for the whole summer."

"Where do you buy the cigars?" I ask.

"In Florida," he replies. "I camp all winter on a cay near the Everglades."

Mike has done a lot of kayaking. I am in awe. He has paddled down the Pacific coast from Alaska to Seattle, on Lake Baikal in Russia and on the Baltic Sea. Maybe when I am seventy-four, Connie and I will have a similar life, spending our time surrounded by water, rock and trees, and well-supplied with the finer things in life – good beer and wine, lots of books and dogs.

Bidding farewell to Mike, I head to Killarney, with dreams of ice cream dancing in my head. The sun is getting low as I cut inside the lighthouse that guards its harbour. Killarney is only about 40 km (25 miles) from where I camped last night, but with all the deking in and out of islands, I

Mr. Perch's Fish and Chips in Killarney, reputed to serve the best fish 'n chips in Ontario.

estimate that I've paddled 64 km (40 miles) into a hard wind. Once more I am pooped.

I tie *Loon* up at the dock outside the Sportsman's Inn where a crowd of men is gathered outside. Strung up from a tripod made of three logs is a medium-sized black bear. A large man dressed in camouflage-patterned hunting attire and holding a crossbow is the centre of attention. A reporter is snapping photographs, and the others are hanging around like puppy dogs. The crowd moves like a single organism to the bar in the Sportsman Inn. I cannot help feeling disgust. I am not against hunting; it is natural that humans hunt. But the spring bear hunt, where bears are essentially trained to come to a specific place for food, is just plain murder. I don't get it.

Walking over to Mr. Perch's Fish and Chips Stand, I order fried perch. It has been said that some people fly here to eat Perch's famous fish and chips.

"I've paddled all the way from Ottawa to eat here," I say hopefully.

But just as at Valois' Restaurant, the server does not flinch. Perhaps I am not from far enough away. The fish and chips are as good as reputed, and I order a second round.

As I leave the sheltered harbour at Killarney and head across Frazer Bay, the wind whips up from the southwest, and I am forced to land in a protected little bay. At first the wind annoys me. Hey! I have a schedule to keep! Even though no one else cares about it, I'm more destination-oriented on this trip than I have ever been. It is like a long canoe race for me. Each day I set a goal, based mainly on the next place where I can get ice cream or French fries or find a television set to watch the hockey playoffs. Definitely, I am happiest when moving fast. It is as if I want to get this trip over with and return to my "comfy" life – walking Peppy, eating supper with Mom (while she drives me crazy in the way that mothers always do to their adult children, and we love them all the more for that), playing hockey, seeing friends, planning new adventures. Maybe I'm just lonely.

*Right: Kitchen on Georgian Bay. All the modern conveniences at my fingertips –
heat, water, unlimited counterspace – and a great view.*
*Inset: These pots, originally from Pakistan, could tell many stories. They have
travelled across more continents than I have.*

This is a lonely trip, much lonelier than a trip that takes one into the
true wilderness, where there really is no one else around. The town of
Killarney is just a few miles back. Although lights along the coast from
where I am are not visible, I know that there are people close by. They are
in their warm homes, watching the hockey game, snuggling up with kids
and dogs and lovers, laughing with friends. The nearness of people makes
me feel more isolated than ever.

But I look around me, and I am awed by the beauty. This is classic Killarney
country – white quartzite rock, twisted pines and clear green water. The full
moon is rising as I fall asleep. An early start is the plan if the wind is down.

I wake up in the middle of the night, on this night, for two reasons: first,
I have to pee, because I drank three cups of hot chocolate before I went to
bed; and, second and most important, it is quiet. There is no sound of waves
crashing in on the rocks, and the quietness woke me. I check my watch.
Three a.m. I have decided to start wearing a watch, rather than relying on
tiredness and hunger as cues to the time of day, as I am always tired and
hungry. I lie awake, with the full moon shining in my face, and then decide.
"What the heck, let's go!" I am on the water before four in the morning.
Breakfast at six (damn that watch!) on a rocky beach.

Today is the first day that the sun shines and the wind is low. The paddling
is wonderful as I course through narrow passages and into the Bay of Islands.
Colonies of cormorants, common terns and ring-billed gulls occupy tiny
islands of pink polished rock. The hills along the shore are covered in

hardwood forests. The trees are just beginning to bud and are tinted with a delicate light green blush. Behind the light green deciduous forest lie the La Cloche Mountains, shining, glinting, sparkling silver and white, covered in open forests of dark pines. I am happy again, not lonely, because I have all this for company.

Only one negative thought disturbs my bliss. The sole of my rubber boot splits this morning, and one foot is wet. Not even duct tape will fix it. I wring out the wet sock, put a plastic shopping bag over it, and put the boot back on.

The North Channel of Lake Huron is big and open. I see the radio tower from the town of Blind River maybe 40 km (25 miles) away, point *Loon*'s bow in that direction, and sing my way there. The quartzite hills fade away behind me, and black, gnarly rock islands rear up in front of me. Grey water meets grey sky. And I am the only thing moving in the whole universe.

I sing up every song I know – Jimmy Buffett, Fred Eaglesmith, Tom Paxton, all the old folk songs that Mrs. Shaw taught us in Grade 5. I paddle and sing and watch the water split around *Loon*'s bow. I can watch her bow for hours. I adjust my paddling technique so that the bow slides through the water as if it is on rollers. No bobbing up and down, no rocking side to side. No sound other than the hiss of water falling off my paddle as I reach forward for another stroke.

Paddling in conditions like these – calm water, big water and a long way to go – for me is like moving meditation. Performing any repeated motion – running, cycling, cross-country skiing, skating, walking or standing on one's head – for a long time puts one in a special state of mind. For me, running makes me think of nothing, except how much each part of my body is suffering. Cycling makes my mind very logical, and I can solve problems on long bike rides. But paddling puts me in a dream state. Strange and silly images pass through my mind. It is a very creative state of mind. When I run out of songs that I know, I start to compose my own. Some of them even sound pretty good. But, like a dream, when I stop to write them down, they just fade away. Sometimes I am left with a chorus or a few lines, just like a complex dream that leaves you with a few strong images after you wake up. And like the images from dreams, a few of these songs have stuck with me:

Paddle away with me,
Paddle or you'll never be free,
I'm the man who can calm the wind on the lake,
But I can't calm the wind in me.

Here are a couple of verses:

A women in white drifts by,
The epitome of grace,
Flowers in her hair,
Vines frames her face,
She offers me peace, she offers me bliss,
She whispers words of love, and tosses me a kiss
Nothing but dust on the Southwest Wind.

And,

One day I'll reach the Sweetwater Shore,
I'll lay my paddle down, I won't travel anymore,
But I'll find that I'm not really at my journey's end,
but at the beginning of beginnings, the source of the wind,
That damned Southwest Wind.

My reveries are broken by the sight of my first lake freighter, heading out with a load of ore from Algoma. Never had I seen anything made by people that is so huge. It moves fast, and I wonder if I will be swamped by the wake. Amazingly, it leaves barely a ripple on the smooth grey water of Lake Huron.

I am looking forward to meeting a friend, Lisa Venier, in the Sault. She becomes incorporated into the dream-songs:

Hold on, Lisa, I won't be too long,
But I'm still 25 miles on the wrong side of Thessalon.

Out here, I feel lonely. One little tiny dot on this huge expanse of water. But there are times today when I can see and hear the Trans-Canada Highway where it dips down near the shore. Cars and trucks whiz by, but here, on the original trans-Canada route, it is deserted. Except for that one huge ore-carrier. I know that Chris Taggart is somewhere ahead of me, paddling in his own loneliness, leaving a line for me to follow, as has Mackenzie and every other paddler who has come this way.

So I head into Thessalon, saying goodbye to the bald eagles, terns, gulls, cormorants, mergansers and Canada geese, and leaving behind the islands of twisted, gnarly black rock and equally twisted pine trees and the smooth pink whale-back islets. I leave all this beauty to find French fries.

Past Thessalon, as Mackenzie said, I stick to the north shore. I leave the big water of Lake Huron behind and enter the St. Marys River, another of the Canadian Heritage Rivers on this route, designated in 1998. This river is the hub of the continent, hydrologically, ecologically, politically and historically. The St. Marys was the key link in the route to the west for fur traders, settlers and the military during the seventeenth and eighteenth centuries. In modern times, it has been and remains a vital link of commerce.

I head upriver, against the usual headwinds and now the current again. The river is split into three main channels, and I pick the centre one, through the United States, as it is the most direct route to the Sault. The river channel is narrow and marked by buoys. How is it possible that a big freighter can fit here? I decide to camp on the river and wait for a lake freighter to pass by, so that I can watch it safely from shore. The only dry spot that I find in the narrowest part of the channel is a U.S. Coast Guard beacon, set on a big concrete pad. I pitch the tent (I am an illegal alien, so I keep a low profile) beside the pad and sit cross-legged on the concrete on a piece of blue foam, sipping hot chocolate. The sun has set. Toads are trilling, geese honking, barred owls hooting, "Who cooks for you-o-o-o-oo?" and bitterns "bonk-wonking." Spring is really here. The stars are blazing overhead, and in the distance the lights of the Sault are twinkling. It is c-c-cold. I put on mitts, a toque, and all the dry clothes that I have with me.

Soon, a deep throbbing can be heard, coming from downriver. A freighter is approaching. I watch in amazement. It seems to fill the entire river from bank to bank. What would Mackenzie have thought? Probably he would have considered this a big improvement over birchbark canoes. Mackenzie was a practical kind of dreamer, and transcontinental trade was his business.

I head upriver against a stiff current towards the Sault. There are many homes and cottages now along the river, and flocks of Canada geese graze on lawns along the shore. As I glide by the east shore, shots ring out. "Probably someone just trying to scare off geese in their garden," I think, but I head out into the middle of the river, far from shore, just in case it is some deranged maniac gunning for paddlers. Somehow, I am always paranoid in the United States. The American channel joins the Canadian at the twin cities of the Sault. I strike out for the Canadian side, expecting the Coast Guard to pick me off before I cross the imaginary line separating two nations. Whew! Safe again in Canada.

Against a strong current, I paddle up the St. Marys alongside a pleasant riverside boardwalk, crowded with lunchtime joggers and cyclists, and I pass the outflow from the hydroelectric dam at the Sault Locks – a Parks Canada National Historic Site. A Parks Canada employee named Randy offers to load *Loon* and my gear into his pickup truck and takes me to the top of the rapids. I telephone my friend Lisa, but she is away for a few days.

Today, the twin cities of Sault Ste. Marie (Ontario and Michigan) are packed with reminders of the voyageurs. There has been a series of communities at the rapids at the outlet of Lake Superior for thousands of years. When Mackenzie came by here in 1793, only about thirty families of Algonquin remained – *"starving one half the year, and the other half intoxicated"* – a sad result of the fur trade, typical of many Native communities across the continent. At the Sault, one of Canada's first canal and lock systems – the lock was built in 1797 – transported the voyageurs' big canoes around the rapids. A reconstruction of the original lock has gone up in its original location, near the rapids. Mackenzie probably portaged on the north side of the rapids along the same route that the pickup truck follows.

This lock and canal system was replaced in 1855, when bigger locks were built on the American side. When the U.S. lock denied passage to a Canadian vessel, the *Chicora,* on the grounds that it was a military craft, the federal government built a set of locks on the Canadian side. Finished in 1895, it was the most advanced in the world. This "high-tech" lock used electricity, generated at the site, to operate the massive gates to fill and drain the lock. The Canadian lock is being rebuilt as I pass through, exactly as it appeared in 1895. The lock opened to recreational boating traffic on 14 July 1998, slightly over a year later.

I walk along the rapids. It is a beautiful oasis in the city. Many tiny overflow channels create miniature Japanese-like natural gardens of marsh marigolds and ferns. A chorus of bird song – yellow warblers, catbirds, and other species (my ears are not attuned to pick out the individual species in this avian orchestra) – rings out from the brush.

I continue up the St. Marys River, past steel mills and industrial sites with huge mountains of I don't know what – white and yellow powder – piled outside. A lake freighter docked at the Algoma Steel Mill lets out a deafening blast as I paddle by. I realize that it has just cast off lines that look about a foot thick and is heading out to Lake Superior just like me. It's 29 May when I head out into Lake Superior.

7

Superior:
The Rugged Northern Shore

Lake Superior is the largest and most magnificent body of Fresh Water in the world: It is clear and pellucid, of great depth, and abounding in a great variety of fish, which are the most excellent of their kind. There are trouts of three kinds, weighting from five to fifty pounds, sturgeon, pickerel, pike, red and white carp, black bass, herrings, and the last and best of all, the Ticamang, or white fish, which is of a superior quality in these waters.

— ALEXANDER MACKENZIE

FROM SAULT STE. MARIE to Grand Portage it is 720 km (or some 450 miles) along the rugged northern shore of the world's biggest body of fresh water (Lake Baikal in Russia has more water, but Superior has a greater surface area). For the voyageurs on the Lachine–Grand Portage circuit, *les mangeurs de lard* (a somewhat derogatory term referring to their diet of pork and peas and dried, crushed corn), this was the most dangerous part of their trip. Lake Superior is feared for its sudden storms and hidden shoals. On the positive side, there are no portages!

I am looking forward to the beauty of the lake, yet am wary of paddling such a small canoe on such a huge body of water. The words in three well-known Canadian songs about Superior scare me. "The big lake, it's said, / Never gives up her dead, / 'Til the skies of November / Turn gloomy" is a line from Gordon Lightfoot's "The Wreck of the Edmund Fitzgerald," his song commemorating that loss of life.[1] I am relieved that it is June. I have seen the lake freighters on the St. Marys River, and it is hard to believe that the waves could be big enough to send one of those behemoths to the bottom.

The sun, wind and icy water cleanse my soul, as well as the rocks along Lake Superior's rugged northern shore.

Ian Tamblyn writes in "Wood Smoke and Oranges": "It tossed the mighty ship around, / Smashed the lighthouse doors, / Sent shivers down my spine, / The rugged northern shore."[2]

Stan Rogers' "White Squall" tells the story of a young seaman who is swept off a big lake freighter to his death by a white squall – a sudden wind that seemingly comes out of nowhere. "Don't take the lake for granted," says the song. "It can go from calm to 100 knots / So fast it seems enchanted," is how I remember the words.[3] I'm not looking forward to one of these. What may have been a white squall nearly killed the Shepardsons on Lake Superior a mere 3 km (about 2 miles) from Thunder Bay. Carl Shepardson describes the experience: "I spotted a blue line on the horizon, no more than 8 miles out to sea. Three or four minutes later I observed that it must be the wake of some giant ship five miles off ... [I]t appeared to be [an] advancing line of breakers. It was no more than another couple of minutes and we could now see an ocean of whitecaps [approaching]. Everything was dead flat calm around us. In less than five minutes the lake around us went from flat smooth to swells. Then came the wind, whitecaps and finally combers five feet tall ... never have I seen things go to Hell so quickly."[4] Heading out on the big lake sent a few shivers down my spine too.

But the beauty of it all! Lake Huron and Georgian Bay are beautiful, but they just prepare you for Lake Superior. On Superior, the colours are deeper and richer, the water is clearer, cleaner, and colder, the air is fresher. Superior is an apt name, for she (I started to refer to the lake as "Mother Superior") truly is a lake of superlatives. With an area of 82,000 sq. km. (49,200 square miles), she is the biggest lake in the world. Twenty-five Prince Edward Islands could fit in her). Superior is the deepest of the

Great Lakes – 405 m (1,350 feet) at its deepest. She holds 10 per cent of the world's freshwater. You could dump all the water from the other Great Lakes into Superior, and she would have room left over for most of the other lakes in Canada.[5]

Of concern to me, Superior is also the coldest of the Great Lakes – "ice-water mansion," says Lightfoot; she is always numbingly cold. Even in midsummer, the average water temperature is a frigid 2.5 degrees Celsius. In sun-warmed lagoons in mid-June, when the sun is strongest, the water is still too cold for a swim. It seems incomprehensible that the water can be so cold, the air so balmy, and the sand so scorching hot, all within the space of a footstep.

Of all the Great Lakes, Superior harbours the biggest trout, is rimmed by the highest cliffs, and is buffeted by the severest storms, and its rocky coasts are pounded by the highest waves. What a lake! Even Mackenzie, usually so objective, waxed poetic about Lake Superior.

I head out on Lake Superior, 29 May, the sky hazy. A solitary tall man on shore, in the cottaged shoreline just west of the Sault, waves at me as if he knows me. Slowly, the lake opens up, as if reluctant to show her immensity. Gros Cap is the first bold granite headland so typical of Superior's north shore. The rock forming Gros Cap is deep pink, covered with bright orange lichens. The cliffs plunge straight down and disappear in the clear, green waters. I look down, maybe 15 m (about 50 feet), and see huge boulders on the bottom. It is too pretty to pass up. I stop for lunch, sitting on the bare rock, and watch the wind pick up from the southeast and the clouds lower. Wary, I continue paddling up the shore. Off my left shoulder, the shore of Whitefish Bay retreats, becoming a thin, dark line separating the grey water of the lake from the grey sky. Then it is gone.

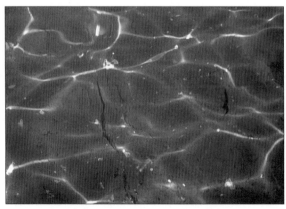

A paddler can gaze down through the pellucid waters of Lake Superior and see amethyst-studded rocks more than 10 metres (about 33 feet) below.

Today, I face my first open water crossing. It's no big deal – between 6 and 10 km (say, three to six miles), depending on how chicken I am and when I decide to leave the safety of the shore. I am in a bit of a hurry – never a good idea on Lake Superior, who dictates her own schedules. I've arranged to meet my friend Karen Mackay at Pancake Bay, at noon on 30 May. Pancake Bay is a provincial park, and the Trans-Canada Highway comes close to the lake there. It is about 77 km (about 48 miles) from the Sault – a long one-day paddle for me. So I have a cushion of half a day. However, I am keen to make this crossing today and have an easy day tomorrow. Or, if it's a miserable day, at least I won't have far to go.

There are whitecaps on the water now, and the clouds are becoming increasingly menacing. I paddle out a mile or so from shore, to see if the wind is much stronger out here. The wind is at my back, and the waves are regular. I surf down a few waves. *Loon* is flying. Under these conditions, 9.6 km (about six miles) will take less than an hour, I figure. Surfing is exhilarating, as you head down a wave diagonally, then catch the next wave. This is really fun, so much fun that, after one particularly long surf, I exclaim to the wind, "Whee, that was fun!" Never, never, never say "Whee, that was fun" on Superior! She is not that kind of lake. I pick up the next wave, and *Loon* skids down it, the spray flying in a white sheet from her bow. But when we reach the bottom of the wave, she keeps going. I watch, frozen in one of those "this can't be happening to me" moments, as the bow disappears into the bottom of the wave in front of us, piercing it like an arrow. I backpaddle furiously. When the icy fingers of Superior have inched their way up the spray cover perilously close to my crotch, *Loon* at last pulls back out of the wave. Despite the leaky spray cover, I am relieved not to feel any water sloshing around my feet.

When the next wave rises under the hull, I backpaddle until the crest has passed beneath us, then tentatively get under way again. The wind is really picking up speed now, and the bigger waves coming in from the main body of the lake on my left are colliding with the smaller, steeper waves on my right coming out of Goulais Bay. I am beginning to feel a little uncomfortable for the first time on this trip. Things are getting a little out of control. I keep *Loon* moving forward, towards the tip of the Goulais Peninsula, which of course now seems very far away, and not getting any closer. I keep fearfully checking behind me for extra-big waves and avoid surfing down more canoe-eating waves.

The waves continue to increase in size, now pushing *Loon* around, as I try to quarter them, to make their angle less steep. I can now see the waves crashing violently onto the point that marks the end of the Goulais

Peninsula. I also see that there is no place to land, so I begin to edge out to sea, to pass the point out of reach of the backswell. Safely past Goulais Point at last, I get shelter from the waves and breathe a sigh of relief. If I had to decide again whether to cross Goulais Bay or not, I would be sitting safe and dry on shore on the other side, near Gros Cap.

The wind is really howling now, but I cruise along the shore, sheltered from the main blast. It's pouring rain too, and I am looking for a place to camp. The shore is particularly uninviting here, all boulders and thick bush. A bay opens up on my right, and some cottages are in view. I cross over, buffeted now by the wind, which is whipping the water into a white froth. But there are no killer waves. As I cruise the shore, and am about ready to head back out into the lake, above the sound of the wind and waves I hear a shrill whistle. I turn and look back, certain that I am imagining things. I see two people on the shore, dressed in dark, shiny rain gear, waving their arms wildly. Puzzled, I paddle over.

"No way you're spending the night out here in this," a big man orders me. "You'll stay with us."

His female companion, water dripping from her sou'wester, continues: "We would have driven up the shore to pick you up if you hadn't seen us."

"I didn't see you," I say. "I heard a whistle. Who whistled?"

"That was me," the woman says, looking a little embarrassed. "I haven't whistled like that since I was a teenager."

It's nice to be adopted sometimes. Vince and Carol Casey offer me their guest cottage to stay in. Carol throws my wet clothes in the dryer, and they cook up a huge supper. Vince heads up the Search and Rescue unit for the Sault. I still have the black corduroy baseball cap that he gave me, emblazoned with the emblem of Sault Search and Rescue in gold and red.

"How did you see me out there?" I ask, relaxed now after a hot meal and sipping fine rum.

"Word travels fast here. One of our neighbours saw you and telephoned us about some crazy kayaker out in the storm," says Carol.

Vince points out the window of their cosy cottage: "That's where the *Edmund Fitzgerald* went down. Some of the wreckage was washed up on the shore here, life preservers and stuff like that. A few of our neighbours were here that night and saw her lights disappear."

He continues: "We've seen some strange things out there. One day there was a big mushroom-cloud explosion over the lake. The U.S. military came by the next day and told us that it was just a big bonfire out of control. Later that summer, all the kids got a strange skin rash after swimming in the lake. Very strange. We think an experimental nuclear-powered airplane went down, or something hush-hush like that."

"Wow! X-Files stuff," I think.

I'm on the water at six the next morning. A brisk breeze is already blowing. I boogie along, worried that soon I'll be forced to shore by *la Vieille* (the old woman), as the voyageurs called the wind on Lake Superior. As is usually the case when you leave early, the wind never does come up, and you could have slept 'til noon. I arrive at Pancake Bay at 10 a.m., in dense fog, wet and hungry (as usual). A few hours later – after a few cups of hot chocolate, two bowls of oatmeal porridge, and three pita and cheese and jam roll-ups – I see Karen's station wagon, with a bright green-and-white sea kayak tied on top, pulling off the highway.

I like these rendezvous in the middle of cross-continental canoe trips. They seem simpler to organize than meeting a friend for dinner on a Friday after work. Karen has taken a week off her job at Trailhead, an outdoor equipment and clothing store in Ottawa, to paddle up the coast with me. It will be a nice change after paddling alone on so much big water. But I am also concerned that I will have a hard time adjusting to fitting someone else into a life where I do what I want to do all of the time, if the weather lets me. I get up when I want to, paddle as fast and far as I feel like, eat when I'm hungry, and wait for no one.

"Karen!"

"Max!"

We hug each other.

"Boy, it's good to see you," I tell her. "It's been a long trip here."

"Sixteen hours to drive here," Karen says, "and a lot farther by water. That is a long trip. Hey, how's Sir Alex?"

Karen had given me Sir Alex, the little stuffed teddy bear, just as I was leaving, on a day that now seems so long ago and far away.

"He's a little windblown and waterlogged," I reply.

"What? Max! You've tied him to the deck. I thought you'd keep him warm and dry in your sleeping bag."

Karen is really upset. "He's an explorer," I reply. "He likes it this way. Trust me."

Karen plans to paddle with me for a week. June is the month when the westbound voyageurs usually got to Lake Superior. One of the hazards that they faced was fog. It's the 31st day of May as Karen and I head out into a dense fog – a solid wall of white. We can't see 15 m (50 feet). Heck, we can hardly see each other paddling side by side. We navigate by the sound of the waves on the shore and the occasional transport truck rumbling along

Karen Mackay cools off on a snowbank on Superior's shore near Cape Gargantua. It is the first of June.

the Trans-Canada Highway, which parallels the lake here. But by noon, the sun breaks through. That evening, as we set up camp, I realize that at the end of the day, for the first time on this trip, my ass is dry!

Karen has brought the sunshine, both literally and figuratively. We paddle on calm waters, through warm sunny days. The peace and beauty of Lake Superior seep into our souls. We camp on beaches the colour of wheat and watch the long, lazy sunsets paint the sky with hues found only inside clamshells and the dying embers of camp fires.

Lake Superior constantly amazes and entertains us. We take cheese-cake photos of each other posing on huge chunks of ice grounded on the shore. We paddle our craft through an ice tunnel, the ceiling gleaming glacier blue, dripping icy water drops on our heads. Then we paddle through holes worn in the towering black sea stack known as Devil's Chair. We are awed by the sheer cliffs of Cape Gargantua and by Old Woman Bay, where Bill Mason's ashes were scattered – his favourite place. Bill Mason was famous for his films, paintings, writings, and his love of canoeing and the Canadian landscape. One night, we see a wolf and two cubs on the island adjacent to the one we are camping on. We see a lone caribou at the mouth of a river. Each evening, we are lulled to sleep by a chorus of frogs and the flute-like trills of wood thrushes.

But if anything defines Lake Superior, it is the rock and the icy clear water. Our craft float on the pellucid skin of the lake like autumn leaves. Paddling on Superior is like flying over an alien planet. The bottom of the lake flows by, green-black in deep water, gradually lightening and bright-ening to lighter shades of green as the bottom slopes up to meet the shore and sky. The rocks are infinite in their colours and patterns. One day, I imagine that I am flying a spaceship over Jupiter. Below, the rocks are banded in stripes of ochre-red and cream, looking like the contours on a map and sculpted in smooth curves, like the lines on a Prospector canoe or like a woman's thigh (I wonder what metaphor is in Karen's mind?). A

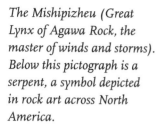

The Mishipizheu (Great Lynx of Agawa Rock, the master of winds and storms). Below this pictograph is a serpent, a symbol depicted in rock art across North America.

series of potholes is ground into the bedrock 4 or 5 m (10 or 15 feet) below the surface, the grinding stones still there. I see where Henry Moore, the famous sculptor, got his inspiration.

At Agawa Rock, we stop to ponder the pictographs painted in red ochre on the vertical cliffs. I wonder if the red ochre came all the way from the Mattawa? It is easy to imagine standing in a canoe, where the teal-green water meets the cliff, the sun warming the rock canvas. You hold a birchbark pot of red ochre mixed with oil rendered from sturgeon and with other unknown (to us) ingredients. The pictographs here are over a thousand years old. There are water snakes or sea serpents, bolts of lightning, canoes with many paddlers and canoes with only two, and a creature reminiscent of classic Loch Ness–style sea monsters, called Mishipizheu, whose backbone protrudes through its skin.

Pictograph sites from one end of the country to the other share many common elements. Often they portray animals such as moose, caribou, and bison. I saw bison depicted on the Bloodvein River in Ontario, making me wonder if they had once lived there or if the artist had perhaps travelled from the prairies. Many mythological and spiritual figures and designs are also common to sites across Canada. It makes you realize that the country has been knitted together by canoe routes for millennia, and to travel these ancient highways gives you a connection with those who have gone before.[6]

Connections. Increasingly, in our society, we are becoming disconnected – from the land, from the past, from the future, from our heritage. We live for ourselves, for today, in isolation, and measure our lives by our accomplishments and possessions. But these, as we all come to grasp eventually, have no lasting value. In the end, it is our connections, our relationships, that have meaning – with family, planet, spirit, universe. Even our art, music, and literature now tend to look inward, rather than outward, examining the self, instead of celebrating – as art used to in earlier times – the wonder of creation, the glory of God, the mysteries of the universe. Perhaps it is time for art to celebrate the earth, before it is too late.

We look at the art gallery at Agawa, created by so-called primitive people a thousand years ago. It is timeless in its beauty, and although we do not understand the meaning of the figures, their power comes through. They may just be graffiti, but if they are, they are exquisite graffiti, much more beautiful than the spray-painting of one's name on a rock, which is how people seem to decorate, or desecrate, rocks today, in both Native and non-Native communities. We give thanks that the pigments that the residents of this land mixed up a millennium ago last much longer than modern spray paint.

My mind keeps returning to the concept of beauty as a valid criterion, the most valid criterion, to judge any kind of development or project. It's so simple. If it adds beauty to the world, then it is good. If it takes away beauty, then it's bad. Everywhere, I see the loss of beauty. It is being displaced by money. Money is now the most powerful god. Society judges everything and everyone by their ability to generate monetary wealth. It continually sacrifices beauty in the interests of economics, which has led to endless repetition, uniformity, and predictability. But why not live in a world of beauty *and* wealth? The two concepts are not mutually exclusive. But we treat them that way. We cannot afford beauty, cry the politicians and the developers.

But beauty nurtures the mind. Beauty percolates like water, seeping into the minds of those who live in beautiful places. A beautiful world, a vibrant society and a healthy environment go together. But in our society, a healthy economy is always at loggerheads with a healthy environment. We can't afford it, say the money-mongers. If we don't clear-cut vast swaths, we'll close the mill. It's not economical. We can't afford to leave the trees, say the developers planning a new subdivision. It's not economical. The houses all have to look like army barracks. Otherwise, it's not economical.

I am sure that it was not economical for the Ojibwa to paint these images on the cliffs of Agawa, when they could have been trading copper to the Iroquois. It comes down to a question of spirituality. If I flatter myself as qualified to express an opinion (and clearly I do), I would say that society is heading for a spiritual crisis, is on the road to spiritual anarchy, at the same time as our species is pushing the world towards – shall we say? – major environmental imbalances.

All this reflection comes from my looking at a few old rock paintings. Check them out yourself, and see how you feel. A trail leading from the

Trans-Canada Highway in Lake Superior Provincial Park will take you there, if you would rather not paddle there.

Michipicoten, our next stop, used to be a major fur-trading centre. From here, a route led up the Michipicoten River and down the Missinaibi River (nominated as a Canadian Heritage River) to the Moose River and thence to James Bay. It is a quiet village today; most of the activity has moved a few miles east to Wawa on the Trans-Canada.

We arrive in Michipicoten early in the day. My friends Peter and Sandra Labor are there to meet us. Peter spent five summers with the Lakehead Expeditions, paddling voyageur canoes across the continent. He's been on the trail of Mackenzie from Montreal to the Arctic and the Rocky Mountains. I soon learn, much to my disappointment, that there is no hockey game on television tonight.

Karen and I are ready to leave the next morning, when she notices that I am having a difficult time packing. "What's the matter with your hand?" she asks.

"Ah, it's just an infected hangnail," I say. "Too much cold and abuse."

However, hangnails are windows to the soul, and a seriously infected hangnail is not to be ignored. Karen grabs my hand for a closer look.

"Max, that looks like more than a hangnail," she says. "I think you should get some antibiotics while we're here in a town with a hospital. The next one is Thunder Bay, and it could get nasty before then."

Karen is usually right. So we borrow Peter's car and drive to Wawa. I have a sneaking suspicion that something is seriously wrong. The end of my middle finger on my right hand is tender and red. A little more than a year ago, I had been stuck by a scorpionfish on that finger when I was in Honduras on vacation. I had to endure a four-hour boat ride to the nearest hospital to get medical help. I sang Jimmy Buffett songs all the way to take my mind off the pain. I feared that I was going to die, and I am sure everyone on the boat was wishing that I would, or at least pass out. At the hospital they filled me with painkillers and anti-venoms. The doctor warned me that there was a danger of infection later, but I didn't think that she meant a year later.

I waggle my finger for the emergency doctor at the hospital in Wawa. He says, "Hmmm," and fetches a colleague. He too says, "Hmmmm," and brings a third doctor. I hear the word "surgeon" mentioned, and I'm starting to sweat, with three guys in green smocks staring at my finger and all chanting, "Hmm."

I am told to come to the hospital every six hours for a shot of antibiotics for the next three days. If that doesn't work, they will have to operate. The surgeon gives me a textbook that describes the possible procedure. I begin to read it before I leave. Peel back this layer, drain the fluids out of that sack – and "ooooh" – I suddenly don't feel very well. A nurse asks me: "Are you OK? You look pale. I think you should lie down."

"Just take this book away from me," I say. I'm really not very good in hospitals.

I recuperate slowly at Peter and Sandra's, while Karen heads off alone farther up the lake to Dennison Falls. The antibiotics work. My finger turns all kinds of colours, like a Lake Superior sunset, and swells up. That's a good sign, the surgeon says – I will probably be able to continue my trip in a week or so.

"Stuck in Wawa for a week!" I say to him. "I thought that only happens to hitchhikers!"

"At least you'll be able to watch the playoffs," he replies.

Bonus. The Detroit Red Wings, my favourite team since the glory days of Gordie Howe, win the Stanley Cup.

Karen returns from her solo excursion, brimming over with enthusiasm, and revelling in the solitude of paddling such a big lake on her own, but her vacation is over and she has to head back to Ottawa. With the playoffs over, and a big hole in my finger where the surgeon has drained it, I have no reason to hang around any longer. I put on a big bandage, cut the end of the finger out of my paddling glove, thank my incredibly generous hosts, and head out for Dennison Falls.

Dennison Falls is on the Dog River, a couple of miles in from the coast. An army of sculptors could not produce in a lifetime a waterfall so beautiful. Words fail miserably to describe it. If there are "power points" on the planet, where lines of force as yet undefined by physics meet, surely this is one of them. It is not just the beauty of the falls. The feeling of well-being that one has standing beside it or, better yet, under it is – um, well, it's orgasmic. Perhaps standing on the top of Kilimanjaro or Everest might compare. I am serious. Go there and see for yourself.

I play hide and seek with the fog and tag with the wind all along the coast of Pukaskwa National Park. While Mother Superior sleeps, I try to put miles behind me. I pass headland after headland. Waterfalls tumble like white curtains into the lake. I paddle inland on the Swallow River and get treated to the most beautiful waterfall of all. Back on the lake, on my left, the ghostly cliffs of Michipicoten Island, 20 km (12 miles) out, change shape, appearing like thunderheads and then dissipating to a thin, dark

Every river and stream entering Lake Superior on the northeast shore does so in dramatic fashion. This is the Cascade River in Pukaskwa National Park.

line. Every campsite has a vista of the lake and the setting sun. I stop to investigate the ruins of the logging camp at Pukaskwa Depot. I wallow in the Pukaskwa Pits, ancient depressions made on a gravel beach, waiting in vain for visions. One night soon afterwards, I hear the far-away, lonely wail of a train whistle.

I am closing in to Hattie Cove, where a road has been built to the coast in Pukaskwa National Park. As a long-time Parks Canada employee, I'm looking forward to meeting the park staff. A few miles south of Hattie Cove, a group of kayakers can be seen heading my way. I change course to intercept them.

"Hi, Max!" floats over the water from a two-seater kayak.

"Oh, hi, Dan! Hi, Dianne!" I reply, a little stunned.

Dan Malette and his wife are from Ottawa. Dan and I paddled together on the Soper River on Baffin Island. We often train together in Ottawa for canoe racing. I had no idea that they were coming here. But they knew that I was heading up the coast.

"We wondered if we'd run into you. We rented the kayaks from Peter Labor in Michipicoten, and he told us all about your infected finger," Dan says.

No time for much talk. The wind is picking up. I head north for Hattie Cove; Dan's group heads south towards Michipicoten. Neither of us can predict that we will all be windbound for the next three days. But I am lucky. In Hattie Cove, Bob Reside, the park warden, and his wife, Cathy Widdowson, take me out to dinner and give me space in the staff residence to stay, while the wind and rain thrash the lake and Dan and Dianne huddle in their tent.

Bob and I talk of some of the problems facing the park. Pukaskwa is a wilderness park, bordered on the west by the wild, rocky shore of Superior, cut by tumbling rivers and cloaked in dense boreal forest. The only road into the park is at Hattie Cove. A 60-km (37 1/2- mile) trail runs along the coast. The only other way to see the park is by boat, canoe or kayak. The park is big – 1,878 sq. km (1,127 sq. miles). Yet the wildness of this remarkable area is in jeopardy. Only about forty woodland caribou survive in the park today. Members of this species require extensive, undisturbed old-growth forest, where they can find the lichens that they live on festooned on the trees. When the park was set up in 1978, it was a protected wilderness within a much larger unprotected wilderness. Today, it is an island of wildness surrounded by roads, mines and clear-cuts. Big as it is, it is not large enough to contain all the elements needed to support wide-ranging creatures such as caribou and wolves.

On my trip, I see at first-hand all across Canada the fragmentation of our remaining wilderness. There are many places that look just as they did when Mackenzie passed by, but underneath there have been fundamental ecological changes. More disturbing, the changes are taking place at an ever-increasing rate. Logging is the most obvious incursion into the wilderness of the Canadian Shield. Although computers were predicted to create the "paperless" office, the world's appetite for wood fibre to make paper seems insatiable. Logging roads penetrate deep into the Shield's boreal forests. One mechanical harvester takes the place of forty-five men with chainsaws and scars the forest much more deeply. Deep forest creatures, such as caribou and pine marten, are disappearing. The wilderness that Mackenzie knew exists only as isolated vestiges of landscape.

At noon on my third windbound day at Hattie Cove, I finally build up the courage to leave, sneaking cautiously up the coast, tight to shore. Mother Superior is still restless, but the storm has blown itself out. I have been so fortunate to be able to watch it from shore. At the northeast corner of Lake Superior, the railway dips down to the lake. Red rock cliffs alternate with black cliffs here. The railway track runs below the cliffs for a short distance, disappears in a tunnel blasted through the cliff, continues over a trestle where a river tumbles in, and then retreats back into the boreal forest. The train whistle that I heard several nights ago must have been from here. Could I have heard the whistle blow a hundred miles – just as in the song made popular by Peter, Paul, and Mary?

I'm looking forward to Rossport, a small community on the north shore. I pull up to the dock at the Halcyon Haven, a little store that sells groceries and fishing gear and, most important, French fries, fried lake trout and ice cream. I eat on the dock and watch the lake trout jump out in the bay. The setting seems idyllic.

Then I go back inside for another cup of coffee.

Rose, the owner, asks the usual questions: "Where you heading?"

"Saskatchewan," I answer casually. People usually don't know how to react to that.

"When do you think you'll get there?"

"End of July."

"When d'ja leave Ottawa?"

"May 7."

"Ya tired?"

"You bet I'm tired. And hungry. Where's that pie and ice cream?"

"Who do you work for when you're not paddling?" Rose asks, probing a little too pointedly.

"I work for National Parks," I reply, a little hesitantly, "for a program called Canadian Heritage Rivers."

There's silence from Rose and the other customers. Something is up.

"Boy, do we want to talk to you," Rose says. "Don't go anywhere. I've a few phone calls to make."

Soon, a group of townsfolk gather in Rose's restaurant. The topic is the National Marine Conservation Area (NMCA) proposed by Parks Canada for a large area of Lake Superior near Rossport. I am in the hot seat. An NMCA is an area managed for ecologically sustainable use. The townspeople are concerned for the future of commercial fishing, tourism and their own traditional recreational pursuits. They worry that motorboats could be prohibited and that they will not be able to go to their favourite islands.

A fellow named "Joey" plunks in my lap a copy of the *Parks Canada Policy for National Marine Conservation Areas*.

"See," he points. "It says right there that motor boats may be prohibited."

"Well, that's true, but it doesn't mean they will be," I stammer. "You have to work out this kind of stuff with the planners from Parks Canada."

"Yeah, but can we trust them?" He lists all the Parks Canada people who have been to Rossport recently. There's clearly a lot of distrust of government in this town, and there's a lot of angry murmuring from the assembled folks.

"You'll just have to make your own judgment about what's best for you and the lake and your community, but I think the NMCA would be a good thing. Those guys from Parks Canada wouldn't be here if they didn't think it was a good thing. This isn't a government land grab."

I am exhausted by the time the crowd grows tired of grilling me about all the words in the policy book and what an NMCA really means. I assure them that it is not part of a world-wide conspiracy to take over all the world's coastlines and rivers. (There's some mumbling about me, as an employee of the Canadian Heritage Rivers System, being part of this conspiracy.) No, their homes will not be expropriated and their families relocated to the far north. Most of their concerns, however, were well-founded and centred on maintaining their way of life.

"That is exactly what an NMCA would ensure," I tell them over and over again.

I leave the next morning, feeling that I should be paid overtime and a per diem for travelling so far to discuss Parks Canada issues. I thread *Loon* through the islands fringing Nipigon Bay. The rocks here are amazing! Native people mined copper here for thousands of years, but I am fascinated by the amethysts and agates. Some of the gravel beaches are made of agates! Every handful of beach gravel contains gems! Through the clear waters, I can see purple amethyst crystals embedded in the lake bottom. On one point, boulders of amethyst lie scattered about. I pick up the smallest and throw it as hard as I can against a bigger one, but only tiny fragments break off.

I am on the water again when I hear a motorboat heading my way. In minutes, a black-hulled speedboat pulls up beside me and the driver says, "I want to talk with you about the marine conservation area. Why don't you follow me to my cabin for lunch?" I have the feeling that this is an order.

I shrug and look forward to free beer. By the time I tie up to a dock in a sheltered cove on a nearby island, Tim is in the cabin and has the kettle boiling on the wood stove, and the soup is hot. Over steaming coffee and thick pea soup, he explains that he runs outfitting and fishing camps and is worried about how the NMCA might affect his business. I reassure him that his kinds of activities would surely continue, but I feel that he may not be revealing all his future plans. I worry about jet ski resorts and that kind of tourism. I cannot imagine a more beautiful area for jet ski touring, but try to banish the thought from my mind.

I head southwest along the outer edge of the Black Bay Peninsula towards Silver Islet and the cliffs of the Sibley Peninsula. I keep The Paps, two high hills reminiscent of breasts (have I been travelling alone too long?), on the point of the Black Bay Peninsula on my right, the open lake on my left. A dense wall of fog is out on the lake, sliding closer to shore, then back out to sea. As it comes shoreward, I watch islands disappear one by one, as if they are eaten up by the fog. I wonder if it's coming to eat me?

On a tiny island between Magnet Point and Magnet Island, I see an old red "Drink Coca-Cola" sign, on a shed beside a dock where two commercial fishing boats are tied up. Never one to pass up a Coke, I tie up beside the fishing boats. A woman, obviously friendly, comes out of a small white house, with a beer in her hand. She introduces herself: "Hi! I'm Donna, and this is Ron Gerow," she says, as a large, friendly looking, middle-aged man follows her outside.

Ron is a fifth-generation fisherman. He tells me that all the buildings on this island were built over a century ago. He takes me into the shed and shows me his father's linen fishing nets and ice chisels that ring like tuning forks. It is like a museum of commercial fishing.

"I've dragged up all kinds of things out of this lake," Ron tells me, "including a Sony video camera." He shows it to me. "But the most interesting stuff is all the Native artifacts. I think lake levels must have been much lower, and I set my nets along old shorelines that are now shoals."

When I ask him about the fishing, he tells me: "The fishing is as good now as it was in my granddad's time, but it takes four times more fish to support a fishing business. My granddad hired six men to help him. I fish alone, 'cause I can't afford to hire anyone."

I wonder if it would be more economical to go back to smaller boats and pay for hired help.

The next morning, heading over to the Sibley Peninsula, I pass a commercial fisherman hauling in his nets. I paddle over to see what he has caught. He yells at me: "Hi, Max!"

His name is Jim Mackay, and he knows Gail Jackson, the Parks Canada planner in Thunder Bay working on the NMCA idea. Word travels fast, faster than I can paddle. Jim gives me a nice five-pound lake trout for supper.

I poke around the tiny island off the village of Silver Islet where silver was mined under the lake over a century ago. It was one of the richest silver deposits known in the world at that time. I can see the opening to the mineshafts through the clear water. I wonder how they kept the water out? I paddle over to the mainland, to the village of Silver Islet, a cluster of brightly painted wooden homes, reminiscent of a Newfoundland outport. Accompanied by the local dog, I walk up to a store, but it's closed. I'm just leaving when a woman comes to the door and says, "You look like you need a coffee."

"And pie and ice cream," I add, hopeful. As I devour four-berry pie that rivals the raspberry pie at Valois' Restaurant in Mattawa, she tells me that the miners used a big coal-fired pump to keep the water out of the mineshafts. But the pump broke down (it's rumoured that the foreman was drunk, she adds coyly), the mine flooded, and it never reopened.

The wind is high and getting higher, so I don't linger. I head for the tip of the Sibley Peninsula, where there is a bird-banding station and a cabin owned by the Canadian Wildlife Service, and maybe someone to share my lake trout with.

I am awestruck as I paddle. The cliffs rise up almost 300 m (1,000 feet). Nestled on the point in a grassy meadow is a cluster of wooden cabins, with the cliffs of the peninsula rearing up behind them. This is a nice place to band birds, I think to myself.

There are three biologists at the main cabin – Dan, Euell and Cole. I offer to contribute a fresh lake trout for supper, and they provide a pizza. These guys have a great setup here. In the tradition of Scandinavian people who settled this part of the country, there is a sauna, which is heavenly after weeks of icy cold water. I sweat out the chill of Lake Superior water and fog and fall asleep in the guest cabin (for visiting scientists, I suppose), lulled to sleep by the sound of a porcupine eating the cabin and the mice partying. Tomorrow, I'm going to take a full day off paddling and hike the cliffs of the Sibley Peninsula.

Some day off! I get up at dawn and hike all day. I am exhausted! I climb up and down those cliffs four times. I just can't help myself! I am amazed to see the lake from the perspective of a peregrine falcon (falcons, reintroduced to this area, nest on these cliffs), especially after having been stuck on its surface for so long. The only negative thought that keeps wriggling into my brain is that I should be paddling. From the cliff top, I can see across Thunder Bay all the way to the city of the same name, and the water is dead calm all day. I have a 25-km (15 1/2-mile) crossing tomorrow – the longest of the trip so far – and I'm hoping for a day like this.

The trails of the Sibley keep me jogging all day long. My knees ache after climbing up The Chimney, at the very tip of the peninsula. I've been sitting in a canoe for a long time. The Natives call the peninsula the Sleeping Giant, or Nanabosho; I climb up his chest and nose. Nanabosho was a giant who had led his people to this peaceful haven. When he found silver, he swore his people to secrecy and made them bury the precious metal under water. But one warrior made himself weapons of silver, and when he was killed in battle with the Dakota – his people's traditional enemy – the search was on to find the source of the silver. Nanabosho saw a canoe with Dakota and two white men coming, and so he raised a storm. The canoe capsized, and all the men drowned. This angered Manitou, the Great Spirit, who turned Nanabosho to stone. He can still be seen, stretched out on his back.

I am ready to head out before dawn for the crossing to Thunder Bay. I first call Gail Jackson, the NMCA planner, on the radiophone from the cabin, and she is to meet me for breakfast the next day at the harbour in Thunder Bay. I try not to think of the Shepardsons' experience with a white squall on their approach there. It's a beautiful, star-lit morning as I point *Loon*'s bow towards the lights of Thunder Bay twinkling in the west and set off. Soon the sun paints the thin morning clouds blood-red and rose pink, violet purple and every shade in between. When halfway across, a brisk wind out of the west springs up, slowing me down. The big grain elevators do not seem to be getting any closer. But three hours after setting out, I pass the lighthouse that marks the entrance to the harbour. I notice that the word "lighthouse" on the very official-looking sign erected by the Coast Guard is missing the "t."

Gail is there as I pull into shore. Halfway to Saskatchewan. Whew!

Gail and her family treat me royally. I call up Bill Ostrom, pack-maker extraordinaire,[7] and he whips me up a new spray cover for *Loon*, so I can keep my ass dry. I get cleaned up, wined and dined and resupplied. Gail, her husband Mike Fratell, and the kids take me on a picnic, and we swim in a lake with warm water. Now that's a treat.

I leave Thunder Bay from Old Fort William, the reconstructed historic site set 10 kilometres (six miles) up the Kaministiquia River. The main inland headquarters of the North West Company was moved to the original Fort William from Grand Portage in 1801. The Nor'Westers knew that the Grand Portage headquarters was in U.S. territory, and it was only a matter of time before taxes and duties would make business there untenable. Fort William served as a trading post until 1878.

The Canadian Pacific Railway levelled the original post to make way for the train lines to pass along the north bank of the river. Today, the rebuilt post proudly stands as it did in its heyday in 1815, when the "lords of the lakes and forests" – as fur trade chronicler Washington Irving coined the top officers of the North West Company – held court here in sumptuous banquet halls with all the amenities that one could find in the palaces of Europe.

I head down the murky Kaministiquia towards the lake for the final dash to Grand Portage. One more night camping on Mother Superior. I am sure that she has some surprises left in store for me.

What a night! The thunder is booming, and I can hear, not far away, the cracking of boulders as they bounce down a slope. But by dawn, the sound and fury of the storm give way to the sound of veeries singing up a storm – a beautiful, musical storm.

I am right. Mother Superior does not want to let me go. To add to the matter, I'm a little disoriented, as my map, of course, stops at the U.S. border. I have sketched the islands and points on the way to Grand Portage from a map that Peter Labor showed me back in Michipicoten. But I always get lost crossing over the edge of map sheets.

When I think I must be near Grand Portage, the wind suddenly picks up from the west, trying to blow me out into the maw of the lake. The wind almost rips the paddle from my hand, it's so strong and sudden. I skirt the shoreline, making a giant 19-km (12-mile) detour to avoid a short open crossing, and sneak up along the peninsula to what I think may be Hat Point. Here, the voyageurs traditionally put on their hats and finest, most colourful shirts and sashes, to make a grand entrance to the post at Grand Portage.

It's wild at the end of the point, with "Duluth Rollers" crashing in. Taking a deep breath, I pull my hat down and head out. I make hardly any headway against the wind. But wind is always strongest at the end of a point, and inch by inch, I work my way towards the tip. There it is, at last, the big wooden stockade of Grand Portage, with a gambling casino, built in Las Vegas style, beside it. Praise be, I must be in the Good Ol' U.S. of A! I paddle up the dock and can barely crawl out of the boat. Brenda Beck and Eric Harris are waiting for me, and they support me as I stand and sway on the dock. I've been on the water too long. I'm land-sick. I manage a weak "Ya-hoo!" But somehow, my arrival is anti-climactic.

Brenda and Eric take me to the reconstructed fort. They plan to video-tape me crossing the 15-km (9-mile) Grand Portage – the historic trail to the west. I am too tired to party. We celebrate by booking a room at the casino next door to the fort (I'm sure that gambling is a traditional activity, but this casino has all the neon and tackiness of Las Vegas) and sleeping.

I have mixed feelings about leaving Lake Superior. She has shown me many faces. She is a lake of extremes and contrasts. The most rugged, most beautiful, most exhilarating lake; she is friendly and frightening, gentle and violent, never boring. Her infinite variations on the theme of rock, water, and forest create the most beautiful of scenery. But most of all, paddling Superior is an emotional experience. A relationship is forged between paddler and lake. Like your first love, this relationship stays with you forever.

I've now travelled about 2,000 km (1,250 miles) since leaving Ottawa.

8

The Boundary Waters

*The river [Pigeon River] continues to be shallow, and requires
great care to prevent the bottom of the canoe from being injured
by sharp rocks.*

— ALEXANDER MACKENZIE,
ON THE PIGEON RIVER

MUCH OF MACKENZIE'S ROUTE across Canada feels abandoned
today. It is the same feeling as walking the deserted streets of a
ghost town. Along the route, tumbledown trapper's cabins and overgrown
portage trails speak of a much busier time when this was the route of commerce and life, travelled by the fur trade canoe brigades and Native people.
When David Thompson went this way in 1797 – first moving eastwards to
Grand Portage, to change employment from the Hudson's Bay Company
to the North West Company, and then heading back out west again – he
described meeting brigades of canoes and passing Native encampments
and villages almost daily. Hardly a wilderness experience!

To this point, except for a few sea kayaks paddling the coast of Pukaskwa,
I have seen only one other canoeist, just upstream of Ottawa. But this section
of the route will prove different. It is still a busy place for canoes. In fact,
it may just be the busiest "wilderness" canoe area in the world.

It is 500 km (300 miles) from Grand Portage to Lake of the Woods.
Grand Portage is the eastern terminus of the Boundary Waters–Voyageur
Waterway, which follows the international boundary westwards for 250
km (150 miles) from the mouth of the Pigeon River on Lake Superior's

western shore to Lac la Croix at the western boundary of Quetico Provincial Park. This part of the route consists of narrow river channels and convoluted lakes. Most important, from here the water drains in three distinct directions. From an almost imperceptible height of land, in a boggy portage between North and South lakes, one trickle heads to Lake Superior, and another, to Hudson Bay, while water a little way south is soon heading to the Mississippi. Less spectacular than the Columbia Icefields of the Rockies, this is one of the continent's most important watershed divides, where a random gust of wind can determine if a drop of falling rain flows to the Arctic, the Atlantic, or the Gulf of Mexico.

In 1999, the entire length of the Boundary Waters–Voyageur Waterway was designated by the Canadian Heritage Rivers System for its legacy as a fur trade route, for its unspoiled wilderness, and for its incomparable value as a canoe-tripping mecca.

Conservation is not new here. In fact, this was one of the first areas in North America where wilderness conservation was an issue. The year 1909 saw the establishment of Quetico Provincial Park in Ontario and of Lake Superior National Forest across the border in Minnesota. This is Sig Olson country – a name that I would run into again on the Churchill River in Saskatchewan, more than 2,000 km (1,250 miles) west. Olson was one of the continent's most outspoken and effective conservationists. Here is where Sig found his "singing wilderness," in the lake country, where people still travel by pack and canoe over the ancient trails of the Natives and the voyageurs.[1] Olson led the way to protect the area from logging and hydro-electric development. The Boundary Waters Canoe Area in Minnesota, boasting over 2,400 km (1,500 miles) of canoe trails, is the legacy of his commitment to preserving this treasured land. What better legacy could anyone leave? The route also runs through more recently established pro-tected areas – Ontario's Middle Falls and La Verendrye provincial parks, along the Pigeon River, and Minnesota's Voyageur National Park, west of Lac La Croix.

Grand Portage is named after the gruelling 15-km (9-mile) trail bypassing the Pigeon River's plunging cascades and canyons. I must admit, I am feeling a little smug about this portage. Brenda and Eric, my faithful video crew, have brought my canoe wheels. I plan to roll *Loon* and all my gear over the portage. Verlen Kruger described the trail in *One Incredible Journey* as "wide enough to drive a jeep down." That was in 1971.

Before hitting the trail, I have a crisis to resolve. I have a sore throat, a sniffly nose and do not feel very energetic. But worse, the insides of my thighs are chaffed. I'm walking like a cowboy who has spent too many days riding a fat horse. This rather embarrassing condition is the result of paddling for hours in soaking wet underpants in very wavy conditions on Lake Superior. Seemingly I use my legs to paddle and to balance in the big waves more than I imagine. So, rather than feeling like celebrating after my arrival at Grand Portage, my first priority is to find a tub of Vaseline.

Grand Portage is situated at the eastern end of an ancient portage. By the mid-1730s, it had become the main approach west to the vast fur lands of the interior. The first fort was built here in 1778, to protect the fur trade from the U.S. army. From then until 1802, it was the main inland headquarters of the fur trade. That year, the North West Company moved its headquarters north to Fort William, to keep the fur trade route entirely in Canadian territory. Here, the brigades of 36-foot *canots de maître* delivered their cargoes of trade goods that had come all the way from Lachine (now part of Montreal). The voyageurs would party and rest up for the return trip, laden with furs from the north and west brought by *les hommes du nord* – the traders who lived in the *"Indian country."*

Today, the fort has been reconstructed, complete with the Great Hall, warehouse, kitchen, fur press, lookout tower and palisade. Grand Portage National Monument is staffed by interpreters in period costume. But in olden times, the Great Hall would sometimes spill over with a hundred partners and clerks of the fur trade, the tables laden with venison and fish, the wine and spirits flowing, and Scots, Frenchmen and Native men and women all dancing together to the bagpipes and fiddles. The bourgeois of the North West Company would gather to feast and discuss plans for expanding their fur empire. The list of people who sat at the great table reads like a "Who's Who?" of Canadian history – Alexander Mackenzie dined here, as did David Thompson, Alexander Henry the younger, Roderick Mackenzie, Duncan Cameron, Cuthbert Grant and Duncan McGillvray. I ask a young man dressed as a voyageur in a blue-striped shirt and corduroy trousers about the trail. He asks where I have come from and where I am going. I see his eyes cloud over in that faraway, misty look that I have seen many times before. "Gee," he says. "I'd love to do something like that some day, but I haven't even been over the Grand Portage Trail yet."

The voyageurs from Montreal each had to carry eight *pièces*, each weighing 41 kg (90 pounds), over the portage. I should have realized from Mackenzie's journals that my wheels might not work as well as I had hoped. He reported that both horses and cattle had been tried without success.

Nevertheless, I set off, with *Loon* strapped securely to the "wheels" and my pack stowed inside. The voyageurs normally did not take canoes over the portage. Canoes were waiting at the other end, at Fort Charlotte on the Pigeon River. These were the smaller, more nimble *canots du nord*, paddled by four, five, or six men and able to carry thirty-five *pièces*.

In 1922, members of the Minnesota Historical Society cleared the route of the old portage that I am about to follow. I set off jauntily, rolling along the trail, but do not get far. I run into an obstacle that the voyageurs would not have to face – a boardwalk. The boardwalk over a swampy section of the trail is too narrow for the wheels. I unstrap *Loon* and carry my packs and canoe over the boardwalk in two trips, then tie everything back on. A short distance farther along, there is another boardwalk. I repeat the procedure. Then I run into another boardwalk, and another, and another. Then there are the logs across the trail that I have to lift the canoe and pack over. Not to mention the boulders that tip the load over on its side repeatedly.

Add a ka-zillion mozzies and deer flies to the mix, and steamy temperatures. A few days ago, I had wished for summer to come, and all of a sudden, it is here in all its ferocity. I haul my ungainly load up a steep hill, my head pounding with the heat and exertion. I glance down at my sweaty body. Not a single square centimetre is not soaked with sweat, right down to my ankles. My head starts to spin, or at least that's exactly how it feels. At the top of the hill, there is a road. I decide to ditch the wheels in the bush, but at that moment Brenda and Eric drive by, ready to film the triumphant modern voyageur.

"Water," I gasp. "I need water." Brenda already has their camp stove going, brewing up a pot of coffee. "This will perk you up," she says. I sit in

Starting out with enthusiasm on the Grand Portage. A few minutes after this photograph was taken, I was no longer smiling. Boulders, logs across the trail and narrow boardwalks over swampy areas rendered my canoe wheels useless on the trail.

the shade of a tree, sip instant coffee, and then carry on in the traditional way, without the wheels. They finish the portage in Brenda and Eric's van.

Some hours later, I arrive at the Pigeon River, tired, bug-bitten and not feeling in the least triumphant. Little do I know that the worst is yet to come.

Brenda and Eric are able to drive to the site of Fort Charlotte at Partridge Falls – another 400-m (1,330-foot) portage. I do not even remember the falls, which Mackenzie describes as *"considerable, over a perpendicular rock of one hundred and twenty feet."* Except for the portage trail, all traces of the glory days of the fur trade are quickly left behind at Grand Portage. Not a trace here of a fort – only a clearing at the end of the road where Brenda and Eric have parked their van. We paddle together up the little Pigeon River, looking for the *"Prairie"* that Mackenzie mentions, where we hope to camp. The land along the river is low and swampy, and we end up camping in a "mozzie-pozzie," perhaps the dreariest campsite of the entire trip across Canada. We set our tents up in a wet, "hummocky" sedge meadow, where each footstep leaves behind a little puddle of water, a breeding pool for more mosquitoes.

My diary entry reflects my mood:

> *What a change from the fresh breezes of Lake Superior. It's hot and muggy and my whole body is itching from bug bites. There are no-see-ums crawling all over me, and I'm looking at several thousand black flies, about a dozen deer flies, and one moose fly on the roof of the tent. Outside, there's a ka-zillion mosquitos trying to get in. I put earplugs in to drown out their whining (I wondered why I brought them). Just a few days ago, I wished for summer to hurry up and get here. Now that it is here, I wish it would hurry up and go away. Once again, I ask myself why I am doing this?*
> — Max, 27 June 1997, on the Pigeon River

The next morning I continue upstream, while Brenda and Eric return to their van, promising to meet me at Mountain Lake, what looks like an easy day's travel for me. But like a boxer on the ropes, I find that this part of the route just keeps slugging me, not giving me a break.

"Oh, man, what a day!" "This is really tough." "God, what a route!" "This country sucks!" These are just a few excerpts from my journal of 28 June. I walk *Loon* up the shallow, fast-flowing Pigeon River, watching carefully for a small clearing that marks Fowl Portage. It should be called "Foul" Portage, I remark. *"Two thousand, four hundred paces,"* says Mackenzie. Since his time, about two thousand, four hundred trees have fallen over the trail, which I think has not been cleared since he walked over it. Direct descendants of the mosquitoes and black flies that tormented Mackenzie swarm around me. On the next portage, a muddy trail to Moose Lake, the sole of one of my trusty old running shoes peels off. Not even duct tape will reattach it. As I launch *Loon*, her rudder cable snaps. "I'll fix it later," I mutter to myself. On the next portage – Portage de Cerise, or the Great Cherry Portage – the zipper to my bug jacket breaks. My mood is not improving. As I portage into the first muddy little water lily-covered pond before Mountain Lake, it's getting dark, and I realize that I've been travelling in a bad mood for about fifteen hours. Waiting, watching for me, at the muddy little pond are Brenda and Eric, in bug-suited finery, with their video cameras rolling. We paddle together in the gloaming down lovely Mountain Lake, to a roadside campsite where they have parked their van.

As I lie awake that night, itching from head to foot, the no-see-ums tormenting me, I seriously contemplate hopping in Brenda and Eric's van and driving back home with them. I need a holiday. However, with quite a bit of encouragement from my friends, I decide to continue. It can only get better. Right?

Wrong! I get lost. Paddling along the international boundary presents some unexpected challenges – like trying to follow the route on my 1:250,000 topographical maps, which have a shaded line along the boundary that obscures all the details along a swath about 2 km (1.2 miles) wide. At the end of Mountain Lake, I will take Watap Portage, which was a newly opened route when Mackenzie passed through. It leads to the Long Portage, which Mackenzie refers to as *"the new Grande Portage, which is three thousand, one hundred paces over very rough ground, which requires the utmost exertions of the men, and frequently lames them."* Needless to say, I am not really looking forward to this!

It is early morning, the sun is already "stinking" hot, and the bugs are out in force. I carry *Loon* and my gear over the portage. I have just loaded the canoe and am getting under way when two men paddle towards the portage. They have no packs in their canoe, have no bug-jackets, and are wearing bathing suits and nothing else. Watap Lake has no access to it other than the Long Portage. How did these two guys get here, I wonder?

"Hello. Did you come over the Long Portage?" I ask.

"Nope," one drawls. "Just paddled from the lodge."

"Um, is this Watap Lake?" I ask, tentatively.

"Nope, this here's Clearwater Lake," the other replies. Both look remarkably the same.

I take out my map, and we all peer at it. Sure enough, there's Clearwater

Lake, south of Mountain Lake. I have taken the wrong portage. So I lug my pack and canoe back over the portage to Mountain Lake and search the shore for another portage. I paddle all around the western end of Mountain Lake, but no other portage. I look at my map again and can imagine a route from Clearwater Lake to Rose Lake, the destination of the Long Portage. So I haul my canoe and pack back over the portage a third time, determined that this would be the last time!

What a great decision this turns out to be! I paddle to the lodge at the end of the lake, where Bob Marachino, the owner, gives me ice cream, soda pop and a good map. He explains that I am not the first to end up there by mistake and that it is a much better route than the Long Portage.

Bob looks me over and says: "You look pretty darn tired. I'll bet you'd like a night in a cosy cabin. If you want, I'll telephone the Hestons on Gunflint Lake and tell them to expect you in about four hours."

It takes me six hours to get there. Along the way, I cross a major continental watershed, between South and North lakes. It is an anticlimactic traverse. Somewhere along the boggy portage lies the height of land dividing waters flowing to Hudson Bay from waters flowing to the Atlantic. When Mackenzie and his party reached this divide, they held a small ceremony, as was the custom for men crossing it for the first time. It apparently involved their swearing never to kiss another voyageur's wife against her will, firing of a lot of muskets into the air, and everyone drinking an extra dram or two of rum or high wine.

It feels great to be going downstream. There's a perceptible current sweeping me into Gunflint Lake. I paddle into Heston's Lodge just before dark. Barb and Greg provide me a cabin, a shower and a cosy bed, in exchange for stories. I am back in the land of rock and pine, and already I can feel the energy from the Canadian Shield feeding my tired bones. Once again, I am looking forward to seeing what is beyond the next bend.

Sig Olson considered Saganaga Lake the most beautiful lake in the world. Or maybe it's the next lake, Cypress Lake, with its crystal-clear waters and cliffs etched with orange lichens. This is beautiful country, and it lifts my tired soul. Rock, water and pine are the essential elements of this landscape. Who could ask for anything more?

Well, I could ask for a new pair of running shoes. Oh, the gods must be listening, for there, on a tiny, rocky islet in Saganaga Lake, are a pair of running shoes. Washed clean and white by the waves, in perfect shape, they are placed as if someone's feet were still in them. Perhaps the owner has been neatly abducted by aliens, leaving behind only these mementos. I

The canoe route to the west follows the international boundary between the U.S. (Minnesota) and Canada (Ontario) along the Boundary Waters–Voyageur Waterway. Stone cairns mark the boundary, not the portage trail.

paddle to shore to pick them up, scaring a mother loon off her nest. She charges me, her wings beating the water, her loon-voice frantic. "Sorry," I apologize to her, "but I need these shoes." Sadly, they are a size too small. Nice try, gods of Quetico.

Darkness is falling, but I decide to make the traverse to the Cache Bay Ranger Station, on the off chance of a free supper. I can see the light from the ranger's cabin shining across the lake.

"You must be Max," a woman sitting on the dock says to me, as I pull up. "I've been expecting you." She is Janet Matichuk, a warden for Quetico Provincial Park. Chris Taggart had passed by some weeks earlier and told her that I should be along eventually.

Lucky me, I get invited for supper with Ranger Janet and two pretty seasonal rangers. I explain my shoe, or lack thereof, to Janet. She offers me a pair of her husband's running shoes. He's a big guy, or at least his feet are. Three sizes too big though they are, who am I to be picky? We toast in Canada Day, 1 July, the next morning before I head out, with one oversized running shoe.

For the first time in my journey, I begin to meet other canoeists, just as David Thompson did on his travels through here almost two centuries ago. One group asks me if my permits are for the American or the Canadian side of the waterway. I look at both shores, shrug, and tell them that it all looks like one country to me. Besides, I don't have a permit.

It is high paddling season, and Quetico is crowded. I meet a guy in a sea kayak heading east, from Lake of the Woods to somewhere on Lake Michigan. I haven't heard of the place where he is going, and he hasn't heard of Ottawa. He seems kind of surly, and I am sure that he thinks the same of me. I end up sharing a campsite with a nice family from Florida, out for a fifteen-day holiday. I cook up a big bannock for all of us, and they share their main course – noodles with a fancy wine sauce, a nice change from my usual beans and rice, Kraft Dinner or spaghetti. Then the rain and the mosquitoes drive us into our respective tents.

I enjoy paddling with other canoeists through Quetico. I point out faded pictographs along a narrow channel to a group of boy scouts. The sight provides a tangible link to the past. Just as at Agawa Rock on Lake Superior, one can easily imagine the artist standing up in his canoe with his birch-bark or clay pot containing a mixture of red ochre and sturgeon oil. We ponder the images of the Maymaygwashi, mischievous, hairy-faced little men, less than a metre high, who live in the rock faces.

Legends of small, mischievous hairy men occur in cultures all around the world. My own childhood was filled with tales of dwarfs, elves and gnomes, all small and endowed with magical powers. There are also lep-rechauns in Ireland; *Agogwe,* dwarfs with long, red hair, in Africa; and *Nittaewo,* little men also covered with reddish hair, with long claws so that they may disembowel you if they don't like you, in Sri Lanka. Don't forget the *Orang pendek,* a race of little humans with large canine teeth reputed to inhabit the jungles of Sumatra. These legends have even become part of our modern North American culture. The New Jersey Devils hockey team is named after a race of fierce little humans who once lived in that state's Pine Barrens. The legend dates back to before the time of settle-ment and was passed on by the original inhabitants to the English settlers.

It makes some sense that these legends may have a basis in truth, as most legends do. Fossils found by the Leakeys, that famous family of anthro-pologists, in Olduvai Gorge in Tanzania show that the Australopithecus (of which Lucy is the most famous member), *possibly* our direct ancestor, was only 121 cm (4 feet) tall. Perhaps other species of humans lived at the same time as Homo sapiens and survive in our legends. Perhaps in some yet-to-be-explored corner of the jungles of South America, the little men still exist. I like to think so, if only to reassure myself that the world above the oceans still holds some unsolved mysteries.

Perhaps these legends contain more truth that we would like. In April 2001, DNA analysis could not identify reddish hairs from Bhutan, suppos-edly from a Yeti – another legendary human-like creature similar in description to Canada's Sasquatch – as belonging to any known creature. Perhaps such creatures may be behind us as we walk through the woods. Maybe we are not alone. Maybe we do not know as much about the world as we think we do. Mackenzie recorded that an *"Indian"* asked him: *"Why are you so curious about the country? Do not you white men know everything in the world?"* Apparently not.

We also noted the images of large triangular torsos with arms, legs and heads. Were they fierce warriors, or the mythical thunderbird, or a combi-nation of both?

Basswood Falls, one of the scenic waterfalls along the Boundary Waters–Voyageur Waterway.

Later, I meet two rangers in a big 18-foot canoe, and we paddle together for the afternoon. I ask them to videotape me running the rapids on the Basswood River. To make it dramatic, I run close to shore and deliberately aim for some big standing waves. The first wave dumps into my lap, and the force of the water rips open the Velcro closure on the spray cover. The next wave ends up mostly inside *Loon*'s belly. Sheepishly, I bail out at the bottom of the rapid. A lesson that I would be taught (if not learn) more than once on this trip: if it's really important, don't attach it with Velcro. There's a lesson like that about reef knots too, but I'll save that one for later.

I paddle into Lac La Croix in driving rain and whitecaps on 2 July. I am looking for Picture Rock, which Mackenzie and other travellers all remarked on. *"Within three miles of the last Portage* [a muddy trail that Mackenzie doesn't even name] *is a remarkable rock, with a smooth face, but split and cracked in different parts, which hang over the water. Into one of its horizontal chasms a great number of arrows have been shot, which is said to have been done by a war party of Nadowasis or Sieux, who had done much mischief in this country, and left these weapons as a warning to the natives that it was not inaccessible to their enemies."*

There are no arrows in Picture Rock today, but a number of striking pictographs, handprints and a beautiful drawing of a moose.

Voyageur National Park in Minnesota, established in 1975 to protect the routes of the fur traders, honours their legacy as well in the naming of the park, but not in the mode of travel encouraged there – it is a motorboat park. Today is 4 July, and naturally all the campsites are taken. I rather boldly invite myself to occupy a tiny corner of a very spacious site, occupied by two families from Minnesota. The amount of gear that they have boggles my mind. They joke that it took them two trips to get here – one

A pictograph of a moose on Lac La Croix in Quetico Provincial Park. The moose was considered by the Ojibwa to be a difficult animal to hunt. Perhaps depicting the hunted animal in rock art could enhance the hunter's luck.

for the gear, and one for the people. It must make camping such an immense effort, I think to myself, to pack and organize all this stuff, like moving house. I must admit, however, that I am envious of the cooler of beer. Luckily, tonight I get to enjoy the beer without having had to haul it.

The wind on Namikan Lake, a big, wide-open body of water, really kicks up this afternoon. I am anxious to get an early start tomorrow, to paddle the some 65 km (forty-odd miles) of Rainy Lake all the way to Fort Francis. I'm in such a hurry because my finger – the one that got infected in Wawa – is very painful again, and I am looking for antibiotics. I read ahead in Mackenzie's journal and discover that he had a reputation as a good doctor and that he used balsam fir pitch to cure infections! On one occasion, he used a poultice of *"bark, stripped from the roots of the spruce-fir* [balsam fir]*, having first washed the wound with the juice of the bark. In a few days, the wound was clean."* He also made a salve of *"balsam, wax, and tallow."* Anxious to do something, I collect a bowl of pitch from the trees around the campsite, and go to sleep with my infected finger immersed in the goopy stuff.

I wake up at 2:30 a.m. My finger is throbbing. In the sky above, there is an amazing show going on. Eight meteors streak across the sky as I watch, transfixed. Or maybe it's just the infection spreading. I pack up and head out at 3:30 a.m. to take advantage of the morning calm. I wrap my finger in a thick wad of bandages and gauze and make up my mind not to think about it until I get to Fort Francis. I portage into Rainy Lake and head west, but I do not get far. The wind is howling, and there's no way that I can paddle such a big lake today. I check the map on the glossy brochure for Voyageur National Park (I've given up on my 1:250,000 maps and navigate now using place mats and tourist brochures) and see a more sheltered all-U.S. back route via Kabetogama Lake to Black Bay, a large bay extending south of the main body of Rainy Lake, only 16 km (about 10 miles) east of Fort Francis.

I stop for breakfast at the hotel at Kettle Falls. Time-warp! I'm not expecting the hotel to look just as it did in the 1940s, including not only the costumed help, but even the paying customers. Strangely, after I battle wind and the amazingly cold weather for July (there was a frost last night), for half a day my finger is throbbing less, rather than more.

This turns out to be one of my hardest days yet. The wind continues to howl out of the northwest. I curse the wind and paddle on. I feel abandoned and lonely, much lonelier than I have ever felt before. On extended solo wilderness trips, I never feel lonely or forlorn for long; because there is no other human being around, no one can remind me that I am alone. Today, motorboats continually buzz by me. I am struggling on big water, with a long way to go, and I know that in an hour or less, they will be warm, dry, and knocking back a beer with friends, while I am still out here paddling in the rain and wind. Most significant, we cannot communicate. We may as well be in separate worlds. At best, we acknowledge each other's presence with a wave. Often, it seems that I just do not exist at all. And that transforms the solitude, which can be glorious, into loneliness, which is never fun.

The 24 km (about 15 miles) of Kabetogama Lake I paddle with each stroke an effort. The portage to Black Bay, a wide-open body of water surrounded by low bulrush marshes, is a taste of the prairies. As I head out across it, the clouds darken, drenching me with cold, wind-driven rain. I scream at the wind:

"Is this the best you can do, stupid wind. I'm still moving forward. Hah-hah!"

Never mock the wind. It hears my words and notches up a few kilometres.

"Hah-hah!" I laugh. "You're nothing but a summer breeze. My mother could blow you away!"

It hears me again and blows even harder. With the visitor centre in sight, on a swampy bay about one metre deep, I'm stuck. Windbound. But I refuse to give in. Now it is a battle of wills. The last kilometre takes probably an hour, but I get there. I am totally exhausted, but, you know, my finger (remember the finger – the reason I'm trying so hard to get to Fort Francis and a hospital to get antibiotics) does not hurt. I would have thought that after a day of battling cold and wet and wind, the infection would be raging. But it seems to be gone. I wonder if the balsam pitch "sucked" out the infection? I'll never really know, but I won't forget about balsam pitch and its magic – real, imagined, or merely coincidental though it may be.

I leave *Loon* securely tied up to the dock at the visitor centre and hitchhike into Fort Francis with a kindly park interpreter. At the hospital, the emergency doctor looks at me a little strangely, but he agrees with my assessment of the situation and prescribes antibiotics, which I pick up at the local pharmacy. However, I have no intention of taking them now. I'll just keep them for insurance in case the infection comes back. Then I head to the Fort Francis Hotel for a well-deserved and long-overdue beer. The superintendent of Voyageur National Park, Barbara West, has invited me to stay for the night. She picks me up at the hotel, and we drive to her home. Lucky for me, her husband's feet are the same size as mine, and I "borrow" a pair of sparkling white, alarmingly new tennis shoes. I feel rejuvenated. My finger problem and my shoe problem seem to be over.

I whine to Barbara about the terrible weather for July and present her with this simple graphical weather record:

> Since Leaving Lake Superior:
> Nice days: 1.5
> Just plain rainy: 2
> Rainy, windy, and cold: 3
> Howling gales: 2.5
> Stinking hot, humid, buggy, and rainy: 2

But the next day dawns sunny, with a light breeze from the west. Barbara drives me back to the visitor centre, and I paddle the remaining 16 km (10 miles) to the twin towns of Fort Francis and International Falls. In Mackenzie's time, this was the site of an important inland post. *"It is necessary to select from the pork-eaters, a number of men sufficient to man the North canoes necessary to carry, to the river of the Rainy Lake, the goods and provisions requisite for the Athabasca country, as the people of that country, (owing to the shortness of the season and length of the road, can come no further), are equipped there, and exchange ladings with the people of whom we are speaking, and both return from whence they came."* The round trip from Grand Portage to the Rainy Lake Post took about a month. Meeting the *"pork-eaters"* here gave *les hommes du nord* a head start to arrive back at Fort Chipewyan before the frost and ice.

Mackenzie explains *"pork-eaters"*: The staple food for the run from Montreal to Lac la Pluie was corn and melted fat. *"The corn for this purpose is prepared before it leaves Detroit, by boiling it in a strong alkali, which takes off the outer husk, washed and dried. One quart of this is boiled for two hours in a gallon of water ... to which are added two ounces of melted suet; this causes the corn to split, and in the time mentioned makes a pretty thick pudding. If to this is added a little salt, it makes an wholesome, palatable food, and easy of digestion. This quantity is fully sufficient for a man's subsistence during twenty-four hours, though not sufficiently heartening to sustain the strength necessary for a state of active labor. The Americans call this dish hominee."* Corn was the cheapest food available, and a man's daily allowance did not exceed ten pence.

I ask Barbara for the easiest way around the dam at Rainy Lake. Her answer is brief and to the point: "I'll meet you there with my pickup truck."

Barbara lets me off just below the dam and drives back to her considerable responsibilities as manager of a very busy park. My responsibilities are much simpler: eat, sleep, paddle, don't get lost. Before me is a big, placid river, burbling peacefully through a gentle valley of maples and oaks and farm fields. The rock and pine land of Quetico and the boundary waters seems far away. The Rainy River cuts through the bed of glacial Lake Aggassiz, coursing just beyond the edge of the Canadian Shield. Its banks are of rich soil, not the ancient pre-Cambrian rock that I have become used to seeing. Although I love the landscape of the Canadian Shield dearly, and in fact describe myself as a child of the Shield, I find the gentleness of the valley of the Rainy River a welcome change.

So did Mackenzie: *"This is one of the finest rivers in the North-west. Its banks are covered with a rich soil, which ... are clothed with fine open groves of oak, with the maple, the pine, and the cedar ... its waters abound in fish, particularly the sturgeon."*

The Rainy River, though a mere two-day paddle from its beginning to Lake of the Woods, stands out in my memory as one of the most beautiful sections of the entire route. Its strong current carries me past meadows of daisies and brown-eyed Susans, pleasant farms with wooden barns painted rusty red, and lush deciduous forests with spreading oaks inviting me to curl up for a snooze under them.

I pass a pretty young woman, sitting with a little girl in a field, among the high grasses and daisies. They are wearing long dresses, with a blue-and-white checkered pattern that one often sees in paintings depicting farm life in the early twentieth century. My canoe drifts, and my mind drifts. I think of endless summer days lying in meadows just like this, watching the clouds drift overhead and the butterflies and bees busy gathering pollen and nectar from the flowers. I think of those fields today, covered with houses and apartments of Ottawa, the few remaining ones now empty of butterflies and bees. I wonder what children growing up there today will remember? The woman and her child wave at me. I wave back and drift on towards Emo.

Emo. This town may have been just a "Coke Stop" for Alec Ross in his epic journey,[2] but for me, it means home cooking and a soft bed. Buzz and

Louise McComb, the parents of my friend Murray in Ottawa, live here, and Murray has asked them to treat me like one of the family. Buzz and Louise are waiting for me at the dock in Emo, a pretty town on the banks of the Rainy River. They take me home with them and stuff me full of home-made blueberry pie, Nanaimo bars, chocolate chip cookies, and a turkey dinner with all the trimmings.

I have planned to take advantage of their hospitality and take a day off to resupply for the run to Hecla in Manitoba. Here's a typical list of chores to do on a layover day:

> Unpack the box of dried food that I had mailed here from Ottawa – always a treat to see what surprises are there.
> Seam-seal the spray cover (Lake Winnipeg is not too far away, and Lake of the Woods is just around the next bend).
> Mail back film and journal pages to Parks Canada in Ottawa for the web site set up by Wade Hong.
> Mail back videotapes to Brenda and Eric, the video crew.
> Mail back the oversize running shoe that Janet Matichuk had given me in Quetico.
> Buy groceries (peanut butter, cheese, tortillas or pita, and stuff like that).

I don't even have a Coke in Emo. But I do have a great visit with the McCombs, and I leave stuffed with food. It's only 80 km (about 50 miles) to Lake of the Woods. I stop at the Kay-Nah-Chi-Wak-Nung Manitou Mounds interpretive centre, just being built (now completed). This Native centre offers a view of life here over three thousand years ago. It is staffed mostly with First Nations people, all of whom seem excited by the project – heart-ening to see this expression of pride.

At the town of Rainy River, a crowd of kids plays in the river, while their mothers relax by the water. It reminds me of a scene from the 1950s. What sticks in my mind is that everyone seems so relaxed and happy. I get involved in a water fight with local kids and have a great time throwing the biggest ones off the dock.

I decide to camp at a commercial campsite where the Rainy River meets Lake of the Woods. But I find these sites so annoying and inconvenient. First, the attendant charges me $15 just to put up my tent. The tent site isn't even close to the water, so I have to lug all my gear here. I wear my earplugs at night to drown out the noise of the other campers. Clearly, I am getting crabby and grumpy.

On the positive side, I have a nice visit from a young couple (the husband is a doctor, and his wife a nurse, in Rainy River). The wife had seen me in town that day, and they track me down just to talk. We all comment on the noise, and the husband invites me back to their home for the night. But I decline the offer. It is clear to me that I've been travelling too long, because the thought that forms in my mind is: "Sure, I'd love to go back home with you, as long as I can snuggle up with your pretty wife."

The next morning, I set out across Lake of the Woods. It is like no other lake I have seen and, I am sure, like no other lake in the world. It is unique. Like Lake Superior, it is a lake of superlatives. Here's a few. It has more islands than any other lake in the world. Its shoreline is longer than Lake Superior's. In fact, the owner of the Whitefish Bay Lodge tells me that its shoreline is longer than the circumference of the earth!

Lake of the Woods is two very different, very big lakes stuck together. One is a prairie lake, rimmed with bulrush marshes, sandy beaches and sand dunes. Here the endangered piping plover finds secure nesting sites. Its waters are murky and rich. Large warm-water fish, like muskellunge, abound. I paddle to an island sand dune. Terns wheel overhead. Schools of minnows flash through the shallow water. For the first time in my life, I see flocks of white pelicans, drifting gracefully like hang-gliders over the lake. I'm awestruck that such an ungainly looking bird can move with such amazing grace.

The other face of Lake of the Woods is the Canadian Shield. The lake here is peppered with rocky islands and islets (more than 14,000 of them) and shoals, with deep green water and rocky shores. Giant lake trout thrive in its cold, deep waters. In small bays, almost completely enclosed by islands, the water is a different colour. Lakes with lakes within lakes. The line between the lakes can be abrupt.

The fur traders normally followed the "Grand Traverse" – the most direct route, but a long, open-water crossing. I chicken out and follow a more protected, eastern route. A short canal cuts through the neck of the Aulneau Peninsula, eliminating what was once a short portage. On the north side, the water is the deep coniferous green typical of cold lakes on the Canadian Shield; on the south, a pea-soup green typical of prairie lakes.

I navigate through the maze of islands using placemats picked up at fishing lodges. I stay close to islands to avoid the motorboats and to enjoy the scenery. I share a spaghetti lunch with a group of American tourists at the French Narrows Lodge. On the evening of 10 July, I squeeze through

Devil's Gap, buffeted by motorboat wakes, and head for the dock on Kenora's waterfront. My best friend in Ottawa, David Kippen, has telephoned his mother, Doreen, who lives in Kenora, and I know that she is expecting me. A lone sea kayaker, an anomaly in this lake of motorboats, meets me at the dock.

"Hi, you must be Max," he says.

"Uh-huh," I nod. I'm tired and don't feel like talking.

"My parents telephoned me that they saw you paddling by. I see you need a new kayak paddle," he continues.

The wooden blade on my kayak paddle has begun to delaminate, and one blade is now considerably narrower than the other. It makes me paddle with a slight limp.

"Uh-huh," I nod.

"I own a camping store in town. I'll fix you up. Is there anything I can do for you now?" he continues, hoping to get more than a monosyllabic response from me.

"I need a drive," I say. "Do you know where Doreen Kippen lives?"

He drives me to her home in town. I'm ready for a rest, but Doreen has other plans. She has invited her extended family and even an acquaintance of mine from Ottawa, Jamie Benedickson, who spends his summers in Kenora, to a party for me. I am overwhelmed by the welcome. Doreen convinces me to have a little holiday in Kenora. I make an appointment for a massage the next day at the clinic in town. The masseuse comments that she has never seen muscles so tight.

No one can stay in Kenora for long without someone explaining that the name of the city comes from the first two letters each of the communities of Keewatin, Norman, and Rat Portage.

On 12 July, Doreen drives me back to the dock, where *Loon* and I are reunited. Together again, with a brand new kayak paddle, we head for the Rat Portage and the Winnipeg River.

9

Winnipeg: River and Lake

There is not, perhaps, a finer country in the world for the residence of uncivilised man. It abounds in everything necessary to the wants and comforts of such a people. Fish, venison, and fowl, with wild rice, are in great plenty; while at the same time, their subsistence requires that bodily exercise so necessary to health and vigour.

— ALEXANDER MACKENZIE

I N THE ERA OF THE VOYAGEURS, the Winnipeg River ranked with the Ottawa in difficulty and beauty. Mackenzie lists twenty-nine portages over 225 km (about 135 miles). Over this short course, the river drops 100 m (325 feet). But today, seven hydroelectric dams have submerged almost all the rapids, making a series of long (and boring) lakes out of what Eric Morse called in his book "unquestionably the grandest and most beautiful river the Montreal Northmen saw on their whole journey from Lake Superior to Lake Athabasca."[1]

Rat Portage, at the outlet of Lake of the Woods, has a boat elevator, which I take to lower *Loon* and myself gently and effortlessly to the placid bay. For the first few hours, the current of the Winnipeg sweeps me along between smoothed rock chasms, reminding me of the French River. The day is very hot and humid. Still in party mode from my stay in Kenora, I paddle to a fishing lodge and order a beer at the bar. A small knot of fishermen gathers around, asking the usual questions:

"Where d'ja come from?" "When d'ja start?" "When ya gonna quit?" "Geez, I'd sure like to do something like that."

To the last remark, I reply: "You know, from here you can travel by motorboat all the way to Lac la Croix in Quetico Provincial Park, or, if you go the other way, well, if you can arrange for a pickup truck to take you around the dams, I figger you could take a motorboat to Saskatchewan without any problem. What's stopping you?"

"Heck, we couldn't pay for the gasoline! It costs me $2 just to start the motor," drawls one grizzled, beer-gutted fisherman.

I just shrug and wonder why fishing boats are designed to sit still 99 per cent of the time and go like stink for the other 1 per cent. It makes no sense to me.

The next morning, I am heading for White Dog Dam. It rained about 7.5 cm (about three inches) last night, but the sun is shining, and I am enjoying drying out. I hear a fishing boat catching up to me, and soon it pulls alongside. It is piloted by an elderly gentleman whom I recognize from the bar last night.

"I'm Jesse Hanson," he introduces himself. "Mind if I come along with you for a while?"

This is the first time that anyone in a motorboat has actually talked to me.

"Sure," I reply. "Glad to have the company. I've sung all my songs, Alex the Bear and I have nothing left to say to each other, and the days are getting pretty lonesome. I've been on the water for more than two months now."

Jesse comes from California but lives up here half the year. "I love this country, and I love to fish," he says, just as we both look wide-eyed at a muskie rolling on the surface behind us. I don't know what directed our gaze to the big fish. It made no sound, but, fishermen that we both are, something made us look behind us just before it came up. Jesse put-putts alongside me for the entire morning, until we reach White Dog Dam. We have one of those rare conversations that go straight to the heart of every-thing that matters, sliding effortlessly through love, fulfilment, happiness – where we have found them and, more significantly where we have looked for them. At the dam, Jesse helps me carry *Loon* and my packs over the portage.

The Native reserve named White Dog made headlines in the 1980s when residents became paralyzed and went blind because of mercury poisoning. The condition, known as Minemata disease, is named after a Japanese fish-ing village where the effects of mercury poisoning were first documented. The White Dog Reservoir had been polluted by mercury used in the pulp and paper industry upstream at a mill in Dryden, Ontario. In addition, any time a reservoir is created, natural mercury in the soil is released into the water. The mercury passes up the food chain, from microscopic organisms, through insects, small fish, and large, predatory fish, to piscavores such as loons and people. The biggest, oldest fish have the most mercury concentrated in their fatty tissues.

As a child growing up on fish caught in the Rideau River – also, like the Winnipeg, transformed into a series of long lakes by dams – I shudder to think of the concentration of deadly mercury in my fatty tissues. Hmmm, could this explain a lot of my behaviour?

As I paddle by the community of White Dog, built on a hillside overlooking the river, I see no evidence of the terrible tragedy that took place here. I am surprised by the large new schools, the community centres and the bright bungalows with tidy lawns and gardens, all looking very urban and out of place here. Some Native children are swimming off the dock. I join them and invite them to take *Loon* for a spin. As I head downriver (or rather, down-reservoir), I spot several people out in boats fishing. I paddle over to a couple in a Scott canoe[2] (just like I have at home). Nazareth and his wife don't worry about mercury, and, as we chat, he lands a hefty pike for supper.

I continue down the Winnipeg River. As I paddle by a small sign marking the border of Ontario and Manitoba, I let out a feeble cheer. At last, I am paddling in another province. The rain is so thick that I can barely read the sign. After paddling for more than two months in Ontario, I don't feel any sense of elation. It's raining just as hard in Manitoba, and the mozzies are just as thick.

I take breaks at the fishing lodges. Although I am really just looking for a place out of the rain, I get treated with overwhelming kindness. At Eaglenest Lodge, Inge brings me a steaming bowl of oatmeal (I don't tell her that this is the 87th bowl of oatmeal that I've eaten since leaving, and, besides, any food is better if someone else cooked it) and freshly baked oatmeal cookies. Farther along, at the lodge at Kendall Point, Daryll treats me to venison sausage and smoked marlin (the marlin was brought by a client of the lodge).

The weather picks up, and so do my spirits, thanks mostly to everyone's kindness. A Hydro worker in a pickup truck picks me up as I am portaging around the dam at Pointe de Bois (pronounced "Point deboyz"). I stop at a resort to fill my water bottles (the water is now very murky and smells like dead fish, the result of millions of carcasses of "fish flies" that cover the surface).

At a small restaurant, part of the Barrier Bay Resort, I order French fries, a grilled cheese sandwich and a milkshake. When Kevin Nally, the owner, brings the 'shake, he leaves the metal container, full to the brim. Refreshed, I get up to pay.

"That will be forty-six cents," he says.

I look at him, puzzled.

"The cost of a stamp for a postcard from Cumberland House," he explains. I scribble his address down in my journal.

I race a thunderstorm across Natalie Lake, the reservoir of the huge Seven Sisters Dam – a concrete structure miles wide. I wonder about lightning strikes and generating stations and put away my trusty carbon-fibre paddle (an excellent conductor, I'm told). Just moments ahead of the storm, I scoot past the "Dangerous Water – Keep Away" warning sign (I'm getting very nonchalant about these signs after the fifth or sixth dam) and land at the top of the structure. A worker at the dam comes to meet me.

"I've been watching you come for about two hours. I figger you could use a helping hand. I'll get my truck," he says.

That night, I find myself camped in a municipal park in the prairie town of Lac du Bonnet (pronounced "lag-Duh-bonny"). Fields of bright yellow rapeseed (now canola) surround the town. The Canadian Shield lies to the east. Now, at last, I feel like I'm getting somewhere. This is a reason to celebrate. I am a prairie boy now. I walk into town for a beer. Tomorrow, *Loon*, Sir Alex (looking a little bleary-eyed, but still stubbornly holding on to his position as lookout on the deck of *Loon*) and I should reach Lake Winnipeg. The date is 16 July.

Mackenzie does not mention his trip across Lake Winnipeg in his narrative and I am tempted to copy his approach and spare you all the gruesome details. I don't know what happened to him. But I do know that everyone who takes on Lake Winnipeg in a canoe has scary adventures.

Alexander Henry, the younger, describes in great detail his journey with his brigade on Lake Winnipeg from 12 to 18 August 1808. Each day at least one squall threatened their canoes or flattened their tents. He observes on 12 August: "The rain fell in torrents, and the wind blew a hurricane. The land is very low, a very ugly, gloomy country." On 13 August he writes: "Our position was rather unpleasant. The sea dashing with great violence against the rocks, and the extreme darkness of the night, and every appearance of the wind increasing made me anxious to find a convenient place to land."

On 15 August: "We had a most terrible squall of Wind with Thunder and Lightning and a heavy shower of Rain. My Tent was blown down, and we passed a most uncomfortable, wretched night and wet to the Skin." On the sixteenth: "The wind continued to blow hard, we shipped much water, the swell was so high that, in rounding a point, we nearly filled several times."

In the entry for 17 August: "the sea ran so high while were under sail, that at intervals we lost sight of the masts of the canoes not more than 30 yards distant."[3]

Two hundred years later, the weather on Lake Winnipeg clearly has not improved, as the Shepardsons found out. It took them an agonizing three weeks to put the big lake behind them. Carl summarizes the primary rule of Lake Winnipeg: "There is no such thing as an easy day on this lake."[4] The nights can be hard too. A storm hit the Shephardsons as they camped on a beach. Soon tents were blowing away in gale-force winds. "The lake was beginning to go wild ... the water had risen twenty feet. I shall never forget the scene. It reminded me of a hurricane I'd once seen at Cape Cod. The 'ocean' was frothy white and churned up as far as we could see. The water was flinging itself across the sand, the fury of the huge waves was awesome."[5]

Eric Morse, in *Fur Trade Canoe Routes of Canada: Then and Now*, writes: "This is probably the worst lake in Canada for small craft."[6] This is a prairie lake, and on a prairie lake, there are no hiding places. The shorelines are low and rocky, or low and "peaty." Limestone cliffs and boulders lying just below the surface make landing difficult.

My head filled with these dire descriptions, I set out on Lake Winnipeg, the water shimmering silver under a big prairie sky. The sky is alive with motion, ever changing, as restless as the lake beneath the hull of *Loon*. Phalanxes of bright white cumulus clouds appear on the horizon and march across the sky, transforming into menacing dark grey the towering thunderheads. The sky is even bigger here than over Lake Superior. This is a land of sky. To paddle on the prairies, as I am to find out, is to paddle in the sky.

I course north up the east side, sliding among low islands of weathered granite, the last outcropping of the Canadian Shield, which disappears beneath the limestone underpinnings of the prairies. The dense boreal forest stops abruptly at the shoreline, a low wall of dark peat-tangled roots and decaying wood.

I head to shore, where I see a few cabins at the head of a shallow bay. Two boys and a girl, all about seven years old, play in the tall grass. There are boats pulled up on shore turned upside down. A door slams in the wind. I do not see any adults until an old man walks out of one of the cabins. Like many First Nations people, he has aged gracefully. His hair is thick and black. He stands erect. There is physical power in his large, stocky frame. Only the lines on his face, story lines, betray his age.

"I've fished here all my life," he tells me, "and I've really seen the lake change. Of course, there's fewer fish now, fewer pickerel and sturgeon and whitefish. Too many fishermen. But the water is lower too, and it's murkier since they put the dam in up north [at the outlet on the Nelson]. And it stinks more, the water."

By the afternoon, the wind picks up, and I pull ashore on a narrow sandy beach, backed by the ever-present dense spruce forest. I hunker down in the sand and fall asleep.

I realize that I am not only dealing with a difficult lake, but I am also fighting myself. I've been trying hard not to admit it, but I'm just plum tuckered out. I'm "paddled" out. I'm "all-alone-in-the-canoe-all-day'd" out. I'm "beaned-and-riced" out. I'm "peanut-butter-and-bannocked" out. I'm tired of cooking oatmeal. The thrill and sense of anticipation of what lies around the next bend or beyond the next point have faded out. I think back to the words of John, a Native fellow whom I met in Lac La Croix, in Quetico. I was cooking bannock in the ranger station. He took a look at me and said that I needed to slow down. "I see the tiredness in your eyes," he said. "You're pushing yourself too hard." He was right. I wonder how Chris Taggart feels right now, paddling somewhere ahead of me, perhaps on Lake Winnipeg. I wonder what he is thinking at this moment.

The wind is down by evening, and I head out. But soon the wind picks up again, from the north. I realize one of the rules of Lake Winnipeg: When the wind lessens, it is not dying down, but gathering strength to blow from another direction twice as hard. I find a sheltered campsite, the best I've seen all day, and set my watch alarm to go off at 3 a.m., hoping to take advantage of the early morning calm.

Taking a break from the wind and waves on the east shore of Lake Winnipeg.

I am really in a lovely place. The shoreline here is similar to Georgian Bay, made of smooth, rounded granite, with patches of bright orange lichens shining golden in the setting sun. Flocks of pelicans float by, and gulls and terns fill the sky. But camping is not as idyllic here as it is on Georgian Bay. The shore is lined with a thick mat of rotting carcasses of "fish flies." They smell just like rotting fish, hence the name. I strain all the water through a handkerchief, to remove the parts of fish flies, and then run it through my water filter, which, of course, instantly clogs. Titration is more successful. However, my supper of beans and rice definitely has a little scent of dead fish flies. My hands smell like fish flies.

I wake up and shine a flashlight on my watch. 4:45 a.m.! I've overslept! The lake is calm, the full moon playing peek-a-boo through drifting clouds. I scurry around in the dark, stuffing everything into *Loon* and carefully shoving yoghurt containers of oatmeal and rice pudding and a bannock, all of which I cooked up last night, under the seat for easy access. With the mozzies swarming, I'm sure that I'm all packed up and ready to go in record time.

I paddle out as fast as I can, trying to leave my whining escort behind. I head north, using Polaris as my guide. After an hour, I begin to wonder why dawn hasn't arrived. The wind is picking up, and I can see two navigation lights in the distance, marking the route, I am sure, to the community of Manigotagan. I check my watch. It is 1 a.m. I guess I was hallucinating when I looked at my watch before. So here I am, in the middle of Lake Winnipeg, in the middle of the night, with the wind rising.

Paddling at night in Lake Winnipeg is, in general, not a good idea. It is hard to find safe landing sites, and there are many rocks lurking just below the surface, even far out from shore. Often, the pelican just ahead is, in fact, a rock. Sometimes, it's a pelican on a rock. Bumping a rock or two in calm water is no problem, just another indignity, but when the waves get high, it is like running white-water in the dark. I am getting uncomfortable, and when I bump into a rock that is bigger than normal, I decide to pull *Loon* up on it and wait for dawn. The pelicans and terns are laughing, I'm sure, at a guy in a purple rain jacket sleeping on a rock in the middle of Lake Winnipeg.

I leave at dawn, skirting the south shore of Black Island, heading for the community of Hecla. That's where I have directed my final boxes of mailed dried foods and supplies. Also, I was scheduled to give a presentation at Hecla Provincial Park that evening, hence my hurrying. At 9 a.m., I pull into the dock at Hecla. I extricate myself slowly and stiffly from *Loon* and stand on the shore, swaying slightly.

A man and his little girl come over.

"We've been watching you for about an hour," he says. "It looked like the waves were going to swallow you up."

"Yeah," says his daughter. "We'd see you, then you'd be gone and then pop! You're back again. I didn't think you were going to make it."

I do not even remember how I got to the restaurant in Gull Harbour. I do know that someone paid for my breakfast (my third of the day). I do not remember my presentation, but there is a photograph of me beside a hand-written sign saying: "Take a tour in the canoe that has paddled here all the way from Ottawa, only $5.00." I do not remember getting any customers.

The wind blows all the next day, and the next, and I'm happy for the rest. But I am getting into a squeeze. I am scheduled to meet Brenda and Eric in Grand Rapids in four days. They are flying from Toronto to Winnipeg and renting a car there. They plan to follow me by road as best they can and then rent a motorboat on the North Saskatchewan River for the trip to Cumberland House.

There is no way that I can paddle to Grand Rapids in four days. I now face a very difficult choice. Do I wimp out and get a ride to Grand Rapids with Brenda and Eric, or do I continue on and tell them that I'll get there when I get there? Brenda and Eric are paddlers, and they understand that there is no hurrying on Lake Winnipeg. I know that the wind will go down. I also know that I am exhausted, and the thought of another week on Lake Winnipeg, with the big open sections ahead, is not something to look forward to.

I sit by the lake and stare at the waves, hour after hour. Finally, I make my decision. I call Brenda and Eric, and we discuss the situation. They will pick me up on 22 July. I have four days to rest!

"Here's something to keep you safe on the water." Phil Manaigre hands me a necklace made from a black leather thong strung through a water-worn stone, set off by a few beads. "The hole in the stone is natural," says Phil. "It's a symbol of good luck on the water in Icelandic culture." Hecla was founded by Icelandic immigrants, as a fishing community. The provincial park celebrates the Icelandic culture.

I am overwhelmed. Phil heard that I was here and drove up from Winnipeg to meet me. I had heard of Phil because of his love of paddling Lake Winnipeg and his search for amber in Cedar Lake, the reservoir created by the massive Grand Rapids Dam. I promise to keep an eye out for rocks with holes, to search for amber, and to take cigarettes for the elders whom I would probably meet on Cedar Lake.

Brenda and Eric arrive on schedule, and we strap *Loon* on the roof using a child's inflatable water toy to cushion *Loon*'s tender bottom. Kumar Sundaram, eighteen years old, is with them. He came from India a few months ago to live with them and go to school in Canada. Brenda and Eric thought that he should see the country. He has no idea what is in store for him, and no idea how many mosquitoes are awaiting him.

Four hours later, I unload *Loon* into the waters of Cedar Lake, above the dam at Grand Rapids.

10

Grand Rapids to Cumberland House

On entering the Saskatchiwine, the great rapids interrupts the passage.

— ALEXANDER MACKENZIE

WHERE GREAT RAPIDS AWED MACKENZIE, the Grand Rapids Dam, built in 1963, now plugs the mighty North Saskatchewan. The once-awesome rapids, plummeting between limestone cliffs, are merely a trickle. Gone too is the *"excellent sturgeon fishery at the foot of this cascade, and the vast numbers of pelicans, cormorants, &c"* of which Mackenzie speaks in his journals.

There is no trace left of the canoe portage that Mackenzie and his men followed. In the town of Grand Rapids and below the dam, however, there are remnants of the tramway built in 1877 for York boats, the cumbersome wooden craft that eventually replaced birchbark canoes on many of the fur trade routes.

I launch *Loon* in a quiet bay on Cedar Lake above the Grand Rapids Dam and soon learn a lot about reservoirs. When Mackenzie came through here, Cedar Lake was noted for its abundance of fish and wildlife: *"Its banks are covered with wood, and abound in game, and its waters produce plenty of fish, particularly the sturgeon, abound with geese, ducks, swans, &c."* The dam raised the water of Cedar Lake about three and a half metres or twelve feet. This does not sound like a lot, but no trees were cut before the river was plugged, and the rising waters have spread out over the almost-level spruce-forested land, more than doubling the size of the original lake and creating a huge mess. There is no real shoreline, only a gradual transition from shallow open water to shallow water clogged with standing and fallen silvered spruce trees. I remember playing a game when I was young called "pick-up-sticks." You dropped a bundle of skinny chopsticks in a pile and tried to extricate individual sticks without moving any others. It looks like someone has played "pick-up-sticks" here with trees. The submerged trees force me to paddle out in the middle of this 100-km- (60-mile) long swamp, in the full sweep of the prairie wind. It is the worst piece of canoeing water that I have ever paddled.

In the afternoon, the wind whips out of the south, and I head for the shelter of a small island, hauling *Loon* up over the spruce logs piled along the shore like a fallen palisade. Some are anchored in the lake bottom, others floating, most both floating and stuck, making the trip to the solid shore very precarious. Unlike most bodies of water, where the liquid stuff is for paddling and the solid stuff bounding it is good for standing on, Cedar Lake has a third state of matter – neither land nor water, but a mixture of both that can be neither paddled on nor stood on. I quickly learn this when I try to take a "short-cut" and get hopelessly stuck in a ghost forest of fallen trees in the middle of the lake.

I try to follow the old shoreline of Cedar Lake, coursing the edge of the silvered, ghostly, flooded forests to the town of Easterville, marked as Chemawawin Indian Reserve No. 2 on my map. As I pull into shore, there is a crowd of children swimming and jumping off the dock into the water. Their jet-black hair and dark tanned skins glisten in the setting sun. Almost immediately, I am surrounded by smiling, laughing, children, hanging on to *Loon*. I roll out of the canoe into the water, to the delight of the children, and together we push and pull the canoe into shore.

Brenda, Eric and Kumar meet me on the dock, and we drive to Clarence Easter's home. Clarence is the chief. He invites us to stay for supper and shows us a video made in 1965 by Manitoba Hydro about the building of the Grand Rapids Dam. At that time, it was one of the first "mega" hydroelectric projects in Canada. The video extolled the benefits that the dam would generate.

"But nobody cared that an entire people would be uprooted. You know, losing not only our homes, but also our fishing grounds, our trap lines – next to being killed, it's the worst thing that can happen to a community," says Clarence. "We were a wealthy community before the dam was built. Everyone made money fishing and trapping, we had a sawmill. It's all now

Cedar Lake, the reservoir on the North Saskatchewan River, created by the Grand Rapids Dam. Flocks of Bonaparte's gulls feed in the shallow water among the fallen trunks of spruce trees in the now-flooded forest.

under water. Now the fishery is no good, the animals are gone, our way of life was taken from us. We're trying to find ways for our people to make a living, but it's a rough road."

Clarence is concerned about his people. Welfare and unemployment have sapped their spirit. As surely as the waters rose behind the dam, it also created a reservoir of alcoholism, drug abuse and family violence.

The next day, I continue on, paddling the silver-shrouded edges of Cedar Lake, heading towards the old community of Chemawawin, now almost completely submerged. Phil Manaigre, a historian and keen kayaker from Winnipeg who visited me at Hecla, had advised me to search for amber near the old town. Before the dam was built, this was one of the few places in Canada with amber. The next year, while in the Museum of Nature back in Ottawa, I would admire honey-coloured nuggets of Cedar Lake amber containing perfectly preserved ants, over 60 million years old. Along with the spirit of the people of Chemawawin, the dam devastated the amber of the Saskatchewan River and all the information that it contained about life here long ago.

As I grub around in the muck, like some deranged manatee, hunting for amber, the sky above me fills with birds. Bonaparte's gulls mill about in the azure sky and line up on the weathered logs. Red-winged blackbirds

Taking a break from the bugs and sun in the old church at Chemawawin, the only building still standing in this Native community, now flooded by the reservoir of the Grand Rapids Dam.

and yellow-headed blackbirds flit like jewels in the willows. Common terns scream at me, for no reason in particular that I can fathom, and drop like arrows into the lake. Black terns perform aerial kung fu. Greater yellowlegs prowl between the logs, their long clawed feet supporting them like snowshoes on the black muck. Canada geese, a variety of LBDs (little brown ducks that I can't identify), and BBDs (big black ducks that I also can't identify) bob on the waves.

This is the prairies. There is a vibrancy and an abundance of life here like nowhere else on earth. The sky is filled with the movement of wings and the cacophony of birdcalls. I emerge from the waters of Cedar Lake covered in black muck, without any amber. I have been seeking treasure under the water, but the treasure that I find is in the sky.

Later that day, I am sitting on a wooden pew in a lovely old church, built, according to the date inscribed in the concrete step outside, in 1952, the year of my birth. The church stands in a grove of aspen trees on an island where the mighty Saskatchewan once flowed by. Now it seeps by, its banks submerged under the waters of the Cedar Lake Reservoir. This is the site of the old village of Chemawawin. The church is the only building from the community still standing above the water. It is cool and dark inside. Although several windows are broken, and light spills in through cracks in the roof, mysteriously, no mosquitoes dare trespass the hallowed space. For me, this church is a sanctuary, and I stay inside for several hours, enveloped by its womb-like darkness and silence. Voices from the past linger. I hear them rising in chorus, joyfully singing praise to God and to the joy of living. I see dark eyes gleaming with hope, and smiling faces.

Outside the church, beyond the shady aspen forest, lies a large meadow where I set up camp. "Verdant" is the word that comes to mind. Like the meadows along the Rainy River, this one is bright with wildflowers – yarrow, mint, grasses, yellow and white clover, and goldenrod, higher than my head. The meadow drones with the buzz of bees, and formations of iridescent blue dragonflies patrol its air space, gobbling up, I imagine to my delight, mosquitoes.

I sit down on a log by the water, stare out to the northwest across the vast expanse of Cedar Lake, look down at my map, and try to make some sense of it all. "The Pas, 63F," is an amazing map sheet. The entire eastern half of the sheet has but one contour line at 900 m (2,700 feet). Where I'm heading, towards the mouth of the Saskatchewan, blue, green and white intermingle, with those little swamp symbols everywhere, and a mysterious purple dashed line that I have never seen before on a contour map. I read that the information on the map is from 1959, before the dam was built, but the purple line was added in 1967 and "may not be as accurate as original detail." I assume that the purple line is the projected "shoreline" of Cedar Lake. A twisting finger of purple projects out into the middle of the swamp, the mouth of the Saskatchewan River. That's what I'm looking for.

When Mackenzie came through here, the Saskatchewan flowed between high banks built up by periodic floods. In this flat land, the banks of the river are the highest land around. When the dam was built, the banks were flooded, except for the highest points, which remain as islands today, such as the island that I'm camped on now. The river still flows through the submerged, or barely submerged, banks. The trick is to find its mouth, somewhere in the middle of this vast mess.

I set off at dawn the next morning. An early-rising veery is calling. It sounds like an opera singer warming up her voice. The notes aren't quite true. After a few off-key attempts, the bird gives up.

Thunderheads move like battleships in the sky. They scare me. I do not want to be caught in the middle of a 100-km (60-mile) swamp in a raging prairie thunderstorm. I head a little south of northwest, towards a thickening in the purple haze of the shore. I hope that it will materialize into riverbanks. I figure that the mouth of the river should be about 16 km (about 10 miles) in that direction. I decide to paddle for an hour or two, and then we'll see what we shall see.

After an hour or so of hard, steady paddling (I figure that I have covered about nine kilometres, slightly more than half of the anticipated distance), the purple haze that I am heading for turns into vast patches of rushes, taller than my head. Now I can't see anything at all. I paddle north, hoping to see some clue. I yell to the sky: "Where the '...' am I?" I expect to see some real land, but there's nothing but reeds and patches of scrubby willow. The vague purple edge that I could see from the island where I camped has disappeared, hidden by the reeds and willows. I cannot pick out any distinct features. Once again I am lost.

I'm feeling very small and alone. Thunder rumbles, making me feel even smaller. I put away my carbon-fibre paddle, not wishing to test its reported ability to conduct electricity. Small as I am, I'm the tallest thing out here. I continue to paddle through the reeds, heading north on the theory that I will cross the old river channel and somehow know this. At last, I see an anomaly – a lone silvered spruce sticking up out of the water. I paddle over to it and look around me. I see other silvered trunks of old spruce trees to the east and west. If I use my imagination, I can connect them into a curving line.

I paddle to the next old spruce to the west and surmise that I am following the submerged banks of the Saskatchewan River. Then, my line of trees runs out. There is nothing but water and scattered clumps of willows. I paddle to the closest clump of willows, exasperated. What do I do now? Clumsily, I drop my double-blade paddle into the water. It drifts away, rather quickly to the east. "Hey! Get baaaaack here!" I yell to my paddle. And then I notice that the murky waters of Cedar Lake are even murkier here, and I'm drifting away from the clump of willows as fast as my paddle. I'm in the Saskatchewan River!

Soon, two lines of willows and rushes define the river channel. Beyond these two thin, wandering lines, the waters of Cedar Lake spread out for miles and miles. The banks slowly coalesce into a wall of tall reeds, mixed with alders, bamboo-like willows and dogwood. The vegetation is so dense that it reminds me of scenes from the movie *The African Queen*, when Rosie and Captain Alcock (a Canadian in the novel) find themselves lost in the swamps near Lake Victoria.

The current in the river is strong, and I make slow progress upstream. But I am glad to have Cedar Lake behind me. I have never felt so dwarfed by a body of water. On other big bodies of water, one skirts the edges. But on Cedar Lake, there are no edges, and you are always in the middle of it. The North Saskatchewan is my first taste of a prairie river. The current is relentless. There are no eddies, no hiding places. I paddle next to the shore, where the current is slower, but the drag of the muddy bottom and shallow water slows *Loon* down. My normal speed is cut in half.

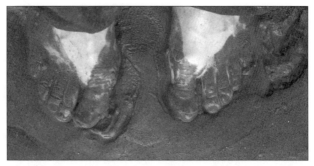

The mighty muddy North Saskatchewan. Likely some particles of mud are still stuck between my toes.

Families of otters, ducks, and Canada geese, along with Brenda, Eric and Kumar in a motorboat rented in The Pas, escort me up the muddy North Saskatchewan. "There's a surprise waiting for you in The Pas," Brenda says, somewhat mysteriously. I paddle on, singing "Going to the Pas, there's going to be a Paw-ty," over and over and over again. They leave me to paddle on my own.

Otters continue to escort us up the river. We stop to investigate a small, sandy beach where the otters have had a party. Crayfish claws, clamshells, and fish scales (I wonder what species?) are neatly piled near the shore. Meadows of clover occasionally break up the monotony of the willow jungle along the banks and scent the air with their sweet perfume. High in the prairie sky, bald eagles soar. When Mackenzie paddled through here, this was buffalo country.

I paddle around long sweeping bends that take forever to complete. The last miles to The Pas seem endless. At last, the highway bridge over the river comes into view. As I pull into the boat launch above the bridge, I see my surprise. A huge banner is stretched over an overturned canoe. In letters two feet high, it reads: "Welcome to the Pas, Max!"

Beside the banner, his long blond hair past his shoulders, and with a smile as wide as his canoe, is Chris Taggart. Another paddler, a young man, slight in build, with dark hair hanging in curls, stands beside him. As Chris and I hug, the mystery paddler introduces himself as Todd Marder.

Chris is on an odyssey to paddle as far as he can in one season along Mackenzie's route. We first met in Ottawa, when he passed through there in April, and I have been on his trail since I left in early May. Todd is from Colorado, and he is retracing the route taken in 1936 and 1937 by Sheldon Taylor and Geoffrey Pope on their journey from New York to Nome, Alaska. His goal this year is Fort Smith on the Slave River in the Northwest Territories.

Three canoes, three paddlers, all heading across a conti-nent, meet on the North Saskatchewan at the town of The Pas.

Here, in the geographic centre of Canada, three cross-continent pad-dlers have all come together. Brenda and Eric treat us all to supper at the fanciest restaurant in town.

The Pas sits in one of the most remarkable areas in Canada for wildlife. Here, the Pasquia, Carrot, and Saskatchewan rivers create a huge network of marshes, one of the largest wetlands in the world. This is a land more of water than of earth. In Mackenzie's time it was a rich hunting ground for buffalo. Today, waterfowl hunters and birdwatchers from all over the world seek it out. One of the richest areas for waterfowl, shorebirds, and raptors in North America, it must have resembled Africa's Serengeti in Mackenzie's time, with vast herds of bison, deer, wolves and grizzly bears roaming around.

In the morning we set off together, with our motorboat film crew escort, up the muddy Saskatchewan. It makes an interesting sight, three solo boats, three solo paddlers, all heading upriver. Each craft is different. Chris paddles a 16-foot Old Town Penobscot, with a hand-sewn spray cover made from a blue plastic tarpaulin. He has christened her the *Nancy Jane* in honour of his mother. His mother may not be pleased to know that he also calls his canoe "The Hate Tank," and, Chris jokes, it has only two speeds: "slow and stop." He hauls away with his long green plastic Carlisle paddle, which has become his trademark. "I've already worn two inches off this paddle," he tells me.

Todd made his own canoe, a 15-foot lapstrake-built boat[1] that weighs a remarkably light 16 kg (35 pounds). He uses a handmade wooden double-blade. His boat is rigged for sailing, and he says that he has done a lot. Perhaps if I knew more about sailing, and was not so chicken, I would not have sent my mast and sail back home when I was in Wawa.

*The North Saskatchewan has a subtle beauty that slowly permeates your soul –
along with the mud that permeates your socks.*

We switch boats along the way, each sampling the virtues and tortures
of different methods of travel. Not even the Muddy Ol' Mississippi can be
any muddier than the North Saskatchewan. With the amount of soil in its
water, it is amazing that there is any left on the prairies to grow wheat. At
every landing, we sink in the muck up to our knees, or even deeper. The
mud sticks to everything – packs, tents, between my toes. I'm sure that I
will still find Saskatchewan River mud on me years from now.

Ah, but the prairie nights are magical. Coyotes howl, and whippoorwills
call out their name, and fish swirl the surface of the river's muddy waters.
Somewhere, sometime, earlier this day, along one of those endless curves,
we crossed the Saskatachewan–Manitoba border. Political boundaries
have ceased to have much meaning for us. We are concerned with watersheds and heights of land.

Our last night together on the river finds us camping on a man-made
clearing on a high bank across from the Tearing River. There is a cabin, an
outhouse and a picnic table, but no one seems to be about. As we are setting
up camp, a pickup truck arrives, and two young Native boys and an elderly
couple emerge. We ask if we can camp for the night, and the old man, whom
the boys call "Grandfather," says that we are welcome, but he politely points
out that he would like to use the picnic table. Soon, a hunk of moose meat is
boiling away over the fire, while the two boys split wood with a hatchet and
toss a spear. I marvel at how these little boys, who look to be four or five years
old, are so adept with these potentially dangerous objects.

They say nothing to us, and the two groups eat separately. Much later, Grandfather comes over and asks where we have travelled from and where we are going. When we tell him, he makes no comment. When he was growing up, long-distance travel in this country was a way of life. "When I was young," he says, "the river was much clearer, and the current stronger." The Squaw Rapids Dam set 80 km (about 50 miles) upstream has changed the yearly cycle of rising and falling water levels. Before the dam went up, meltwaters from the Rockies would cause the river to rise in July and flush away much of the silt. But now, flows are decreased in the summer. I will soon see just how much this has affected Cumberland Lake.

It's 29 July. Todd, Chris and I head up the shallow Tearing River, one of three outfalls of the North Saskatchewan from Cumberland Lake. Brenda, Eric and Kumar take the main channel in the motorboat, to Cumberland House, where they will wait for me. The Tearing River is the route that Mackenzie took. Today, it is very shallow and rocky, another result of the Squaw Rapids Dam. In Mackenzie's time, much more water came down this channel. We cheer at the first piece of granite – a harbinger of the Canadian Shield. I feel a hint of sadness, as I know that Chris and Todd are continuing on into Shield country, while I have decided to end my trip this season here on the prairies. I will not have a chance to let the pine and granite of the Shield wash away this prairie mud.

Where the Tearing River spills over a small boulder dam at its outlet from Cumberland Lake, Chris and Todd head north. I sit on the rocks and watch them grow smaller and replay my decision over and over in my mind. But I made my airplane reservations in Hecla, and it's usually best not to undo decisions that have already been fretted over.

I head west, along the shore of Cumberland Lake, to the community of Cumberland House. I can see the radio antenna only a few miles away. The south shore of Cumberland Lake is a vast marsh, and I paddle mile after mile along the rushes and see no town. The radio antenna fades to the east. I keep paddling, until I round a point and can see the main channel of the North Saskatchewan. I turn back and paddle along the shore again, all the way back to the Tearing River (that's a total of about 25 km, or 15 miles). I turn back to the west and begin poking my way along the rushes. I have not gone too far when I see a motorboat pop out of the bulrushes. It is Brenda, Eric and Kumar. They're wondering what's taking me so long.

"We thought maybe you had stopped for a nap," Brenda says.

"No," I shrug. "Just lost again in the prairie marshes."

"That pole with the gull sitting on top," says Eric, "is the marker for the channel."

"Oh, man," I say, exasperated, "I passed that gull twice already."

We head down the Bigstone River to Cumberland House. In Mackenzie's time, it was on the shore of Cumberland Lake, in full view of arriving brigades. The town is in the same place, but the lake has moved in the last two centuries, so that the settlement is hidden in the alluvial plains and marshes between Cumberland Lake and the North Saskatchewan. Most of the change has occurred since the building of the Squaw Rapids Dam. Without the annual summer flood, Cumberland Lake is disappearing, quickly filling in with silt dumped by the Saskatchewan to become a vast marsh.

I step out on land, and Kumar, all the way from India, shakes my hand. I shake my head, thinking how a young man from India has come all the way to Cumberland House. A month ago, he didn't know what a canoe was, or Saskatchewan, for that matter.

Mackenzie gives us a history lesson from his journals: *"On the west side of these allluvials is Cumberland Lake on the east bank of which is situated Cumberland House. The House was the first inland trading post the Hudson's Bay Company made, remarkably well situated for the trade of fine Furs; it serves as a general Depot for all dried Provisions made of the meat and fat of the Bison under the name Pemmican, a wholesome, well tasted nutritious food, upon which all persons engaged in the Fur Trade mostly depend for their subsistence ... the turbid waters of the Saskatchwine, it has remarkably fine Sturgeon, a fish that requires such water to be in perfection."*

Samuel Hearne founded Cumberland House, the first inland HBC trading post, in 1774, when spruce trees covered the area.[2] Today, cattle graze in pastures on the rich alluvial soils. For several decades, it was the inland hub of the fur trade, and, along with Mackenzie, most of Canada's fur traders and explorers passed through here. I am in hallowed company. From Cumberland House, traders could travel north into the boreal forest to the Athabasca country, west to the Rocky Mountains, and east to Hudson Bay or Montreal. It was truly the crossroads of the continent, and it is a fitting place to end the first leg of my journey.

A real, full-scale York boat mounted on a wooden cradle in the centre of the town and a stone cairn with a bronze plaque remind us of the town's fur trade heritage. Today, Cumberland House is a thriving First Nations community and the home of some of Canada's best marathon canoe racers, including Erasmus Solomon,[3] who for years was the partner of the invincible

A York boat on display at Cumberland House, Saskatchewan. The Hudson's Bay Company favoured these over canoes on major rivers since they could carry more cargo.

Serge Corbin. Together, these two men won most of the major canoe races in North America.

It makes my heart swell to watch Native people, men, women and children, paddling the Bigstone River in marathon racing canoes. I invite some children swimming in the river to take *Loon* out for a short tour. Cumberland House is one community in Canada where canoeing is part of life and a source of pride.

A while later, starting to feel a little empty inside, I walk into town with Brenda, Eric and Kumar. We have a beer in the hotel, I telephone Mom, and we take photographs and video beside the stone monument.

The next morning, we head downriver to The Pas, with *Loon* loaded onto the motorboat. Then I head off to Australia to paddle the coast of Queensland. But that's another story.

Ninety days after leaving Ottawa, at last I arrive at Cumberland House, Saskatchewan – tired but still smiling.

Part II

Bella Coola to Fort Chipewyan, May–July 1998

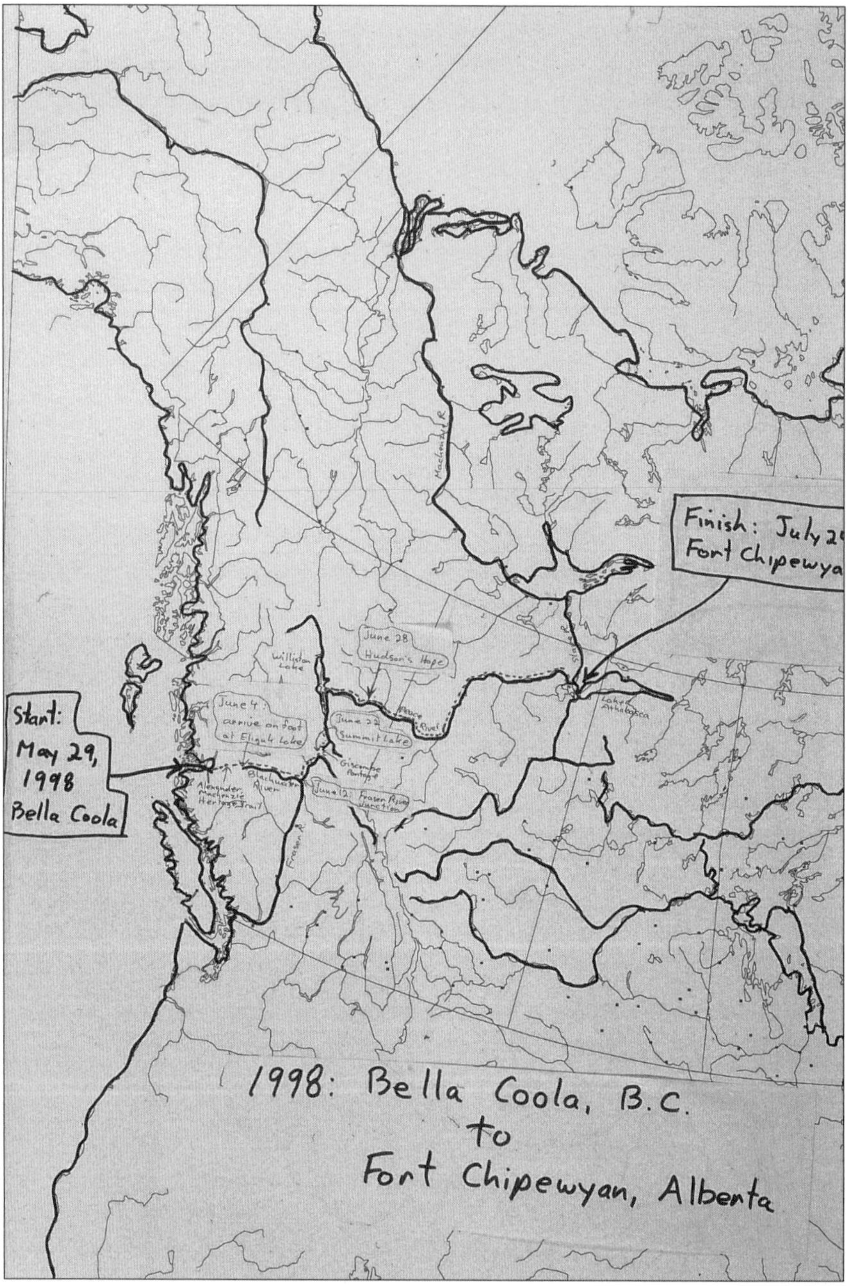

Finish: July 2[?]
Fort Chipewya[n]

June 28
Hudson's Hope

Start:
May 29,
1998
Bella Coola

June 4
arrive on foot
at Eliguk Lake

William
Lake

June 22
Summit Lake

Lake
Athabasca

Giscome
Portage

Alexander
Mackenzie
Heritage Trail

Blackwater
River

June 13 Fraser River
Junction

Mackenzie

Fraser R.

1998: Bella Coola, B.C.
to
Fort Chipewyan, Alberta

Connie and I try to train early in the season, in preparation for the trip.

over mountains covered with snow, there is not time for them to cool." The Pacific is actually about 900 km (about 540 miles) in a straight line from Fort Fork.

Talk runs high between Chris Taggart and me towards spring 1998. Chris had paddled until 15 November, when winter caught up to him in the canyons of the McGregor River, just north of Prince George.

Eventually, we develop a plan. Chris wants to finish retracing Mackenzie's route to the Pacific. We decide to team up and start on the Pacific coast at Bella Coola and follow Mackenzie's route from west to east. Mackenzie walked all the way from the Fraser to the Pacific and back along a Native trading route, now British Columbia's Alexander Mackenzie Heritage Trail. Much of the trail parallels the Blackwater River (which Mackenzie called the West Road River). The Blackwater may have been too steep to travel up, but Chris and I are not going to ignore this obvious water route to the Fraser. We agree that this deviation from Mackenzie's route is justified. Paddling down the river will be a lot more fun than backpacking. We just have to figure out how to get a canoe to the headwaters of the Blackwater.

Chris will go home from Prince George, and I will continue on alone over the continental divide and down the Peace River to the town of Hudson's Hope.[1] There, I will meet Brenda and Eric, the video crew, who will travel with me in motorized canoe to Fort Vermilion, Alberta. Also meeting me in Hudson's Hope will be Connie Downes, a biologist for the Canadian Wildlife Service. She will paddle with me to Fort Chipewyan on Lake Athabasca, a duplication of Mackenzie's route but not the timing. We estimated that this journey would take about three weeks. I'm a little anxious about this arrangement. Will she be bored paddling on a muddy prairie river? Will the bugs drive her crazy? Will I drive her crazy?

Connie and I fell in love over the winter, and I didn't want to blow it. Not this time. We long-distance canoeists don't get to meet a lot of girls, and those whom we do meet usually do not stick around for long – not after they find out that our idea of a good meal is bannock and oatmeal and that dinner at Tim Hortons is our notion of a night out on the town. Our best dinnerware is speckled metal plates and cups from Canadian Tire, wine tastes best for us in a metal mug, and our best leather shoes are moccasins. Lucky for me, Connie already knows all this, and in fact she has some of the same ideas about good times. I needn't have worried.

As spring came, Mackenzie watched the ice on the Peace, and I watch the weather reports on television to find out about the snow pack in the mountains near Bella Coola. By the end of April 1792, Mackenzie noted that the Peace was clear of ice. At the end of April 1998, I speak on the telephone to Andy Motherwell, in Quesnel, British Columbia, about hiking the Alexander Mackenzie Heritage Trail (sometimes known as the Grease Trail) in the spring. He knows the trail over the mountains as well as anyone today. We were concerned about the snow in Mackenzie Pass and about fording rivers swollen with spring meltwaters. "It's been a dry winter," he says. "I figger you can probably leave before the end of May. You'll get your feet wet for sure, but I don't think you'll have any problems."

By the end of April, the plans are set. Mackenzie also was organized by this date. Alexander Mackay was his second in command. Charles Ducette and Joseph Landry were experienced voyageurs who had accompanied Mackenzie on his voyage to the Arctic Ocean in 1789. Other voyageurs included Jacques Beauchamp, François Beaulieux, Baptiste Bisson, and François Courtois. Two additional Native men went along as hunters and interpreters. A large brown dog – known simply as "Our Dog" – became an indispensable part of the team.

The next issue for both Mackenzie and myself is procuring an ideal craft for the trip. Mackenzie's men built a birchbark canoe designed for the journey, *"Twenty-five feet long, twenty-six inches hold, and four feet nine inches beam, she was so light that two men could carry her three or four miles without resting."* Into this craft they loaded 1,364 kg (3,000 pounds) of gear and ten people.

My trusty *Loon* will not be appropriate for this trip. I need a two-person canoe, light, fast, and durable. I shop by telephone, contacting B.C. canoe manufacturers, as shipping a canoe from Ottawa is much too expensive. I finally find a 17-foot duraflex prospector, made by Hellman Canoes of

Nelson. Bob Hellman understands exactly what I am looking for and makes a very generous offer. Michael Greco, president of the Canadian River Management Society, finalizes the deal for me while I am bird-watching with Connie in Point Pelee National Park on Lake Erie. I arrange the logistical details with Bob Hellman from a pay phone at Point Pelee. My canoe will be waiting for me in Williams Lake, at the Red Shred Bike and Board Shed. Now all I have to do is figure out how to get it to the head-waters of the Blackwater River.

I put in more calls from the pay phone. Ben and Donna Davidson, who run Nympo Lake Air, agree to fly the canoe and our gear into Eliguk Lake Lodge. Eliguk Lake is connected by a short creek to the Blackwater River, and the Alexander Mackenzie Heritage Trail runs past the lake. Chris and I agree by phone to meet in Williams Lake on 27 May at the Overlander Hotel. I will fly there; he will arrive by bus. The canoe will get there by truck. This is a lot more complicated than last year, when I just walked down to the river. As Mackenzie did in the spring of 1792.

On 9 May, Mackenzie and his crew headed up the Peace. Those left behind *"shed tears on the reflection of those dangers which we might encounter in our expedition."* Those whom I leave behind shed a few tears too. I pray, just as Mackenzie and his men prayed, that we will return safely.

On the flight west on 27 May 1998, I gaze out the window, 13,000 m (39,000 feet) above the rivers and lakes that I paddled on last summer. The air is Arctic clear. I gaze down at my favourite haunts in Gatineau Park north of Ottawa. The big jet carries me up the Ottawa River, covering in seconds what took me days last spring, past the big dam at Des Joachims, where unknown bodies supposedly lie entombed in concrete, past Oiseau Rock near Deep River. We fly over the cliffs of the Sleeping Giant near Thunder Bay. My knees ache just thinking about the day that I spent climb-ing up and down them last summer. West of Lake Superior, I can see huge clear-cuts, on a scale that would be visible from the moon. The tracery of roads is unceasing. It is the dominant feature of the landscape from the air. Paddling through the boundary waters last summer, it seemed such a wilderness. Yet from the plane there is not one view that does not include several logging roads and clear-cuts between Lake Superior and the prairies.

Other people on the flight seem uninterested in the panorama that is Canada passing beneath them. Most are reading books and newspapers. Yet they could learn much more about their country simply by looking out the window. Only when the captain announced that we were passing over Sudbury did anyone take any notice of what lay below us.

As I stare at the vast clear-cuts, I wonder if our society could have developed any differently. Are we programmed to farm and mine the world? Could we have put together an advanced technology without the drive to amass wealth and populate the world? Could we have computers and space travel and leave the beauty of the world that is our heritage intact? I don't know. But I see that our culture is eating up the beauty and richness of the world, transforming it into commodities that we can eat, live in, sit on, or otherwise use.

I want to shout to the other passengers: "Don't you see what's happening? Is this the world you want for your children?" Maybe it is. Maybe most people do not agree with my simple philosophy, that if something adds beauty to the world, or beauty to your life, then it is worth doing; if it detracts from the beauty of the world, or from the beauty in your life, then it is not worth doing. Maybe that's why I'm the only one on this plane (at least as far as I know) who is paddling across our country.

The days and weeks of paddling last year slip by below as the big jet heads west. I think back to Mackenzie's time, when travelling to the west coast was just a dream, a great notion. Our technology and wealth have given us the means to move around quickly, compared to the paddle. But while gaining speed and ease, perhaps we have not accounted for what we have lost. Destinations we can now reach with ease, but we have lost the significance of the journeys. Are we really any further ahead?

Over the prairies, clouds obscure the view and seem to permeate my brain, bringing my musings to an end, leaving only a mind overloaded with logistical arrangements.

12

Bella Coola to Eliguk Lake: The Long Portage

The fatigue of ascending these precipices I shall not attempt to describe. When we arrived at a spot where we could get water (four hours later), it was with great pain any of us could crawl about.

— ALEXANDER MACKENZIE, 26 JULY 1792

ON THE AFTERNOON OF 27 MAY, I walk into the lobby of the Overlander Hotel in Williams Lake. It is a comfortable, but unremarkable hotel in downtown Williams Lake, surrounded by divided roadways and modern, unremarkable rectangular buildings. It looks like any other modern town in Canada, except for the rodeo grounds across the street. I know that I am in cowboy country. Everyone here wears cowboy boots. I feel conspicuous in my hiking boots.

In the lobby is another man with hiking boots. He is tall and lean, with long blond hair down to his shoulders and a far-away look in his wide-set, grey-green eyes. Our eyes meet:

"Chris!"

"Max!"

We give each other a bear hug and shake hands in the three-stage way that Chris showed me last year. Clasped hands means "business." Thumbs intertwined means "friendship." Hands clasped around the other's wrists means "family." We have not seen each other since we parted at the end of July 1997 on Cumberland Lake. A lot of water, literally and figuratively, has passed under our hulls since then.

We go up to our unremarkable room, spread out our gear and food on the beds. I think to myself how many times I have gone through this scene before, setting out on a remarkable adventure from a very unremarkable hotel room. We sort our food and gear – one pile for the hike to Eliguk Lake, one pile to be flown in with the canoe for the trip down the Blackwater and up the Fraser to Prince George, and one pile to be shipped to Prince George. This pile includes Chris's blue jeans and blue jean jacket, which he always ships ahead to the next town.

Then we walk down to the Red Shred Bike and Board Shed to check on our canoe. It is waiting for us, shiny teal green. I decided to call it *Teal*, staying with the bird theme. We arrange through Beeline Transport to have it shipped tomorrow to Nympo Lake. From there it will be flown into Eliguk Lake at the headwaters of the Blackwater. There is the usual last-minute list of items to buy at Canadian Tire – fuel for the stove, batteries, air horn to scare off the bears, a telescopic fishing rod. Then we go back to the room, with a case of beer and a bag of greasy fast food. We are so excited that we are still up at midnight, talking of last year's adventures, of crossing watersheds and continents.

The next morning we take the Gold Pan City Stage Line to Bella Coola. We stare in fear and amazement into the silty waters of the Fraser where the highway crosses it. The current is swift, pushing the water almost a metre up the upstream edge of the bridge pilings. Brian, the driver, thinks that we are crazy to try paddling up the Fraser. He may be right. There is no way that we could paddle up that current. Our minds cloud over with doubt, but there is no going back now. We ask him to make a brief stop in Nympo Lake so that we can drop off some gear with our canoe and make sure that all the arrangements are in order.

As Brian turns off the highway onto a dirt road, where a wooden sign announces the office of Nympo Lake Air, a dusty pickup truck heads out towards the highway. The truck stops and a woman yells out the window: "Are you Max?" It is Donna Davidson, whom I had talked to several times on the telephone from Ottawa. She assures me that our canoe and gear will be waiting for us at Eliguk Lake Lodge by the time that we arrive there on foot from Bella Coola. She is so excited by our venture that we feel we must be doing something right.

We continue west in the van, catching glimpses of snow-capped mountains through the clouds. Then the road drops precipitously in a series of switchbacks, past sheer rock faces and tumbling waterfalls. "I could piss off the side of the road, and it would fall onto the road below," Chris jokes with Brian. I can feel all the stress of the logistical arrangements dropping away with each switchback.

Before us lies a great valley, its floor nearly two kilometres or over a mile in width. On each side, a row of mountains, covered with snow and dripping with glaciers and waterfalls, rises straight up from the valley floor. To the west, more mountains bar the view to the Pacific. The valley is green – the lush, moist green of rainforests. The road heads down into the valley, where neat farmsteads nestle. To the west, we can see the town of Bella Coola, on the banks of the light green Bella Coola River.

The road continues through forests of giant cedar, orchards and pastures. It is like no other place that I have seen in Canada. It reminds us of photographs of Norway, and indeed, many Scandinavians settled here for that very reason.

The town of Bella Coola lies at the mouth of the swift Bella Coola River. Here Mackenzie, travelling in Native dugout canoes after his long overland trek, described *"a village containing six very large houses ... From these houses I could perceive the termination of the river into a narrow arm of the sea."* Mackenzie at his understated best. Chris and I cannot see the sea. But Steve, who runs the Bella Coola Hotel, says that he will lend us his canoe, and we can paddle to the sea. He will meet us at the government dock in a few hours.

We leap at this opportunity, both of us heading for the bow of the canoe. It's a little crowded up there, and I am sure that Steve wonders how we got this far. We look sheepishly at each other and at Steve, and I explain: "We never get to paddle in the bow. Ever!" I graciously give up the bow seat to Chris, and the swift, thunderstorm-swollen waters of the Bella Coola carry us to the Pacific, about an hour from the hotel. Bald eagles watch us from overhanging snags. Seals bob in the waves. Mackenzie extolled the canoeing skills of his Native escorts: *"I had imagined that the Canadians who accompanied me were the most expert canoemen in the world, but they are very inferior to these people, as they themselves acknowledged, in conducting those vessels* [spoon-bow dugouts].*"*

Where the river merges with the sea, we both cup our hands and taste the salty Pacific waters. We gaze west at the black waters of the North Bentinck Arm, at the dark green slopes of the fjords. Great grey clouds are snagged by the mountaintops. Some 50 km (30 miles) farther out towards the open Pacific, along Dean Channel, Mackenzie left his own graffiti, in vermilion: *"Alexander Mackenzie, from Canada, by land, 22nd July, 1793."* The paint that he used was not as durable as the red ochre pigments employed by the First Nations people. Mackenzie's original message has disappeared. You can still read it, however, as someone in the 1920s chipped the same message into what may be the same rock. We would have to save the experience of seeing the rock for another trip, perhaps one that takes us from Vancouver up the coast to Bella Coola. We take one last, lingering gaze to the west, and then our hearts and eyes turn eastwards. I look at the vertical world around us and make a mental note to buy extra chocolate bars and cheese slices.

The next morning, grey rain clouds cling to the dark green mountainsides. But the clouds have thin spots through which the sun almost shines. These are called "suckerholes" out here, because they fool newcomers into thinking that the weather will clear. Chris and I are anxious to head out. We're meeting Rene Morton and her brother Les Kopas at the Kopas General Store at ten. Rene and Les are the children of one of the legends of Bella Coola, Cliff Kopas. In 1933, Cliff and his new bride, Ruth, set off from Calgary by packhorse, following old trails left by prospectors and traders through the mountains, reaching Bella Coola after four months of hard travel. They stayed – the thought of going back up those mountains may have been just too daunting.

Instead, they opened the Kopas General Store, which is now a historical institution in town. Cliff passed on his deep love of the wilderness, and his penchant for history, to their children. Rene and Les regale Chris and me with stories of the old days, and not-so-old days. They drive us up the Bella Coola Valley, *"hemmed in on both sides and behind [for us, that would be in front] by such a barrier as nature never before presented to my view,"* according to Mackenzie. The neat pastures and hay fields framed by the lofty mountains and sinuous fjords remind me again of photos of Norway. "Norwegian farmers moved here from Minnesota in the 1890s," says Rene, "because nowhere else in the world looks so much like Norway."

We stop to gaze up the trunks of rainforest giants, which, Mackenzie noted, *"were the loftiest alder and cedar trees that I had ever seen."* Ditto for us. No traces remain of the villages that Mackenzie saw along the Bella Coola. But the official trailhead for the Alexander Mackenzie Heritage Trail lies near the site of his *"Friendly Village."* Here, he and his exhausted crew received most hospitable treatment from their hosts: *"We received a large dish of salmon roes, pounded fine so as to have the appearance of cream. Another dish soon followed, the principle article of which was also salmon-roes, with a large proportion of gooseberries, and a herb that appeared to be sorrel."*

Chris and I will not be eating such gourmet meals. Nor will we meet the number of people that Mackenzie did. In many ways, the route over the mountains is more wilderness today than it was in his time. Rene explains: "In 1793, this so-called unexplored land was laced with travel and trade routes. The Southern Carriers from the interior and the Nuxalk people who now live in Bella Coola walked back and forth between the Pacific and the Fraser Valley, visiting friends and relatives in settlements that dotted the route. Dried fish, shells, and eulachon oil from the coast were the main items of trade. The eulachon is a silvery fish the size of a herring. They are so oily that a dried eulachon will burn like a candle, hence the other common name of candlefish. The ancient network of trails from the coast to the interior were often called 'grease trails' because of the trade in eulachon oil."

Each spring, local people scooped the silvery fish, up to a foot in length, in long windsock-shaped nets made of nettle-fibre. They dumped the fish in wooden boxes and left them for several days to stew in the warm spring sun. Then they boiled them, rinsed them with ice water, and skimmed the oil off the surface. They would strain the fish oil several times, and then it was ready to eat, drink, smear on skin, or rub into hair. Mackenzie noted on his third day on the trail west from the Fraser: *"My companion's hair being greased with fish-oil, and his body smeared with red earth, my sense of smelling threatened to interrupt my rest."* I am sure that Mackenzie and his men did not smell so great themselves. By the time that we get to Eliguk Lake, I am sure that our sleep "will be threatened" by our own stench, and we'll be glad for the extra tent packed with the canoe.

Chris and I look at each other as the image of carrying a cedar basket dripping eulachon oil comes into our minds. The smell would draw every grizzly between Bella Coola and Prince George. I guess that those people were not worried about grizzly bears.

Chris Taggart and I pose at the official western terminus of the Alexander Mackenzie Heritage Trail, near Bella Coola, British Columbia, on May 27, 1998. Our trek east started from this point.

The four of us stand by the bronze plaque embedded in a huge rounded boulder that marks the official start to the Mackenzie Trail. The entire trail, from here to its eastern terminus at the Fraser, covers 347 km (about 210 miles). Chris and I will walk only 120 kilometres or about 72 miles to Eliguk Lake, the headwaters of Mackenzie's West Road River (locally called the Blackwater River), where, if all goes according to plan, our canoe, *Teal*, will be waiting for us. We packed for twelve days. It is early in the season to cross the passes, and deep snow and bad weather may slow us. Although we have packed carefully, our backpacks weigh about 27.3 kg (60 pounds) each. When Mackenzie and his men left this place, they each carried about 9 kg (20 pounds) of dried salmon, *"a little flour, and some pemmican."*

The sun is shining strongly down on us as we bid goodbye to Les and Rene and head up the trail. We are so excited to be off, we are almost skipping up the steep slope. Such foolishness soon stops. It is early spring, we are both out of shape, and we are climbing up the side of a very large, steep mountain. Soon both of us are out of breath. The trail switchbacks up the slope through forests of giant Douglas fir and red cedar.

"You know, Max," says Chris, panting and leaning on a giant Douglas fir, "this is the first time I've ever gone backpacking. Maybe I should have told you that before."

"Ah, Chris, backpacking is easy. It's just like portaging. How about a sandwich?"

I take half a Mars bar and wrap a tortilla around it.

"The sandwich of choice for backpackers," I say, handing it to him.

Chris takes the sandwich, laughing: "I thought you were joking when you told me about Mars bar sandwiches. Apparently not. I have a lot to learn."

We continue switchbacking up through the seemingly interminable forest. Our butt muscles are cramping up when the slope finally levels out, and we come out of the forest at beautiful little Hump Lake. A double rainbow frames snow-covered Mount Stupendous, on the far side of the Bella Coola Valley. We have been on the trail five hours and have covered a whopping 8 km (about 5 miles), but have climbed over 1,000 m (5/8 mile). We sit down by the lake and take the cantaloupes out of our packs. Cantaloupes? We packed carefully except for the cantaloupes. These two beauties are worth every sore and aching muscle, as the luscious tropical taste refreshes our tired bones. The setting sun paints the peak of Mount Stupendous the shade of pink seen on the inside of clamshells. Mackenzie too was dazzled: *"Before us appeared a stupendous mountain, whose snow-clad summit* [on 17 July] *was lost in the clouds."* We both fall asleep in front of the campfire, wondering which NHL teams have advanced in the Stanley Cup playoffs.

Hump Lake, 1,300 metres (about 4,000 feet) above the Bella Coola River, was our first campsite on the trail. This little lake, framed by spruce trees and with Mount Stupendous as a backdrop, made for a wonderful bedroom.

We also wonder why Mackenzie's Native guides chose this route to the coast. There were surely better, less steep approaches following the river valleys.

The next day, we follow the edge of a precipice overlooking the Bella Coola Valley. Perhaps this was the very spot that Mackenzie was describing when he wrote: *"Such was the depth of the precipices below, and the height of the mountains above, with the rude and wild magnificence of the scenery around, that I shall not attempt to describe such an astonishing and awful combination of objects, of which, indeed, no description can convey an adequate idea."* Today the entire valley is covered with thick clouds, filling the valley like foam on beer. Mountains rise above the clouds, their snow-covered peaks sparkling (yes, they really do sparkle) in the brilliant sunshine.

We continue to the crossing at Burnt Bridge Creek. Mackenzie mentions fording it *"where the water was three feet deep and very rapid."* He carried across on his back a sick Native companion. I study the tumbling, knee-numbing water, trying to pick out the best route, when Chris yells: "Hey, Max, there's a suspension bridge over here!" We cross without even getting our feet wet but later almost wade through a series of wet meadows, where we sink up to our knees in large patches of mushy snow.

The lush rainforests of the Bella Coola Valley are behind us now, replaced by subalpine forests of spruce and fir. We see tracks of caribou, moose, and wolves. From the patches of forest, ovenbirds and winter wrens call from the spruce woods, mixed with the clear, flute-like calls of hermit and wood thrushes. The sight of a Clark's nutcracker, grey and black and almost as big as a crow, reminds us that we are far away from our homes in eastern Canada. Shoots of Indian hellebore, juicy and tropical-looking, are just pushing up in the soggy alpine meadows, amid the white

Clouds obscure the Bella Coola Valley, but up here it is a sunny day. Mount Stupendous looms above the clouds.

anemones and yellow violets. The beauty of spring in the mountains is ample compensation for our wet, cold feet.

We set up camp at Bluff Lake, a lovely little body of water nestled in the high country, rimmed by forests of sharp-pointed alpine fir and backed by seemingly endless ranges of snowy mountains. Rising trout dapple the lake's surface, and I regret having left my collapsible fishing rod with the pile of gear to be flown in with our canoe.

We continue climbing through alpine meadows interspersed with patches of snow and stretches of brown grass. The patches of snow gradually grow in size. The areas in between are now barren, the soil the same reddish clay that Mackenzie described. Near the summit of the pass, a broad field of snow spreads out before us. To the left and right of the pass, the peaks of the Rainbow Range come into view for the first time. They soar heavenward, completely free of snow, looking like piles of powdered pigment – ochre, rust and an orange that is the same shade as the lichens on the rocky shoreline of Georgian Bay; black, sienna, and purple, the colours found in badlands and desert – all set off by a sky so blue that it appears solid.

A falcon flies overhead, heading north – our direction too. "Let's follow that bird," says Chris, and we strike north over the deep snow. Mackenzie noted that *"the snow was so compact that our feet hardly made a perceptible impression on it."* We find this to be true for us also. We long to climb to the tops of those powdery orange and rusty ridges but feel that we should use

Left: Looking north to the Rainbow Range from the Mackenzie Pass, at just over 2,000 metres (about 6,500 feet), the highest point on the trail.

Right: Chris Taggart, tired but exuberant at the summit of Mackenzie Pass. It was all downhill from here.

the good weather to get over the pass. When Mackenzie and his party came this way in July 1793, a violent storm pinned them down – *"the weather as distressing as any I had ever experienced."* We count our blessings and begin the long descent, vowing that we will come back to this incredible place.

The sharp whistle of hoary marmots accompanies us as we descend back into the forest. We decide to spend the night in Rainbow Cabin, a hunting cabin built in the 1930s, and recently renovated. It's a pleasure to fire up the wood stove and dry out our soggy clothes. We shove hot rocks in our boots to dry them out, but within thirty seconds the next morning they are sopping wet after our first of many fordings of Kohasganko Creek.

The next days blend together in a series of wet creek crossings, clouds of mosquitoes, soggy meadows, swamps and forest. This is truly becoming a walk in the woods, as the trees hide from our view the snow-capped mountains that we just traversed. We hike with our bug jackets on. Tragedy strikes when we leave behind our only bottle of insect repellent. The route crosses several huge wet meadows and passes by the remains of trapper's cabins – testimony to a much busier route in the not-too-distant past.

Several abandoned trapper's cabins are found along the trail. This one belonged to Jamus Jack who hunted and trapped in this area. The cabin was built here because of the large natural hay meadows close by, which provide good forage for horses.

We are relieved to find the new bridge over the Dean River in good shape. Mackenzie and his crew had to cross the Dean in rafts. The river here cuts through a rocky canyon in a series of falls. We set up the tent on a bed of dry pine needles. This was our longest day on the trail – a whopping 26 km (about 16 miles), and our feet are tender. The sound of rapids and the chirping of crickets soon lull us to sleep.

Swamps of spruce, swamps of willow, beaver ponds flooding the trail, squishy boots, and pine forest. Spruce grouse, with their striking red cheeks, stare at us as we walk by. Gatcho Lake is coming up. It's 8 km (about 5 miles) long. The trail skirts the lake. My fantasy is to find a rowboat at the end of the lake. It's not often that a fantasy comes true, but as we head down the trail to the western end, I see an aluminum fishing boat with oars pulled up on shore. I urge Chris to load our gear in the boat, but he is reluctant, feeling that we might inconvenience someone if we move the boat. In the end, I relent, because he is right.

I am glad that we took the trail, which leads to Ulgatcho Village, on a hillside overlooking the lake. Several old log cabins, a church, and a graveyard spread out over a rolling meadow dotted with bright yellow dandelions. It looks like a meadow back in Ontario. There is no one around, although clearly people still use this area. The village was here when Mackenzie walked by two centuries ago: *"At one in the afternoon came to a house. The timber was squared on two sides, and the bark taken off the two others; the ridge pole was also shaped in the same manner, extending eight or ten feet beyond the gable end. The end of it was carved into the similitude of a snake's* head." Geologist George Mercer Dawson[1] travelled over Mackenzie's route in 1876, and he believed that he found the house described by Mackenzie.

The climate here is noticeably drier. The trail winds through mature forests of lodgepole pine. At one of the few vantage points, east of Maliput Lake, we get our last view of the Coast Ranges to the west. This was where Mackenzie first saw these rugged peaks: *"covered with snow, which, according to the intelligence of our guide, terminates in the ocean."* The sight of these rugged peaks must have made him shudder in his moccasins.

At 2:30 in the afternoon of 4 June, our eighth day on the trail, we arrive at Eliguk Lake Lodge. There, shiny green, with graceful curves just like a woman's thigh (gee, such an analogy after only eight days on the trail!) sat our canoe, *Teal*. Eliguk Lake Lodge is a fishing camp, and it looks idyllic. Neat log cabins spread out through an open pine forest. As we walk towards the canoe, a man sticks his head out of the biggest cabin: "Do you guys want a cup of coffee?"

He herds us inside and introduces himself as Moe Schiller, owner of the lodge. Soon we are sitting around a table guzzling juice and beer with Moe and his wife, Jeanette, originally from Quebec (perhaps a descendant of one of Mackenzie's crewmen) and an elderly gent named Gil, a professional fly fisherman. Chris and I ask the question that's been on our minds since leaving Bella Coola: "Who's in the Stanley Cup Finals?"

"We don't know," Moe answers. "This is B.C., and hockey isn't religion out here."

"It's not?" we reply, dumbfounded.

Gil takes me out on the lake that evening, giving me a lesson in fly-fishing. The trout are jumping all over the lake. Some leap a metre or more out of the water.

" I think they just jump for the fun of it," says Gil. "Look for the ones that just swirl near the surface. They're the hungry ones." Eventually I manage to land two nice rainbow trout, which I keep for breakfast. Trail food has been scarce for us; except for a bounty of wild onions, we've eaten only what we carry. We are not like the people whom Mackenzie met, who could, they told him, survive on herbs and the inner bark of trees.

Tomorrow we part from Mackenzie's trail to follow the Blackwater River down to the Fraser.

13

Down the Blackwater:
River of No Return

Canoeing through the canyons downstream from Gillies
Crossing to the Fraser is not recommended – DANGEROUS!
— WOODWORTH AND FLYGARE,
IN THE STEPS OF ALEXANDER MACKENZIE[1]

THE BLACKWATER, OR TOA-THAL-KAS, as the local Carrier people call it, is very special – one of the earliest designated British Columbia Heritage Rivers. During its course of 280 km (about 170 miles) to the Fraser, the Blackwater drops a scary 900 m (3,000 feet). A glance at the topographical maps was even scarier for us than this statistic. As it cuts through the sediments of the Interior Plateau, the river carves a sinuous canyon, dropping at more than 10 m/km (50 feet/mile) for the final 50 km (30 miles) of its course.

Mackenzie dug deep into his soul to make the decision to leave the canoe at the mouth of the Blackwater and walk overland to the Pacific, as the local people advised. In planning our trip, we dug deep in our own souls to decide to paddle the river that Mackenzie walked up, despite dire warnings to the contrary.

"Ah, well," I say to Chris. "If things get really bad, we can always walk." I hope that that will be true. But looking at the depth of the canyons, I realize that walking might not be an option.

On 4 July 1793, Mackenzie and his men began their walk up the

A short one-kilometre portage from Eliguk Lake leads to a small creek that soon joins the Blackwater River.

Blackwater. On 5 July 1998, Chris and I begin our journey by canoe down the river.

"That nice shiny canoe won't look so new by the end of today," or so Gil, the professional fisherman at Eliguk Lake Lodge, sagely tells us. Instead of the bagpipes that bid Mackenzie's expedition farewell, loons wail as we paddle from the dock.

We both are thrilled to be paddling again. For Chris and me, being in a canoe is like being at home. Near the end of the lake, a loon dances on the water, her webbed feet slapping the surface and her wings outstretched. She calls frantically. On the shore, nestled on a bed of dried rushes, are three speckled eggs. We quickly paddle away.

The outlet of Eliguk Lake is choked with logs, and we find ourselves back on the trail, but this time carrying a canoe as well as our packs. We head into a wet meadow after a couple of kilometres, dragging *Teal* through a hummocky sedge meadow.

"Hey, Chris!" I yell, exasperated. "Where are we?"

"Looks like we're in the middle of the grasslands of British Columbia, Max," Chris laughs.

We heave-ho the canoe towards the middle of the meadow and finally find enough water to float her. Lines of current crease the water as it trickles between the rushes and willows. We're heading downstream!

Within minutes, a major tributary enters from the south. More accurately, we're paddling the tributary, Ulgako (Carrier for "branches") Creek, and we soon join the Blackwater River, flowing out of the volcanic Ilgachuz Range. The current carries us over several low beaver dams.

"Yippee! White water! Our first rapids!" I yell, as *Teal* scrapes a rock below the dam. I wince every time her shiny bottom touches a rock. "One metre down, 899 to go to the Fraser."

"I know why they call it the Blackwater," says Chris. "The water is stained so dark I can't see the rocks."

One of the wonderful things in life is to see a river grow. By afternoon, the tiny trickle that was the Blackwater has expanded to a sizeable river – about 15 m (about 50 feet) across, a half-metre (19 inches) deep, and moving about two kilometres (not quite a mile and a half) an hour. We slither down several shallow, rocky rapids before the Blackwater slows down, snaking through grassy meadows.

Weathered log fences are strung along the riverbank. Herds of the happiest cows that we have ever seen follow us. Their rich brown-and-white coats shine in the sun, and their liquid brown eyes appear so peaceful. The young ones gallop after us, gambolling through the willows. Herds of horses – palominos, chestnuts, appaloosas, and greys – also follow us. Never have we seen such healthy, beautiful domestic animals. And no wonder. No domestic animal could have a better home. On both sides of the river spread vast, dandelion-dotted meadows, backed to the south by the snow-covered Ilgachuz Mountains. We stop for lunch at a particularly verdant grassy bank, but when we climb up, we find a huge bull lying there, looking at us in a way that says, "I don't like your looks," and we beat a hasty retreat. The landscape evokes scenes from old western movies.

All these domestic animals remind us that, back in the 1930s, cowpokes Pan Phillips and Rich Hobson brought a herd of cattle into these untouched meadows. They dreamed of building a cattle empire in the Blackwater country – the ranches that we are passing belong to their descendants. Their early hardships and adventures in this isolated country make up as great a tale as Mackenzie's epic journey. The cattle drive through the mountains to the market – through blizzards, hungry wolf packs, angry moose, and unexplored passes – may be the greatest cowboy story ever. The cowboys wore moose hide from their boots and chaps to their coats and hats. This is such a bountiful land, filled with moose and trout, that Chris and I cannot figure out why anyone would work so hard to bring cattle here. I guess that you have to be a cowboy to understand.[2]

That night, Chris and I are relaxing by our fire on the banks of the river. Our fuel is dried cow dung, and we use it also as supports for our pots. In

The upper Blackwater River carries us past several cattle ranches run by descendants of Pan Phillips and other adventurous pioneering cowboys. The rich natural meadows are home for the most contented cattle and horses we have ever seen.

the distance, we can hear the soft mooing of cows. Snipes are dropping out of the sky, the air whistling through their wing feathers. We hear the unique liquid thumping of a bittern coming from a riverside slough. The harsh call of redwing blackbirds fills the rushes. We lie on our backs, sipping hot chocolate, and watching sandhill cranes drift by high overhead, heading north, like tiny black crosses in the evening sky. Slightly lower, bald eagles and hawks soar.

"You know," I say to Chris, sipping my hot chocolate, "I remember about twenty-five years ago when I lived in British Columbia looking at the Blackwater River on a provincial map. The name West Road was written in brackets beside it. I remember thinking that sounded like such an interesting name, and it looked like an interesting river to paddle. Now here we are paddling down it. You just never know where life is going to take you. Or how it's going to take you where it takes you. Like a river."

Chris rolls another cigarette and says: "Ya gotta dream, Max, and ya gotta follow some of those dreams, 'cause ya just never know where they're going to take you."

Boy, Chris is right about that.

It's not long before the Blackwater leaves behind the vast daisy- and dandelion-dotted meadows of dream-ranch country, and the forest of spruce and pine closes in. Moose, deer, and black bears replace the cattle and horses. Rocks and trees replace the weathered log fences.

The peaceful, meandering river begins to pick up speed and power. We pick our way through many rapids, adding only a few scratches to the bottom of the canoe. Not far above Tsacha Lake, the Blackwater begins to cut a deep canyon through the black basalt bedrock, culminating in a 12-m (40-foot) falls, where the river plummets over a vertical rock face in a curtain of white. Below the falls, trout almost a metre long are leaping, trying to swim up this impossible barrier.

"It's just like popcorn popping," says Chris. "I wonder why they keep trying to get up this thing, when it's clearly impossible? They remind me of me sometimes."

As we paddle the last quiet stretch of river through the wetlands above Tsacha Lake, a cow moose with two calves wades across in front of us. Around the next bend, another cow with two calves watches, unconcerned, as we paddle by. Moose were unknown in the Blackwater watershed until 1897, when Old Chief Morris of Kluskus shot the first one ever seen here, according to local lore. Not knowing the species, the local Carrier were reluctant to eat it. By the 1930s, when Phillips and Hobson were driving in cattle, moose were abundant. The cowboys lived on moose and dressed in moose skin, but the Carrier still preferred to eat caribou, their traditional mainstay.

For centuries, woodland caribou had been the most common ungulate in this region. They need large tracts of undisturbed forest for the lichens that they depend on, particularly in winter. These lichens, which grow very slowly, hang in grey-green strings from the branches of old-growth conifers. Moose, in contrast, thrive in forests recently disturbed by fire or logging. Perhaps a series of forest fires created ideal habitat for them and destroyed the old conifers preferred by the caribou. Perhaps logging and settlement to the south were causing moose to expand their historical range. Wildlife populations always fluctuate, but the changes wrought here over the last two centuries have transformed habitat and hence wildlife populations, to a degree and with a rapidity never seen before.

With these thoughts drifting through our minds, we drift onto beautiful Tsacha – the biggest lake along the Blackwater, a 19.2-km (about a 12-mile) stretch of beryl water set in a valley of green and gold. It's high spring. Clouds of golden pollen rise from the pine forests with every puff of wind. Like a golden mist, the pollen clouds move down the valley. Our boots and pant legs are covered with golden-yellow dust. Wind on the lake herds the pollen into lines and patches, like golden-yellow sheets on the water. The pollen is so thick that its fragrance hangs heavy in the air and smells like the smell of sex. No surprise, for that is what pollen is all about.

It is evening, and the lake's surface is like a mirror. Waterfowl calls float across the water – the wailing of a loon, the quacking of mallards, and a medley of grebe calls. Strings of blue-winged and green-winged teal, buffle-head, scaup, and goldeneye whistle in the air over the lake and skid to a splashy stop on its smooth surface. Overhead, several osprey circle, while bald eagles watch from tall snags close to shore. Beaver lodges line the shore like houses in a subdivision. Black "Vs" on the still waters mark beavers making their evening rounds. As we paddle by a wooded island, Canada geese honk in alarm.

"This is some country," says Chris, stretching his arms, paddle grasped firmly in his hands, up over his head.

"Yeah, hard to take," I reply. "But I'm wondering, Chris, who is in the Stanley Cup Finals?"

We find the answer in a sauna. Ken and Sharon are two young people working as caretakers at Blackwater Lodge on Tsacha Lake. The impressive, octagonal log building has smaller, cosy log cabins scattered around for guests. Although the lodge isn't open for business this early in the season, Ken and Sharon invite us in. They have no food, but lots of cold Coke. I cast a beat-up fly off the dock and soon catch enough trout for supper for all four of us. When Ken suggests that he fire up the sauna, we know that we have found paradise. The four of us relax in the sauna, sipping our Cokes and telling our stories. Ken tells us that the final match-up for the Stanley Cup is between Detroit and Washington, and starts Monday. Today is Saturday, and we do not expect to see a TV set for quite some time – not until we reach Prince George, in about ten days. The 1998 Stanley Cup will be history by then.

We leave late the next morning, gliding effortlessly across the twelve-mile expanse of Tsacha Lake. Below the lake, the river really begins to drop quickly into an impressive canyon cut through layers of black basalt. We work *Teal* down the canyon, lining a couple of steep drops, and running others. Near the bottom of the canyon, the river is squeezed, bunching up like a cougar about to spring. We ride down the narrow channel, bouncing through big standing waves at the bottom. Huge, rounded black boulders whiz by us on both sides.

At a small pool of calm water, we pull out to empty the water that has splashed in. Chris grumbles that we did not do that run very well. His cigarettes are soaked. He pulls them out of his breast pocket and lays them in the sun to dry.

The canyon ends with a 6-m (20-foot) vertical drop into a round pool surrounded by black basalt cliffs. We both get the feeling that we are dropping down to the centre of the earth. It is so breathtakingly beautiful that we decide to stop for lunch, so as not to leave all this beauty behind too quickly. Two casts – two fat rainbow trout. Chris already has the fire going and the Kraft Dinner on to boil. Freshly caught rainbow trout, wild chives, and Kraft Dinner – kings could eat no better.

The rainbow trout in the Blackwater are plump, averaging about a half-kilo (one pound) and 35 cm (13 to 14 inches) in length. Below the falls, in the foam-flecked pool, so feisty are they that several leap at a fly at the same time, and it's difficult *not* to catch a trout. They are as beautiful as any tropical reef fish or bird-of-paradise. Their sides are silver, with an iridescent pink stripe running from head to tail. Delicate jet-black dots speckle their flanks, sprinkled most thickly on the dorsal fin and upper lobe of the tail. Looking down from above, we see their mossy green backs, covered with a series of black "Xs." They are almost too pretty to eat. But not quite.

Seeming tragedy strikes on the run down the Echineeko Lakes, really just a 40-km (24-mile) long widening of the river. The sun is shining brightly, and I decide to take off my T-shirt to get some sun. A few blissful minutes pass before I realize, with the instincts developed by long years of living on the edge, that something is amiss. I feel behind me, in the stern, where my shirt should be stuffed. Nothing is there. I look behind, on the quiet waters, and there is my shirt, barely afloat, looking like a pale jellyfish. Now, this is no ordinary shirt. This is my favourite T-shirt, listing the names of all the ski trails in my beloved Gatineau Park. These names have been used for generations and are part of the heritage of Gatineau Park. Then some bureaucratic genius decided to replace all the signs naming the trails with numbers.

Chris and I race back. Just as we are almost ready to rescue the shirt, it disappears beneath the water, sucked down as if by a giant Dolly Varden trout. Like the names of the ski trails, my favourite T-shirt is lost, but not forgotten.

Well, soon forgotten, as we stuff ourselves with fresh-baked cookies and bread at the Echineeko Lakes Ranch, long a destination for big-game hunters and fishermen. In the 1970s, it was run by "Bunch" Trudeau, a licensed guide and expert rider and horse wrangler and the best cook in the area. Bunch was a legend in her time, part of the history of this region. David and Maureen Harrington purchased the ranch from her son, Ted Williams.

Chino Falls on the Blackwater. With every rapid and falls we pass, we get a little closer to the Fraser.

They are proud that the Alexander Mackenzie Heritage Trail runs through their front yard and have dreams of making the ranch a haven for wilderness hikers and adventurers, as well as for fishermen and hunters.

It's a roller-coaster ride downriver from the ranch. In the middle of a rapid, we see a black bear feeding on the carcass of a deer. We wonder if the bear killed the deer. We have seen plenty of black bears on the river, but no signs of *"grizzled and horrible"* bears, as Mackenzie termed grizzlies. We reach crescent-shaped Kluskoil Lake, with spruce-covered hills on one side and large meadows on the other. Just below Kluskoil is Chino Falls – a trout-laden series of unrunnable rapids dropping through huge black basalt boulders and ledges. We bypass it on an easy portage via the Mackenzie Trail. From here, the river really starts to cut through deep beds of gravel, carving a route down to the Fraser.

At the junction of the Echineeko River, we stop to set up camp on a gravel bar, not paying more than glancing notice of the frantic "PEEP!" of a sandpiper. After the tents are up, we find four brown, mottled eggs in a small depression in the middle of our gravel bar. We settle into our tents, but as darkness falls, the mother still does not seem to be around. With rain imminent, we cover the eggs with a fleece jacket. In the morning, a tiny sandpiper peeps in alarm as I crawl out of my tent. We pack up quickly and leave the gravel bar to the sandpiper. We hope her eggs are OK.

Now we are getting into interesting water. William Hillen's book *Blackwater River: Toa-thal-kas* describes his 1970 trip from the junction of the Echineeko River to the Lower Blackwater Bridge: "From the Echineeko to the lower bridge, the Blackwater is evil and dangerous .... Like a dark and furious serpent, the fast, constricted water hisses and thrashes past rock outcropping, lava flows, slick canyon walls and past slides of silt and gravel."[3] My map shows canyons hundreds of feet deep, with sheer walls, ahead all the way to the Fraser. The contour lines are so bunched up that I need a magnifying glass to count them. My topographical map shows a sinuous course, with cross-hatches at each bend, indicating rapids.

The names of the rapids are scary – Slide Rapid, Limping Wolf, Slash Gulch. However, Mackenzie's Native guides told him that *"the river was navigable for canoes, except for two rapids,"* and so it should be for us too.

We find some vicious "S" turns, and the river is getting "pushy." We have to perform some "hairy ferries" to get to the "right" side of the river, but each rapid is runnable. By Slash Gulch, we are exhausted. Besides, it is a beautiful place to camp. The river here funnels between sheer rock walls hundreds of feet high. We cannot see the end of the canyon and decide to scout it. From the top, the water in places is not visible, for the walls are so sheer and the river is so narrow. But what we can see and hear looks and sounds encouraging. We can spot only one significant drop within the canyon, and it looks runnable. The put-in is a little anxiety-producing, as the entire river squeezes to a width of just six metres or about 20 feet, piling up big standing waves.

But once we are inside the canyon, it flattens out and is eerily quiet. At one point, the entire river surges through a slot only one metre or slightly more than three feet across. Chris jumps across the entire Blackwater River. Below Slash Gulch, the canyon walls turn from solid rock to gravel and sand. Given the gravel riverbed, the drops of 12 to 15 m (40 to 50 feet) per mile can be smooth and regular, just a giant waterslide.

All this changes where the road to Prince George crosses the river at the Lower Blackwater Bridge. Local lore recounts that Jonass Jonquin was the last Native person to paddle the lower reaches of the Blackwater. He did it successfully in a spruce-bark canoe around 1900. Hillen, in *Blackwater*, recounts the story of Dr. Baker, who shot the lower Blackwater and declared that "any man who would try it in a canoe must be crazy."[4] Hillen goes on to declare: "From the lower bridge to the Fraser, I want no part of the Blackwater at all."[5]

Crazy or not, we're having a good time. But we are scared as we launch. Once committed, we cannot turn back. If we change our minds, climbing out of these canyons will not be easy. The river sweeps us down, down, down, past black cliffs of solid basalt. At each curve, we see the river disappear downhill, as if carrying us down – again – to the centre of the earth. We try to stop at each bend and listen for the rumble of falls or big rapids. If we can't get any clues from the water, we land and scramble over the steep, sharp volcanic rock to see what lies ahead. We come back from these

For the final 50 kilometres (about 30 miles) to the confluence with the Fraser, the Blackwater flows through a continuous twisting canyon, dropping at a rate of 50 feet per mile.

scouting expeditions scraped and bloodied and agree that scouting is more dangerous than running the river.

The Blackwater is as nice to us as it can possibly be. Only twice do we gasp. Once, a sweeper (a tree that has fallen into the river) blocks the entire channel. It is huge – a Douglas fir, I surmise. This species is found only in the lower reaches of the Blackwater, and I take this as a sign that we are close to the Fraser. The river here is narrow, about 17 to 23 m (about 50 to 75 feet) wide, surging and boiling between sheer rock walls, with eddies so strong that the eddy lines are watery walls about a foot (30 cm) high, over which a canoe could fall and flip. Cross these eddy lines at your peril. Luckily, where the sweeper blocks the river, we are able to clamber up the solid rock bank and portage the canoe below.

We may be running the river, but it feels more like stalking the rapids. We creep around every bend, leaning forward and craning our necks to see and hear if this is where the fatal drop lies. We make *Teal* go around each bend on tiptoes, if a canoe can float on tiptoes. Well, you know what we mean. A little farther on, we hear the deep-throated rumble of a waterfall coming from around the ever-present next bend. We creep around the bend as usual. A landslide blocks the river, creating a small waterfall. On river right is a sheer cliff. But we think that we can portage over the landslide. It is steep and unstable, but we clamber over, wobbling under the unwieldy canoe.

"Say, Chris?" I ask. "When do you s'pose this slide came down?"

"Well, Max," he replies. "Looking at the sap oozing from these broken branches, I'd say a couple of hours earlier today."

Just then gravel and dust start to pelt us, and we launch *Teal* just as fast as we can.

"Geez, Max, this is like paddling down the headwaters of the Amazon or something! Or paddling in an Indiana Jones movie!"

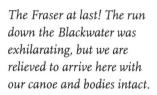

The Fraser at last! The run down the Blackwater was exhilarating, but we are relieved to arrive here with our canoe and bodies intact.

"Shut up and paddle," I reply. We are both already paddling for all we are worth.

We spend perhaps our most memorable night camping on a gravel bar in the depths of the canyon, not far below the landslide. We lie on our backs on the soft gravel, facing a 150-m (500-foot) cliff of crumbly rock across the river. We can hear the occasional rumble of landslides in the distance, and small mini-slides of gravel occur frequently across the river. On our side of the river, a steep forested slope extends almost to the bottom of the canyon, and we feel reasonably secure that we will not be squashed by a falling rock in the night.

We stalk the final few bends of the Blackwater, feeling like John Wesley Powell on the Colorado.[6] At each bend, I mentally count down the number of metres of drop left to get down to the level of the Fraser. We let out a collective sigh of relief when we see its silt-laden waters. We stop on a gravel bar and celebrate our safe descent with the last of our rum.

"Snickers or Mars?" I ask Chris. "Kind of melty. I've been saving these."

"Good thing I didn't know about these, or they wouldn't still be around," Chris laughs. He holds out a plastic bag of squishy, multi-hued glop. "I've been saving something too. Ah, nothing but the best for us ... gummy bear, Max?" The individual "bears" are all stuck together.

We toss the empty bottle of rum behind us: "To Simon Fraser!" we shout in unison. The bottle, made of plastic, clatters, instead of shatters, on the gravel behind us.

When Mackenzie and his men returned to the place that they had left a month earlier, on the shores of the Fraser – about 5 km (about 3 milea) upstream from where Chris and I now rest, sipping the last of our rum – they celebrated their safe return. Mackenzie: *"We now pitched our tent, and made a blazing fire, and I treated myself, as well as the people, with a dram."*

The next phase of our adventure was about to begin – paddling up the mighty Fraser.

14

Up the Fraser:
A River of Liquid Mountains

We ... proceeded with continual and laborious exertion.
— ALEXANDER MACKENZIE, 8 AUGUST 1793

THE FRASER IS A BIG RIVER. Its entire length is designated as a Canadian Heritage River, the first of Canada's big rivers to be completely included in the Canadian Heritage Rivers System. To the Natives whom Mackenzie met, it was simply the Great River, and that name is an apt description.

The power and beauty of the Fraser make us catch our breath. This is a big river for two small people in one small canoe to take on. Not only big, but also mean. If it made the indomitable Mackenzie turn back, what will it do to us? Simon Fraser, in 1808, was the first European to descend the river that is now named after him, but it was decades before anyone else tried. The river gobbled up several canoes of Fraser's expedition, and he had to keep borrowing canoes from the friendly inhabitants of the country.

The Fraser begins in Mount Robson Provincial Park, in the northern Rockies, and rushes 1,360 km (about 820 miles) to the Pacific. No dams impede its course. Mackenzie thought the river down which he was travelling to be the Columbia, then known to him as the Great River of the West. In 1792, Captain Robert Gray had surveyed its mouth, but no white men had ascended it in Mackenzie's time. Mackenzie calculated that to paddle to its mouth and back would be too much to allow him to return to Fort Fork in one season. The people on the way also convinced him to turn around, telling him that *"its current was uniformly strong, and that in three places it was altogether impassable, from the falls and rapids which poured along between perpendicular rocks that were much higher, and more rugged, that any we had yet seen"* – a very accurate description.

Chris and I start up the Fraser with trepidation. This is a river with a mean reputation, well deserved. It runs fast, continuously fast. There are no pools below the rapids, just that relentless current, flowing about 16 km (about 10 miles) per hour in the centre, far too swift to paddle against. The Fraser does not flow, in the sense of a normal river. It seethes, it fumes, it roars. The eddies are like whirlpools, flinging *Teal* back into the force of the current like a piece of driftwood. The water is yellowish brown from the silt that it carries. The silt-laden water hisses against the hull of the canoe, the death cry of mountains being carried to the sea. When we met Ron Thompson, an outfitter familiar with the Blackwater, in Williams Lake, he told us: "I think you boys will do fine on the Blackwater, but I don't know how you're going to get up the Fraser."

The Fraser twists and winds in a never-ending series of curves. Chris and I constantly argue over which side of the river to paddle up. On a normal river, we would paddle up on the inside of the curves, the shortest distance and where we can take advantage of the eddies and quiet water. Rivers deposit sediment on the insides of the curves, making lining and tracking easier. But on the Fraser, this logic fails. To paddle across the river, which is about 100 to 200 m (330 to 660 feet) wide, so as to stay on the inside of the twists and bends is not a decision to be taken lightly. Once we are in the centre of the river, the current quickly overpowers us, sweeping the canoe back downstream. Also, the inside of the bends is not always the best place to be. The eddies are powerful and dangerous. Eddy lines – the borders between the water flowing upstream in the eddy and the water flowing downstream in the main current – must be crossed with caution, if at all. Often the eddies are about 30 cm (about 1 foot) lower than the main river. Paddling up these watery steps is exhausting – and dangerous. However, every water step that we conquer – and I choose this verb deliberately, for that is what it feels like to us – gives us a sense of satisfaction that we have ascended another foot of elevation.

We try tracking, with me on shore pulling on a rope attached to the bow seat and looped under the hull, and Chris in the canoe paddling, poling and steering. But the rocks along the shore are rounded and slippery, and it is like walking on ball bearings. Also, walking along the shoreline of the

Fraser is like negotiating an obstacle course, with cliffs, fallen dead trees and boulders blocking the route. It is futile!

We come to one very difficult corner, where the main current slams into a solid rock face. We park *Teal* in the eddy below and clamber over the rock with lining ropes. Chris finds a secure spot close to the water level, and I leave him there with the bow rope, attached to a rope bridle looped around the front seat of the canoe, so that the pull is from the bottom of the canoe, reducing the risk of broaching in the current and filling it with water. I clamber back to the other side of the rocky corner with the stern rope, ready to "pendulum" *Teal* into shore if things go badly. The river here roars like a waterfall. It is the sound of currents colliding and water slamming against solid rock. In fact, we are attempting to pull the canoe up a horizontal waterfall. Because of the sheer rock face, it is difficult to pull at the most advantageous angle, and the current threatens to pin *Teal* against the cliff.

Chris carefully inches *Teal* up the current but has to let her drop back. The river is surging and sloshing back and forth, from side to side, and one surge almost swamps us. When the river sloshes back the other way, Chris quickly hauls *Teal* past the corner into calm, safe water. We both heave a sigh of relief and wonder what Mackenzie did here. Perhaps this was his carrying-place, where *"the great body of water ... rolls through this narrow passage in a very turbid current, and full of whirlpools."*

Travelling up the outside of bends brings a different set of difficulties. Here, the powerful current erodes the bank, exposing the silvered trunks of long-dead trees now protruding horizontally into the river like the bones of prehistoric creatures, forcing us to paddle closer to the main force of the current. We wonder how old these dead trees are. How long they have been buried in the silt before being exposed by the Fraser's relentless scouring?

Some of the cut banks are hundreds of feet high, forming vertical walls of yellow silt and gravel. Tiny landslides rattle down to the river constantly, thickening the soup of pulverized rock that passes for water in the Fraser.

Despite the effort, the Fraser awes us with its beauty, on both a grand and a tiny scale. The colours are vivid – cut banks of brilliant yellow and orange, skies so blue that it looks like we could scoop up the blue in our hands and make "skyballs" out of it, solitary, tiny yellow daisy-like flowers with purple centres, defying the river's relentless scouring. Bald eagles laugh at us from riverside snags, and deer watch us peacefully from the forested banks.

Despite its ferocity, the Fraser is, and has been, a lifeline for people for millennia. The Fraser is the world's greatest salmon river. Salmon have long supported the people who live along it. Mackenzie was awed by the salmon as he ascended the river: *"The salmon were now driving up the cur-*

The Fraser has cut a deep canyon in its rush to reach the Pacific. Erosion continues before our eyes as we watch dust and gravel rumble down the steep "cut" banks.

rent in such large shoals, that the water seemed, as it were, to be covered with the fins of them." He observed that salmon were not only the favourite food of the Carrier whom he met along the Great River but were absolutely necessary to their survival. He uses this fact to coerce local people to return several stolen articles: *"I gravely added that the salmon ... came from the sea which belonged to us white men; and that as, at the entrance of the river, we could prevent these fish coming up it, we possessed the power to starve them and their children."* His ruse apparently worked, but one has to wonder if this is Mackenzie telling the truth or his ghost writer embellishing the great white explorer, leader and hero.

Although the Fraser is flanked by both the Trans-Canada Highway and a railway, there are few signs of civilization along the river. At night, we can hear the roar of trucks gearing down and the wail of passing trains. But other than these intrusions, it looks and sounds just as it did to Mackenzie. But there have been a few changes. On a rainy day we pull into a dock – the first sign of human life that we have seen in three days on the river. There is a motorhome parked near the dock, but no one seems to be around. We set up a tarp to cook lunch under and to dry out our cold, wet, tired bones.

Soon a man in his fifties walks down to the dock. He is dark-skinned and weathered and very suspicious. We introduce ourselves and show him the note that we have already written and tucked into the door of the motorhome, thanking the owners for their hospitality and explaining who we are and what we are doing.

"Call me Glen. I've lived here for more than twenty years," he says.

"Glen," I say, taking out Mackenzie's journals, "Mackenzie mentions that he did a long portage around Fort George Canyon, where" (I search for the correct entry) *"the rocks contracted in such a manner on both sides of*

the river, as to afford the appearance of the upper part of a fall or cataract ... how-
ever, there did not appear to be any fall as we expected; but the rapids were of a
considerable length and impassable for a light canoe."

Glen looks thoughtful. "You know," he says, "the river isn't as bad as it used to be. Even in my time here, the banks have eroded, the channel is wider and shallower. I think you fellows will be able to work your way up the canyon staying on the water."

Heartened, we set up camp just below the canyon. A sign by the Trans-Canada Highway announces that we are at The Great Canadian Campsite. Two other people are here – Brian, a master's student, and his undergraduate assistant, Craig. They are studying drumlins.

That night, 15 June, storms dump buckets of rain, and the wind howls all night. The next day will be no good to travel. In the morning, Brian and Craig offer to drive us to Red Rock, where there is a small restaurant and gas station. Chris and I stay all morning, drinking coffee and Cokes, talking with the other customers. All seem to have nothing to do and nowhere to go. The talk is mainly about the big storm last night. It was much more severe than we realized, and sections of the highway were washed out. We walk the 8 km (about 5 miles) back to the campsite and sleep all afternoon.

The next morning is foggy, but the storms are past. We cannot see across the river. I have a bad headache, and my stomach is queasy. I fear that I ate something bad at the restaurant yesterday. It's only 34 km (about 21 miles) from here to Prince George, and Chris is determined to get there today. I take some Kaopectate and Tylenol and hope that I can survive.

At Fort George Canyon, we manage to paddle up the rapids, taking advantage of eddies created by huge jagged hunks of black volcanic rock fallen into the river from the cliffs above. We feel as if we are spawning

We paddled up the Fraser through Fort George Canyon without portaging, which makes us feel quite triumphant. Mackenzie had to portage three times here on his return trip up the Fraser.

salmon – hopping from eddy to eddy is like climbing stairs. Each eddy is a step; the more steps, the smaller the height of each one. We find that we can paddle *Teal* up steps more than 30 cm (1 foot) high, if there is a haven of quiet water above to tuck into and rest. We are ecstatic as we furiously paddle *Teal* up to the final eddy. Our celebration is with our last Mars bar, carried all the way from Bella Coola. The wrapper is wrinkled, and the chocolate skin cracked, but it gives us renewed energy. The Natives of Chile chew coca leaves for energy; we rely on chocolate and caffeine.

It is hard to believe that sternwheelers once plied these rushing waters. Iron posts in the cliffs beside the river were used to winch steamers up the river. Passengers were required to help the crew haul on the cables. In 1910, the steamer *BX* was launched. She was the first ship to navigate the canyon under her own steam. She spelled a new, but brief, era for river travellers. She had hot and cold running water and steam heat. Even better, passengers didn't have to work as deck hands and haulers. But roads eventually spelled the end of steamers on the Fraser, and in the rest of Canada, early in the twentieth century.

Above the canyon, the Fraser runs a straight course to Prince George, before it takes a long and hard turn to the east and south. At 7:30 that evening, we arrive. A train passes beside the river. "There goes the no-caboose," I say to Chris. "I remember when I was a kid we always waved at the caboose. I guess kids today won't even know what a caboose is," I lament.

We paddle up a quiet side channel to a grassy bank and haul our canoe up the bank, lean back against our canoe packs, and heave a great huge sigh – of relief, fatigue, exhaustion and exhilaration. Chris finally gets up and walks across the road to a Coke machine. He wobbles and sways, as if the land was rocking back and forth. We've both been in the canoe too long.

Chris comes back with two drinks. "Chris," I say, "It looks like you can hardly stand."

"Yeah, I've got canoe legs," he says, wobbling his hips before plunking down beside me. "I remember last year in Lake Winnipeg when I was on shore and I was just swaying. I'd been out in the waves for days and I could hardly stand up."

We sip our drinks slowly. "You know," says Chris, "it was really good, because there was just this communication between us as we were coming up the Fraser. I mean, I could just tell what you were doing. I just sort of felt: Yah, OK, he's over there, just doing this, and I'll do this now. And it just felt, I mean the communication was just from the feel, the lean of the boat. Like, I'd lean over to one side of the canoe to paddle and you'd do something to make it all work, and it's hard to explain, but it was fantastically fun."

Chris's eyes are shining. We will miss each other. Chris has to go back to Ontario from here, to work on a caribou research project in the north, and I will continue on alone.

We are in a municipal park. Soon the security guard comes over to see what we're up to. His name is Roger. He can't believe that we came up the river.

"I've gone down the river," says Roger. "But to go up. That's unbelievable."

"I'll never do it again," I tell him.

Another fellow named Dorely comes by. He has a box of donuts and offers us some, which we gobble up greedily. Then we remember the Stanley Cup playoffs!

"Is there a game tonight?" we both ask Dorely.

"You're too late," he says. "It's all over, and Detroit has won it again."

Long canoe trips are very bad for watching hockey playoffs, as well as for relationships, we conclude.

Chris telephones his friend Rick Brine to pick us up. Soon we are relaxing with Rick and his wife, Alain, and their two sons. Chris met Rick last autumn when he arrived in Prince George on his epic cross-continent canoe journey. Rick has a heritage of cross-Canada canoeing. His father, Ralph, led an expedition in 1967, taking a freighter canoe with a 20-hp outboard, loaded with mail, from Vancouver to Montreal.[1]

I am really sick, with cramps and diarrhoea and no appetite. Rick and Alain are splendid hosts and nurses. I stay with them for four days.

Luckily, I recover in time for the Willow River Wildwater Paddlefest. Here, Chris and I paddle with some of North America's best white-water playboaters and kayakers. We both try out solo white-water playboats and kayaks. We are even on the winning team for the canoe/kayak relay race. After the paddlefest, Chris hops a bus to head back to Ontario and his caribou research.

My plan is to continue on solo over the continental divide and into the Peace River, to Hudson's Hope, a distance of over 400 km (about 250 miles). Hudson's Hope will be a momentous meeting place for me. Not only will Brenda and Eric be there on 2 July, but I will also see my one true love, Connie. The complexion of the trip will change, as the four of us will continue down the Peace River.

I give myself ten days to travel to Hudson's Hope – an average of about 40 km (about 25 miles) per day.

15

Over the Continental Divide: Paddling across the Roof of the Continent

Here two streams tumble down the rocks from the right, and lose themselves in the lake which we had left [Arctic Lake]; *while two others fall from the opposite heights, and glide into the lake which we were approaching* [Portage Lake]; *this being the highest point of land dividing these waters, and we are now going with the stream.*

— ALEXANDER MACKENZIE,
ON CROSSING THE CONTINENTAL DIVIDE

ALEXANDER MACKENZIE TOOK a very difficult route over the continental divide – up the Parsnip River to a series of three small lakes, now called Arctic, Portage and Pacific, and then a small steep stream, now called James Creek, to the McGregor River and then to the Fraser. Mackenzie was trying to follow the advice of an old man with whom he had talked that winter in Fort Fork, way down on the Peace River on the other side of the Rockies. This man claimed to have been on many war expeditions over the mountains. His advice was sound, but he didn't say (or perhaps Mackenzie misunderstood him) to take a right turn up the Pack River. In fact, Mackenzie does not even mention the mouth of the Pack River in his journals. Simon Fraser later mocked Mackenzie in his own journals for "sleeping" while he paddled by the easy route over the divide.

Why people whom Mackenzie met along his journey showed him this difficult route is hard to know. Perhaps it was a fine route for hiking, but not for an 26-foot canoe. Certainly the Native guide who suggested that direction had no intention of joining the canoe for the downstream run on James Creek, which Mackenzie named *"Bad River."* It was hard work getting over the divide. But it was suicidal going down the other side. The expedition ran into big trouble and almost came to an end on James Creek, where it almost completely wrecked its canoe. Mackenzie's crew patched it up and continued. After another wreck, the men halted to build a new canoe – *"a stronger, better boat than the old one."* In only four days, they were off again. The resourcefulness and skill of these paddlers in all facets of canoe travel put us to shame.

Few have followed this route over the divide since Mackenzie. In 1959, Ben Ferrier found the creek a tangled morass of beaver dams, log jams, and fallen trees.[1] His party members suffered terribly. Their legs were bruised from falling on rocks and numb from wading in the icy water. A knee injury forced them to give up the attempt.

In 1993, the Lakehead University Expedition, retracing Mackenzie's journeys, took two fibreglass replicas of fur trade canoes along this route. Expedition members reported that "the two days spent traversing this 17-km section ... was quite intense and dangerous. The water was COLD!"[2] It was almost constant portaging or lining. The group found the lower part of James Creek much like Mackenzie's description: *"the river before us was so full of fallen wood, that the attempt to clear a passage through it would be an unavailing labour. The country through which we had passed was morass, an almost impenetrable wood."* The Lakehead expedition also damaged one canoe on a rock that punched a hole through the fibreglass.

Chris Taggart also followed this route in 1997 – after the onset of winter. He crossed the continental divide on 13 November, after waiting a couple of days for the ice on Pacific Lake to thicken enough so that he could pull the canoe across it. He then successfully descended James Creek. "The river was a blast. I was really clipping. I can hear the *Nancy Jane* [his canoe] right now: 'Don't you ever do that to me again!' " A day later – his 214th day of travel – Chris was frozen in on the canyon of the McGregor River. "I have come as far as I could. I'm proud!"

Given all these unnerving experiences, I decide to follow the route taken by Simon Fraser, and by all the fur traders and prospectors and canoeists who followed. I will go over the Giscombe Portage to Summit Lake and down the Crooked River and the Pack River to the mighty Peace River – now backed up 300 km (180 miles) by the W.A.C. Bennett Dam to form Williston Lake, the largest "lake" in British Columbia.

The Giscombe Portage takes its name from a prospector of African descent, John Giscombe, who opened the 7.5-km (about 4 1/2-mile) route to connect Summit Lake to the Fraser in the 1860s. The route was busy during the Cariboo and Omineca gold rushes. Giscombe's squared log home was restored in the 1980s, and the portage cleared again. A provincial historic site, the Huble Farm, marks the Fraser River end of the portage.

On 22 June, I set off from Summit Lake. I'm sitting on the front seat, paddling *Teal* stern-first, with all my gear stuffed under the stern seat. She is still a little back heavy and handles a little "piggishly." The Crooked River begins as a series of long, narrow, lily pad-studded ponds connected by short gravel riffles that the canoe barely skids over, with the gravel tickling her hull. Soon the little stream increases in volume and meanders through a flat valley of spruce and willow swamp. It is hard to believe that I'm in the Rockies – the mountains look to be very far away. The stretch above Davey Lake seems interminable, as the river almost loops back on itself several times.

The Crooked River is a lively place above the water. There are many beaver dams to drag *Teal* over, and the turns are so tight that I constantly bump along the shore trying to crank this big ol' canoe solo. Mother moose with long-legged calves watch as I paddle by. Mother Canada geese float in the current, with trains of goslings behind them. I can hear the snipe winnowing high above, like flutes wobbling in the air. The ever-present bald eagles and osprey keep the fish on edge. Bald eagles are pirates and will steal fish from the smaller, more timid osprey. There are so many bald eagles that I start to wonder if they are affecting the populations of osprey.

The Crooked River is lively below the surface too. The water is crystal clear and I am fascinated watching the gravel and waving waterweeds pass beneath the hull of the canoe. As *Teal* approaches, schools of minnows flash in the sunlight and larger fish disappear into the shadows. The river is filled with fish – suckers, minnows, squawfish and at least one rainbow trout, which I cook up for supper.

I camp at Davey Lake, about halfway between Summit Lake and McLeod Lake, and try to catch a trout for breakfast. Out of trout-sized lures, I have only one tiny Mepps left, with a single barbless hook, and yesterday I broke the tip on my trusty $7 telescopic fishing rod. Even with the single barbless hook, I keep hauling in squawfish, up to 45 cm (18 inches), but no trout.

Late that afternoon, 23 June, and helped by a strong crosswind, I cruise north up McLeod Lake – which is about 25 km (15 miles) long – in two hours. *Teal*'s size and her light load let me use the length and depth of her hull like a sail. From the lake, I can see some hills in the distance, but I have to keep reminding myself that I am in the Rocky Mountains, at the roof of the continent.

At the south end of the lake is Fort McLeod, a cluster of three restored log cabins with red-shingled roofs. An interpretative sign tells me that this is the oldest continuously occupied settlement in British Columbia, founded by Simon Fraser in 1805. The post closed its doors in 1952, the year I was born. I ask the sign: "Hey! What about all the villages occupied for thousands of years by British Columbia's First Peoples? We white people are just the most recent in a series of human migrations of continental proportions."

I'm actually more interested in the lodge at the south end of the lake, where I figure I can buy pie and ice cream.

At Fort McLeod is the outlet of the Pack River. The Pack is a delightful river. It flows quickly in a continuous series of gentle, rainbow trout-packed riffles. I am not the only one fishing. I watch a pair of western grebes fishing, apparently successfully. They dive simultaneously, and both are gulping down something when they emerge. On the river below me, a cow moose and a calf swim across the river. A coyote yips at me from the bank. The wildlife along the Crooked and Pack rivers seems as abundant as it must have been in Mackenzie's time.

All too soon, my ride down the Pack River comes to an end. The current slows, and all the trees on both sides of the river have been cut down. The Pack is now a long, sinewy lake. The water has changed from crystal clear to an opaque, unhealthy-looking yellow-brown. An hour passes, and then the vastness of Williston Lake opens up before me. Huge "snags," weathered silver, stand in the lake near the entrance of the Pack River, like a giant picket fence. On the tops of several of these snags, perhaps 20 m (67 feet) high, are osprey nests, untidy platforms of sticks. I can see the silhouettes of the chicks in the nests, their bare heads and scrawny necks poking up over the edge.

Williston Lake is huge. It seems to go on forever. So much sky. I have not seen this much sky since last summer on the prairies. Some 20 km (12 miles) up the lake, smokestacks belch grey clouds at the mill complex in the lumber town of Mackenzie, named for the famous explorer. In the farther distance are misty blue mountains. After paddling in canyons for so long, I find this huge expanse of water impressive.

I gaze through binoculars across the bay at the end of this arm, Parsnip Arm, of the lake and pick out two pickup trucks parked near the water. I paddle over there and talk with two fishermen, both of whom live in Mackenzie. They give me a recreational map of Williston Lake, which is much more detailed than my 1:250,000 maps. I'll bet that Mackenzie would have been thankful to meet someone with a map like this.

I camp on an island close to the town of Mackenzie. It is a perfect campsite, with a gravel beach for sleeping, plenty of driftwood for a fire, and no bugs. If I turn my back to the smokestacks, the scene seems pristine and peaceful – silver water, misty blue mountains, pink clouds. The ever-present bald eagle soars overhead. Loons, grebes, and a variety of diving ducks float on the calm water. I'm relaxing with a cup of hot chocolate when I hear the throbbing of a big engine. A huge barge, the *Williston Queen*, is heading for town.

The area has changed beyond recognition since Mackenzie's time. He and his party *"proceeded against a rapid current* [up the Parsnip River] ... *the water ravages the islands in these rivers ... by driving down great quantities of wood ... the men were oppressed with fatigue."* Later, prospectors and dreamers later mucked for gold on the gravel bars. Trapper's cabins, trading posts, and little Catholic churches were built, and long narrow riverboats sailed, with rivermen standing at the stern holding the handle of a roaring outboard. All this is gone now, along with dinosaur bones embedded in rocks along the cliffs, now submerged in dark waters.

In 1968, the W.A.C. Bennett Dam went up on the Peace River fourteen miles upriver from Hudson's Hope, creating Williston Lake reservoir – 225 miles (340 km) long. The T-shaped lake consists of three flooded river valleys – the stem of the "T" is the Peace, and the horizontal line of the "T," its two former tributaries, the Parsnip (the South Arm) and the Findlay (the North Arm). The Peace Arm cuts across the Rocky Mountains; the Parsnip and Findlay arms lie in the Rocky Mountain Trench.

The Parsnip Arm, where I am now paddling, is about 120 km (about 75 miles) long. This could be a long, hard paddle. *Teal* is a big canoe, and already I am getting blisters on my hands. That tells me that I'm trying too hard.

Clouds. Clouds. Clouds. "I really don't want clouds at all."[3] But these are beauties – great big, puffy, white ones. Clouds in the sky, clouds in the water. The murmuring of the mountains. Later, there are dark and foreboding clouds, veined with lightning and carrying the grumbling of thunder. The wind is light, but blowing from all directions. I seem to be in a rain shadow, as none of the wandering thunder squalls reaches me. Nevertheless, I stay close to shore, with thunderheads shadowing me and scaring me by tossing the occasional lightning bolt my way.

Williston is amazingly lake-like for a reservoir. It has no "draw-down" – the dead zone caused by fluctuating water levels. When I paddle it, it is filled to the brim, and it has lovely, natural-appearing gravel beaches. I wonder how these have formed. I hypothesize previous "Williston Lakes," perhaps during the melting of the continental ice sheets, when landslides might have blocked the Peace. But on the whole, I am bored by this arm of the lake. The forests flanking it have been clear-cut, and a dense jungle of aspen encroaches the shore. The mountains are worn and rounded, but they are getting higher, steeper, and closer as I head north.

I am ready for a break when I hear the throbbing of engines. The *Williston Queen* too is heading north. "What the heck?" I figure. "Why not try hitching a ride?" I plan my strategy carefully. Timing is everything. At the narrowest part of the arm, I paddle out to the middle of the lake, stand up in the canoe, and stick out my thumb, in the classic hitchhiking posture – hand on hip, insouciant slouch – trying to look cool. To my amazement, the engines slow down. "Jackpot!" I shout to myself.

A crewman walks out on the deck, which is about 8 m (about 27 feet) above me, and shouts: "Are you OK?"

"I'm just heading to Hudson's Hope," I reply. "I was wondering if you'd give me a lift?"

"We're just heading to the North Arm," he says – that's the Findlay Arm.

"That's OK," I answer. "I'll just get off at the Forks" – about 80 km (50 miles) north.

"Hold on, I'll check with the captain," he says, and he disappears into the superstructure. In a few minutes, he's back: "Captain says we're not insured to carry passengers. Sorry."

Sadly, I paddle on. But strangely, the barge circles back towards Mackenzie. Maybe the captain feels guilty about not picking me up.

I picked a destination before I left this morning – a campsite called Wilson Creek marked on the recreational map of Williston Lake that the two fishermen gave me yesterday. It's about 64 km (about 40 miles) from last night's campsite, but I'm curious to see what's there. Apparently the B.C. Ministry of Forests made a commitment to provide recreation as part of the deal to build the dam on the Peace and to log the mountains.

The storm clouds are mustering when I finally reach my destination. Not seeing anything from the shore, I climb a high, steep wet clay bank. At the top is the end of a logging road, a decrepit picnic table, and a fire pit made from an old truck wheel well. The mosquitoes are terrible, and there is no easy access to the water. It is just about the bleakest place on a bleak lake. I retreat to *Teal* and paddle a mile back to a nice gravel beach with no mosquitoes and plenty of giant driftwood logs washed up like the carcasses of long-dead whales. It has all the conveniences that a lone paddler about to get dumped on by thunderstorms could ask for – access to water, firewood and big logs to lean against and anchor the tent.

The far shore of the lake disappears as the storm approaches, but I am snug in the tent, with a steaming cup of hot chocolate, a bowl of Kraft

The Peace Arm of Williston Lake cuts through some of the most rugged ranges of the Rocky Mountains.

Dinner garnished with dried spaghetti sauce, and bannock smothered in butter and honey. But the bannock tastes strange, and I wonder if I used Aunt Jemima pancake mix by mistake. Tomorrow, I should turn the corner into the Peace Arm, heading out of the Rocky Mountain Trench and into the mountains.

Surprise. The next morning, a lynx comes down to the water's edge, clearly curious about this apparition moving clumsily on the water. The lynx sits by the shore, as I struggle to get my video camera focused on it, looking very calm and collected, as if canoeists come by here every morning. The lynx kindly waits patiently as I roll the camera and then loses interest in me and disappears into the aspen jungle.

I am getting excited as the mountains close in and I approach Findlay Forks, where the three long arms of the vast reservoir come together. Here, where the Findlay and Parsnip rivers come together to form the mighty Peace, Mackenzie had to make a difficult choice: *"If I had been governed by my own judgement, I should have taken the former* [the Findlay, the branch running from the west] *as it appeared to me to be the most likely to bring us nearest to the part where I wished to fall on the Pacific Ocean."* But Mackenzie followed the advice of the old man with whom he had spoken during the winter at Fort Fork. In his journal entry of 12 May he relates:

"This man had been at war on another large river beyond the Rocky Mountains, and described to me a fork of it between the mountains; the Southern branch of which he directed me to take." Although the southern branch – the Parsnip – is smaller and steeper than the Findlay, Mackenzie followed his advice. Too bad for Mackenzie that the old man did not give a few more details, and he might have followed the Pack River/Crooked River route. Now the meeting of these streams is submerged under 83 m (250 feet) of water.

The forks are still impressive. Here is the largest expanse of water in the Rocky Mountains, where winds from any direction could pin me on shore. As I paddle east into the Peace Arm, I see a cluster of cabins at the end of a wide bay, with a big white sign that says in huge black letters: "CAFE."

What can a poor cross-continental paddler do except paddle a mile out of his way to have a cup of coffee, and perhaps a second breakfast. I tie *Teal* at the dock and walk up the hill to a building where smoke is coming out of the chimney. Inside, three young men are lighting into three huge stacks of pancakes. Peter Kyllo, the chef, and his family have been guiding in this area for more than half a century. His family recalls the days before the Bennett Dam plugged the river like a gigantic thumb in 1968, when they took sportsmen and women up the Peace in long narrow motorboats made specifically for running the rapids. Peter shows me a 1965 article in the *Western Producer* about this region: "She offers everything ... trout, bear, deer, scenery, rapids, cascading waterfalls, mountains of a thousand colours that rise starkly from the Peace."[4]

"Enough romanticizing, Peter," I say. "Can I have some of those pancakes?"

"Anything but pancakes," he replies. "How about some French toast and coffee?"

I paddle out into the Peace Arm with a belly full of French toast and sloshing with coffee. As I turn the corner to head east, an amazing and magnificent scene slowly reveals itself before me. Grey limestone mountains rise up dramatically from both shores, sheer cliffs 1,000 m (3,330 feet) high. The Peace Arm snakes through the skyscraping mountains, like a gigantic fjord as spectacular as any in Norway or Newfoundland or on the B.C. coast.

I detour up a long side-fjord to the Wicked River, which falls in a racing, cascading torrent through a solid rock gorge so narrow that the tops of the cliffs flanking it almost meet in places. The water in the Peace Arm is crystal clear here, and I decide to try a cast, with my broken rod and barbless single hook. A huge Dolly Varden trout sucks the spinner into its mouth. I watch the great fish swimming in the pool below the falls. I can see the white edges of its pectoral fins, and the blue spots on its back, in water at

The Wicked River roars through a narrow canyon as it enters the Peace Arm of Williston Lake in the heart of the Rocky Mountains.

least three metres (about 10 feet) deep. Three harlequin ducks watch as I battle the big fish. Happily, the barbless, rusty hook pops out, but not before I have played the big fish until it is close to the canoe, where we stare at each other, eye to eye. I wonder how big this big Dolly Varden really is?

There are many mysteries and surprises in the waters of Williston Lake, in addition to the size of the one that got away. In the pool where the Dolly Varden is now resting, there lies the submerged homestead of an expatriated Russian, Nicholas Ignatieff who, as a young man, was one of the few fortunate noblemen to escape the Russian Revolution. His new home became Toronto, but at one time he regularly travelled west into the mountains, a refuge from the dreariness of Bay Street. When he was guided up the Peace to the junction of the Wicked River, in the shadow of Mount Selwyn, he was certain he had found one of the most beautiful places on the planet. I am now floating over this place, and still find it beautiful, but I try to imagine it as it once was.

R.M. Patterson (best known for his book *The Dangerous River*, which tells of his adventures on the fabulous South Nahanni) describes this meeting of the rivers in pre-dam days: "This place where the great river [Peace] enters the mountains has magic to it. The mind is caught and held by it, and the weight of countless ages during which the Peace cut down the Rockies as they rose in its path can almost be felt here. It was a place ... where nothing could ever change ...."[5] How wrong he turned out to be!

In 1949, Nicholas Ignatieff built a home here. He also dreamed of creating a settlement for European refugees from war-ravaged countries in the rich valley soils of the Rocky Mountain Trench. But his dream was never realized. He died unexpectedly in 1952, at the age of 49, apparently of a heart attack. Now his home and his dream lie submerged in the icy waters that rose up behind the W.A.C. Bennett Dam.[6]

There are even the ruins of an old mansion hidden in the icy waters of the reservoir. "All's Well" was built by Jack Adams, an adventurous, and clearly very successful, prospector, for his actress-socialite wife, Lucil. For years, she was the only white woman in this area. Mail was delivered infrequently by boat from Hudson's Hope and usually consisted of letters from her relatives and friends full of concern about her lonely life in the wilderness.

Above the water, high above, is the Cave of Winds, a gaping black hole, like a malevolent eye, near the top of a mountain on my left. Legend has it that the original inhabitants of the country would not pass this strange-looking cave. Swiss mountaineers climbed up to the cave in the 1940s and found that it extended to the top of the mountain and made a weird, whistling sound when the wind was strong. I paddle by the Cave of the Winds quickly, but I cannot help looking back several times.

As I head east on the Peace Arm, the mountains gradually grow less spectacular, and small patches of prairie begin to appear on raised benches above the lake. They look like carpets of green laid on top of the thick layers of fine sediments making up the shoreline. The big lake is dead calm. I play with the reflections of the mountaintops on the water, paddling *Teal* along the line on the water where the reflection of the mountains meets that of the sky. The water surface is not perfectly still, and the reflections of the peaks lengthen and shorten, like fingers reaching for me. Everything seems to be happening in slow motion. But, as in all big lakes, progress is surprisingly rapid. A mountain that was barely a concept an hour ago is now a looming reality. Soon it will just be a memory, lost in the blue mists of distance and time. But another vague concept to head for will appear in front. And so it goes, hour after hour, point after point. Big lakes make you kind of crazy.

I stop for a tea break where there is a particularly pretty little patch of prairie perched like a golf-course green on a flat, football field-sized area on top of a bluff squeezed between limestone cliffs and the gravel beach.

"Here's my perfect campsite," I think to myself. "Fire down by the water, sleep on the prairie. Perfect view of the setting sun. High and breezy."

I set up my tent and sit on my very own private prairie overlooking the lake. I watch schools of whitefish swimming by not far from shore. Bright green and yellow grasshoppers crawl and hop on the screen of the tent. I feel completely relaxed and at peace. It is 9 p.m., and my shadow extends across my prairie. I spend some time talking with my shadow, because I know that he will soon be gone.

I leave at four the next morning, woken by the wind. Big rollers are, well, rolling in from the west, but there's gentle, if not smooth, paddling. In two

The view from inside my tent on the shores of the Peace Arm of Williston Lake. This was one of my favourite campsites of the entire trip – framed by water and mountains, with prairie turf for a mattress, and the colours of the prairie all around.

hours, the end of the lake begins to materialize in the distance. It is hard to make out what I am looking at, and I don't know exactly what I am looking for. The entire end of the lake looks like a dam. But soon I can see the hydroelectric power towers and the huge towers in front of the dam at the water-intake tunnels, and that's where I head. I have no idea how I will portage around this "Mother of All Dams," but surely I will have an easier time than Mackenzie did at this spot.

Where I see a dam, this is what Mackenzie saw: *"the stream rushed with an astonishing but silent velocity, between perpendicular rocks ... it was really awful to behold with what infinite force the water drives against the rocks on one side, and with what impetuous strength it is repelled to the other: it then falls back, as it were, into a more strait but rugged passage, over which it is tossed in high, foaming, half-formed billows, as far as the eye could follow it."* Mackenzie and his party had just completed a three-day, 19.2-km (about 12-mile) portage around the Peace Canyon, cutting a trail wide enough to carry their canoe up the side of what is now called Portage Mountain, following a narrow existing trail. A paved road to the dam now follows their route.

Drifting in *Teal* on quiet, wind-sheltered water above the dam, I can see sunlight glinting off the windows of a modern-looking building on a hillside 30 or 40 m (100 or 125 feet) above the lake. I beach *Teal* below the building, pulling her in over big, slippery driftwood logs, and clamber up the hillside through a shrubby forest of serviceberry, birch, and aspen. I emerge from the bush onto a large paved parking lot. A big bus is just pulling out. The driver looks my way, opens his window and shouts at me: "Do you want a tour?"

I shrug, nod and jog over to the bus. The driver opens the door, and I step in. The bus is filled with people. Lots of them. I haven't been this close to this many people for a long time. There is only one vacant seat, beside a very pretty young woman, dressed in dapper navy blue slacks and jacket. Suddenly, I am very aware of my dirty clothes and unwashed, no doubt smelly, body. The bus drives down a big hill to the base of the dam. Massive doors silently slide open, and we drive inside the dam.

The scale of the dam is overwhelming. While not a big fan of dams, I can't help being amazed and impressed by this project. Someone had a big dream to bring electric power to all of British Columbia, to create the largest lake in the province, to plug a mighty river, and it all happened as planned, and it seems to work. There's a kind of beauty to bringing any big vision to fruition, a testament to human ingenuity, determination, and perseverance. If Mackenzie were alive today, perhaps he would be thinking of projects like this.

I learn a lot on the tour from Rheannan Bach, the young woman from the bus, who is the tour guide.[7] The W.A.C. Bennett Dam, named for the then-premier of British Columbia, is one of the largest earthfill dams on the planet. The dam is 2 km (1.2 miles) long, almost 200 m (670 feet) high, and 850 m (2,830 feet) thick at its base, and it weighs approximately 100 million tonnes. I cannot really conceive how big it is until a truck drives across it, and it looks like a dinky toy. A staircase runs partway up the face of the dam – six hundred steps. The dam backs up the Peace River more than 362 km (226 miles). The reservoir took five years to fill with water, which it catches from a watershed as large as New Brunswick. All this water is channelled through ten concrete intakes – the towers that I have just seen upstream of the dam. From these, the water falls at 22.5 km (14 miles) per hour, through ten steep penstock shafts, to the underground powerhouse. There its force spins huge turbines, which rotate the generators that produce the electricity. Simple, eh?

The W.A.C. Bennett Dam plugs the mighty Peace River to form Williston Lake, the largest lake in British Columbia.

The generating station, which is built inside the dam, is cut out of solid rock and looks like a perfect set for a Star Wars movie. It is like a huge cave, 15 stories high, .5 km (1,670 feet) long, and brightly illuminated with lights that cast a weird yellow-purple glow on the walls and machinery. I stare into the horseshoe-shaped tailrace tunnel – the manifold – which returns the water to the river downstream of the dam. I ask Rheannan if I can launch *Teal* in the manifold. She shakes her head.

While I stuff myself with doughnuts in the cafeteria, Keith Cheyne, the bus driver, Rheannan, and the other staff members at the visitor centre (the building with the big windows that I had first seen from the water) discuss how to get the canoe and my gear around the dam. Two strapping young lads from Alberta, here on vacation, help me drag *Teal* and my gear up the hill. The next tour is not full, and Keith decides to load the canoe in the tour bus. We slide *Teal* in between the two rows of seats after all the passengers are on board. Keith explains that there will be a slight detour while he drops me off at the tailrace just below the dam. Rheannan video-tapes me as I load up. I can hear the whirr of the generators and glance furtively over my shoulder at the wall of gravel that holds back 74 billion cubic metres (96.9 cubic yards) of water relentlessly pushing against it. Rheannan waves as I paddle off.

I gaze back at the bulk of the dam and at the channel blasted through solid rock and wonder about the wisdom of it all. Although it is hard to argue against a non-polluting source of power, I'm reluctant to support such huge projects, which cause such massive changes to the land and water. I have a deep mistrust about having so much power concentrated in one place.

My mistrust may not be unfounded. While I stay tonight in Hudson's Hope, I will learn that someone hacked into the computer system that controls all the B.C. dams. There was brief panic, but no threats to flood the province came through, and operations soon returned to normal. The provincial government told the public nothing about the problem. But the situation did add credibility to my gut misgivings and mistrust.

Below the dam, the current sweeps me into a deep canyon of red and grey rock, with shiny black patches of coal. A waterfall pours over the cliff, falling in an intricate white tracery. Delicate ferns grow on the cliffs beside the falling water.

The current soon slows and stops, as *Teal* slides into the still waters of Dinosaur Lake, the reservoir of the Peace Canyon Dam, 24 km (about 15 miles) downstream. Dinosaur Lake winds through a landscape like no other I have seen. Imposing cliffs of shale and high banks of fine grey sediment

Around 14 miles (about 23 kilometres) below the W.A.C. Bennett Dam, the Peace Canyon Dam backs up the Peace River to form Dinosaur Lake, named for the fossilized bones found in the soft sediments that comprise its banks.

rise up over 100 m (about 330 feet). Aspen forest and grassy meadows cover the tops of the banks, as if someone has unrolled a prairie carpet over the sediments, creating instant aspen forest and grassland.

The box canyon of the Peace revealed many secrets of the earth's past before the Peace Canyon Dam flooded it in 1980. Fossilized bones of plesiosauruses were found here in 1976. These long-necked marine reptiles, up to 12 m (40 feet) in length, swam in the ancient seas that covered this area 100 million years ago. Many fossilized footprints were found in the canyon, including the world's earliest of birds, discovered in 1979, and the tracks of herds of duck-billed dinosaurs. Who knows what other finds are now hidden below the water?

The lake is dead calm. The reflections of the trees, the high cut-away banks of soft grey sediment, the lone birch trees, the towers of harder sedimentary rock in the water are like Japanese paintings. The colours are soft and muted. Nothing moves. It is so peaceful. I like the Peace.

Mackenzie did not. Instead of a calm lake, he saw a raging river. After lining their canoe up rapids for days, things got worse: *"We proceeded to where the river was one continued rapid .... Here we again took every thing out of the canoe, in order to tow her up with the line .... At length, however, the agitation of the water was so great, that a wave striking on the bow of the canoe broke the line, and filled us with inexplicable dismay, as it appeared impossible that the vessel could escape from being dashed to pieces, and those who were in her from perishing. Another wave, however, more propitious that the former, drove her out of the tumbling water, so that the men were enabled to bring her ashore ... the river above us, as far as we could see, was one white sheet of foaming water."*

Whereas Mackenzie wondered how to proceed up this raging river, I calmly paddle past an island where five people are having a picnic. They wave me over.

"Do you have a match?" a man asks me. Of course, I have matches stuffed in all my pockets.

I toss a packet of paper matches to him. They introduce themselves. I tell them about my experiences at the dam, and it turns out that I am speaking to Rheannan's mother. Two of the others, Bob Fequet and Greta Goddard, generously invite me to stay with them while I wait for the rest of my crew in Hudson's Hope. We make arrangements for Bob to meet me at the Peace Canyon Dam. I'll be there in about two hours.

As I paddle the final few kilometres to the Peace Canyon Dam, about 3 km (about 2 miles) from Hudson's Hope, I think about all the landscapes that I've passed through since I left Bella Coola: snow-capped mountains, vast meadows, basalt, shale and silt canyons, silt-laden rivers, a huge reservoir, and a mind-boggling dam.

To see the landscape change at the speed of a canoe fills me with a sense of anticipation as each new vista unfolds, to give way to amazement as each new landscape engulfs me. The slow speed of the canoe, like walking, eases me into new vistas. It is so much more fulfilling than zooming at the speed of sound or at the speed of a pronghorn antelope running full out. It gives me a chance to be a part of the landscape, to ease myself into it, to sleep on it, walk on it, float on it, and to carry some of it with me under my fingernails and in the cracks in the worn skin on the sides of my index fingers. More than anything else in my life so far, watching landscape pass slowly before my eyes brings me a profound peace and joy.

Bob and Greta meet me at the Peace Canyon Dam. We load up *Teal* and my gear in the box of Bob's 1974 pickup truck. I am ahead of schedule and have four days before Connie, Brenda and Eric will arrive. In that time, I become part of Bob and Greta's family and part of the community of Hudson's Hope. On 1 July, Canada Day, I take part in the celebrations and have my photo taken with the two RCMP officers in town, Mike and Mike. Employees of B.C. Hydro, museum personnel, shopkeepers – everyone knows me. It's just the holiday I need.

16

Down the Mighty Peace:
A Long and Winding Road

From the place which we quitted this morning, the West side of the river displayed a succession of the most beautiful scenery I had ever beheld.
— ALEXANDER MACKENZIE, 10 MAY 1793

L IFE IS CHANGING, and transitions make me nervous. Well, I'm really nervous about meeting Connie. This is her summer holiday, and I feel obliged to ensure that she has a good time. What if the Peace River is boring? What if the bugs are terrible? What if the weather is terrible? What if she doesn't get along with Brenda and Eric? What if she doesn't get along with me? I've never been on a long canoe trip with her.

On 2 July, Brenda and Eric and Connie all arrive at Bob and Greta's home. Connie has been in southern Saskatchewan doing surveys of prairie song-birds. She is a songbird biologist for the Canadian Wildlife Service. An old friend and canoeing buddy, Elaine Nepstad, drove Connie here from her home in Valleyview, Alberta. Brenda and Eric have driven here in a rental car from Edmonton, where they flew from Toronto. They have their Grumman canoe with them and a 2-hp outboard. Once again, we have made a ren-dezvous in another part of Canada, on another leg of Mackenzie's long, thin trail across this vast country.

On 3 July, we bid goodbye to Bob, Greta, their two-year-old son Christopher, and their dogs, Wiley and Captain Crunch. Christopher gives us his favourite stuffed dog, which he tells us is named Christopher after

I meet Connie, my future wife and mother-to-be of Isaac, in the town of Hudson's Hope, British Columbia, as we had arranged before I left Ottawa. She has just completed songbird surveys in southern Alberta and Saskatchewan.

himself. Yesterday, at the local Thrift Store, Connie and I bought a teddy bear that we have named Mackenzie. Mackenzie is a surrogate for Sir Alex, my faithful partner of last summer, whom I had somehow misplaced. We felt that we needed a travelling companion. Now we have two. We place Mackenzie in the bow and Christopher in the stern.

We launch our canoes, Brenda and Eric, the film crew, in their canoe with a "kicker," just below the Peace Canyon Dam. B.C. Hydro employees allow us to drive down to the river on a service road normally closed to the public. They promise not to open the dam and flush us down the river. Compared to the W.A.C. Bennett Dam, this structure is minuscule. But nothing about these power projects is small. The turbines and generators for this dam's powerhouse are among the largest ever installed in North America. Manufactured by the Leningrad Metal Works in Russia, the four 200-tonne turbines got here on a journey of Mackenzian proportions – a total of 20,000 km (some 12,000 miles). They are so large that trucks could not transport them along highways. A road was built for them through the wilderness from the British Columbia coast to Ootsa Lake, whence they were floated across the province. Ilya Klvana, the kayaker who crossed North America in 1999, followed the British Columbia route of these Russian turbines, portaging his kayak on wheels along the turbine highway.

Below the dam, the Peace flows quickly between imposing cliffs of shale. The water is translucent light green. Waterfalls decorate the cliffs in narrow curtains of white, dropping over 100 m (330 feet) in streams, trickles, and torrents. The river swirls around "flowerpots" – top-heavy columns of resistant sandstone. Springs gush from the cliffs, their mineral-laden waters painting the cliffs in rich shades of cream, sienna and gold.

The Peace River near Hudson's Hope was much more scenic than we had expected, flowing green and clear, past cliffs, caves and "flowerpots" as shown here.

The Peace, the mighty river of the north, is one of the oldest and deepest rivers on the continent, having flowed east out of the Rocky Mountains for perhaps as long as 60 million years. During this time, it has been covered by glaciers and blocked by deposits of gravel and rock and, most recently, by the W.A.C. Bennett and Peace Canyon dams. Below the Peace Canyon Dam, the Peace travels for 1,991 km (about 1,200 miles) to its confluence with the Slave River near Lake Athabasca.

We pull over and climb up to a grotto in the cliffs. Water falling from springs above creates a screen of silver in front of the mouth of the cave. Brilliant green icicles of algae, water dripping continuously from them, hang down like long stalactites. Tiny white stalactites hang down from the ceiling. Connie and I crawl in between the dripping water and cuddle in the cave. It is a magical place. The Peace is a magical river.

The current of the Peace soon sweeps us under the bridge where the Alaska Highway crosses and into the prairies. Just downstream, the Pine River enters the Peace with a river-full of silt, changing the green water of the Peace to brown. High bluffs and shale cliffs rim the river. Above the bluffs, we know, there are roads and ranches and towns, but there are few signs of civilization down here. The air is fragrant with the sweet smell of clover and the aroma of mint and chives, which grow in profusion close to the water's edge. Thick beds of white and yellow clover about two metres high cover the low islands that break the Peace into shifting channels. There was no clover when Mackenzie came this way – it arrived with the ranchers and farmers. Deer graze along the river and run up steep slopes with incredible ease, but the herds of elk and bison that Mackenzie reported are gone. We see magpies – my first on this trip – a sure sign of the prairies. Predatory cries alert us to the presence of red-tailed hawks, soaring in slow circles high in the cerulean sky. Their cries have a primal, prehistoric quality – the sound that I imagine a pterodactyl would make. Flocks of Bonaparte's gulls and California gulls float in the eddies and

Clover, taller than my head, covers the low islands and shore, scenting the air with its sweet fragrance.

stand on the mud flats. The ever-present bald eagles keep watch from riverside bluffs.

The current sweeps us across the British Columbia/Alberta border, just downstream from the Clayhurst Bridge, the first obvious intrusion of modern civilization after the Alaska Highway. At the bridge are the foundations of a house. The house is gone, but the gardens that once adorned it are doing just fine. Oversize daisies and lilies in full bloom grow in profusion around the old foundations. Connie picks two wonderful bouquets – purple and pink lupines, yellow Shasta daisies with maroon centres, purple and pink asters, orange and white lilies. We put the flowers in two yoghurt containers and secure these to the bow and stern decks of *Teal*. Mackenzie (the teddy bear) moves back to share the stern deck with

The Peace River becomes a true prairie river as it crosses the border between British Columbia and Alberta. This is the area Mackenzie described as: "the river displayed a succession of the most beautiful scenery I have ever beheld ...."

Christopher (the stuffed dog, remember?). Everyone seems happy, and we set off downriver with our newly decorated canoe.

Below the Clayhurst Bridge, the scenery becomes ever more prairie-like. The once-green water of the upper Peace is here opaque with silt. We hear the hiss of silt hitting the hull of *Teal* – a sound that I haven't heard since battling up the Fraser. We decide to stop and camp on an island a few kilometres downstream from the bridge. This may be the island where Alexander Mackenzie camped on 14 May 1793, when he wrote that *"it* [the current] *became very rapid, and* [the river] *was broken by numerous islands."* On the north side of the river, prickly pear cactus and prairie grasses cover the steep slopes. On the shadier south bank, the dark green of spruce and the bright green of aspen forests cling to the crumbly soil.

Connie and I paddle across the river and climb up the north bank late in the evening. Many of the cacti are topped with bright yellow blooms. Serviceberry trees are heavy with juicy, dark blue berries. We fill our hats with berries and take them back to camp to sweeten our breakfast oat-meal. We climb to the top of the bluffs, about 300 m (about 1,000 feet) high, as the sun is setting. The river appears as a curving silver snake, as if made of glass. Two coyotes call back and forth to each other, before a chorus of yipping animates the darkening sky. Before turning in for the night, we fill a bucket with river water to settle the silt overnight. But in the morning, our water filters clog up almost immediately. We give up on this system and start to look for springs for drinking water.

As we drift down to Dunvegan (once a fur-trading post), where a sus-pension bridge crosses the river, the scenery is breathtaking. The slopes covered with dry bunchgrass invite us to climb them, but it is too hot during the day. Hoodoos – eroded spires of soft sediments glued together – create the silhouettes of castles. Mackenzie observed: *"the West side of the river displayed a succession of the most beautiful scenery I had ever beheld. The ground rises at intervals to a considerable height, and stretching inwards to a considerable distance; at every interval or pause in the rise, there is a very gently-ascending space or lawn, which is alternate with abrupt precipices to the summit of the whole, or, at least as far as the eye could distinguish. This magnificent the-atre of nature has all the decorations which the trees and animals of the country can afford it: groves of poplars in every shape vary the scene; and their intervals are enlivened with vast herds of elks and buffaloes."*

We walk along the muddy bed of Fourth Creek. The creek, now just a trickle, has carved a steep canyon. Aspen and cottonwood grow along its bed. Hoodoos, some with larger, flat rocks balanced on top like hats, have formed on the dry, steep canyon walls. Our footprints mix in the soft goopy mud with prints of bears, deer and coyotes. Back at the Peace, we stand in the shallow water to cool off. The water is so opaque that our legs appear to stop at the waterline. We cannot see even one centimetre below the surface.

When Brenda and Eric help us unload the canoes to camp that night, my feet sink into the mud. Everyone laughs. Then my ankles disappear, my knees, my thighs. I'm completely stuck. "Help!" I call out. "I'm stuck." No one moves to give me a hand. No one wants to get muddy. At last, relaxing completely, I slowly wiggle one leg out, then the other, and slither like a pre-historic mud-man up the bank. By this time, everyone has given up the idea of staying mud-free, and we slither and slide into the river, swimming in the surprisingly refreshing opaque waters, whooping and hollering.

That night, the river rises over one metre in height, reminding us that, despite appearances, this is a dam-controlled river, harnessed for power production. The W.A.C. Bennett and the Peace Canyon dams have changed the river's annual cycle of high- and low-water levels. Peak flows have gone down, and high winter demand for electricity has resulted in higher flows in winter than in summer – a reversal from pre-dam days. Before the Bennett dam was installed, the Peace froze for about six months a year. The release of more water in winter has delayed freeze-up, especially near Hudson's Hope. Elders on the lower Peace tell us that the ice is thinner now, and there is less scouring of the banks during spring break-up. The mouths of tributaries are shallower and overgrown with vegetation, affecting spawning and rearing for many species of fish. There are more serious implications for the vast Peace-Athabasca delta, the world's largest freshwater delta, but I discuss these when we get there – still more than 1,000 km (625 miles) downstream.

Alberta's largest suspension bridge, (550 m or 1,833 feet long) crosses the Peace at Dunvegan. Here we see our first buildings along the river – a lovely log church weathered silver grey and the log rectory beside it. These structures and the house of the Hudson's Bay Company's factor have been restored to their appearance in the 1890s, along with the St. Charles Roman Catholic Mission Church and Rectory. Costumed interpreters help bring the days of the fur trade back to life.

The North West Company established Dunvegan as a fur trade post in 1805, to replace Fort Fork – which Mackenzie had built – as the main post for developing the fur trade in the far west. Its location was ideal, on a flat fertile benchland, perfect for vegetable gardens. Herds of bison blackened the surrounding prairies and hills, providing a reliable source for pemmican – the fuel of the fur trade. Here North West Company fur trader Daniel

Harmon wrote his meticulous journals, which depict fur trade life so vividly.[1] In 1821, the new, amalgamated Hudson's Bay Company took over the post, which remained in operation until 1918.

We enjoy our tour of the buildings, but the highlight of our visit is the tea room and market garden. We belly down to a sumptuous supper of fresh salad picked from the garden, home-cut French fries, and strawberry short-cake and ice cream. After our hottest day on the river, under an unrelenting prairie sun, we are ready to pamper ourselves. Ron Friesen, the owner, gives us a sack of potatoes and a bucket of strawberries to take with us.

Ron recalls when Alec Ross, who has recounted his canoeing experiences in *Coke Stop in Emo,* spent a few days here on the final leg of his epic journey in 1989. We ask Ron about the scaled-down replica steamboat sitting high and dry beside the greenhouse. "We had an idea to use it as a floating hotel and restaurant, running tourists up and down the Peace, just like in the old days," he says. The river is so beautiful, we wonder why the idea didn't catch on.

We are thankful to have the whole river to ourselves, but in the not-too-distant past it was a much busier place. Brigades of birchbark fur trade canoes soon followed Mackenzie up the Peace. After fur trade amalgamation in 1821, York boats made their first appearance here. These craft, much heavier than canoes, could carry much more cargo. In addition to having long sweep oars, they could be rigged with a sail. But I can't imagine how such clumsy craft navigated the swift, shallow waters of the Peace. They must have been tracked up much of the river, with several crew members pulling with a heavy rope from shore, while a steersman remained on board.

In 1882, at Fort Chipewyan, the HBC built the first steamship in what is now northern Alberta – the SS *Grahame.* But that vessel ran up the Peace only as far as Vermilion Chutes, below the town of Fort Vermilion. The intrepid black-robed priests of the Oblate Order of Mary Immaculate (the OMI) modernized river travel in the isolated Peace River country. Bishop Grouard bought a steamboat in Peterborough (better known as the centre of canoe building in Ontario).[2] The boat was portaged in pieces from Lesser Slave Lake over what is now known as the Grouard Trail to the Peace, where it was reassembled at St. Augustine's Mission, near present-day Shaftsbury, the ferry dock. Named in memory of Bishop Charles Eurgene de Mazenod – the OMI's founder – the *St. Charles* was 60 feet long. Launched in 1903, the steamboat was operated by the OMI, with Father Leteste as captain, until 1911. The trip upstream from Fort Vermilion to Peace River Crossing took six days, and a round trip cost $30.

Not to be outdone, the HBC in 1905 built the *Peace River* – a 110-foot sternwheeler, which started the glory days of steamer travel on the Peace. The year 1916 saw the launching of the largest and most luxurious boat – the *D.A. Thomas*. This stern-driven paddlewheeler, 161 feet long and 37 feet wide, accommodated 160 passengers. The staterooms had hot and cold running water and electricity. The dining lounge boasted white linen and the finest silver. This floating luxury hotel operated in country considered wilderness, where most people lived in tents or log cabins.

The U.S. army used sternwheelers in 1940 to transport materials for the Alaska Highway and for the bridge over the Peace River at Taylor Flats. Roads into the Peace River country ended steamer traffic; the last commercial run took place in 1952. Now, with the fur trade canoes, York boats, and sternwheelers gone, we have the river all to ourselves.

Brenda and Eric get up early, fire up their little outboard, and head to the town of Peace River. Connie and I sleep in until ten. I feel guilty about our late start. Connie and I munch on strawberries as we paddle downriver. The valley of the Peace is widening, and the bluffs along the river are not as high.

Connie reads from Mackenzie's journals as we paddle. We are looking for the site of Fort Fork. To jump-start his expedition to the Pacific, he built this fort in the autumn of 1792 as an advance post, just 10 km (6 miles) upstream from *"forks of the river,"* where the Smokey River joins the Peace. He had sent crewmen here in the spring *"for the purpose of squaring timber for the erection of an house, and cutting palisades, &c. to surround it."* When he and his men reached the post on 26 October 1792, the river was freezing over. The advance crew and about seventy local Natives fired a volley of welcome to greet them. Mackenzie wryly noted: *"If we might judge from the quantity of powder that was wasted on our arrival, they certainly had not been in want of ammunition."* He set out for the Pacific on 9 May 1793.

We land where we think that the old fort was located. There are no obvious traces left today, but archaeologists have recovered many artefacts from Mackenzie's time. From Fort Fork, Mackenzie would have had a panoramic view up the Peace River, which cut a great trench to the unexplored lands to the west. Out of sight lay the Rocky Mountains, which he knew he must cross to achieve his goal.

That evening, we meet up with Brenda and Eric in the town of Peace River, which is nestled at the foot of rolling bluffs and offers a spectacular view of the river. There are beautiful riverside homes, ugly square apartment blocks, and enough fast-food franchises to fulfil our wildest junk-food fantasies. The town lies at the heart of the most northerly grain-growing area on the continent, on top of great underground reservoirs of natural gas and oil, and at the edge of the boreal forest and its seemingly inexhaustible supply of wood. The biggest business in town is the huge bleached Kraft mill, belching white smoke and perhaps making the paper on which this book is printed. A Beaver legend printed on souvenir mugs says that if you drink the water of the Peace, someday you will return. However, given all this industrial activity, none of us will be drinking any more water from the Peace. No way.

The next day, a short distance downstream, Connie and I head to shore where we see a small waterfall dropping into the Peace. We are thinking: "clean, clear, cool water" – one thing that we are beginning to miss on the "mighty muddy" Peace. But as we approach the bank, we see something strange about the little stream. Its water is milky grey. White globs of goop coat its polished rocks, and shiny black patches of oil float in its eddies.

"Black gold, Texas tea," Connie says. "It's kind of beautiful, in its own way."

I wet my fingers in the stream and touch them to my tongue. The water is cold and saltier than the ocean. We follow the rivulet up the bank and see a remarkable sight. The water is burning. Just above the bank, the water gushes out of the ground from a rectangular concrete well. A bright orange flame, about three metres (about 10 feet) high, dances in the breeze. It looks like a scene from hell. I take photographs of Connie through the flame.

"It stinks here," she says. "I don't know if I can get much closer. If the wind changes, I'm going to get fried."

"Wow! Connie, we could camp here on a cold winter night and toast marshmallows."

We retreat to the peace and serenity of the river.

The scenery is still beautiful, but changing. The valley continues to widen, and the prairie is being replaced by forests of birch and poplar. In the late afternoon sun, the white and cream-coloured bark and bright green leaves of the aspen seem to glow, as if illuminated from within.

"Connie, I wonder where Brenda and Eric are?" I ask. They have gone on ahead, with the help of their outboard, to look for a campsite. "It's stinking hot, and we're out of strawberries." I whine.

There's a small cluster of homes by the river.

"I wonder if one of these houses has cinnamon buns?" I continue. "I'd really like a good homemade cinnamon bun-bun-bun."

Connie replies: "That's the trouble with civilized canoe trips. You're always thinking cinnamon buns rather than saying 'forget it, we're not going to see a cinnamon bun for a month.' It'll be a relief to get away from those potential Coke stops."

All the way down the river, Connie would pick out a name of a long-gone community on the map, and we would stop there in the hope of finding a Coke machine. We stopped even at provincial campsites marked on a recreational map of the Peace, but they were invariably deserted. We didn't even find a Coke machine at the Shaftsbury ferry. Connie has a minor addiction to Coke, and the pickings have been slim.

Then we see a sign on a riverside birch tree that would lift the heart of any hot, thirsty paddler: Something even better than Coke – BEER, 2 KM.

Soon we arrive at Peace Island Camp. Brenda and Eric are already there, sipping beer. This is a private camp on an island in the middle of the river. Rarely have we seen such a peaceful, bucolic, idyllic place. We certainly didn't expect to find something like this on the muddy Peace. But this river, as we are finding out, is full of surprises.

The site has eight little cabins with green-shingled roofs, a small main lodge made of wooden planks, outdoor washbasins filled with warm water and oil lanterns already lit to guide clients who have had too much beer. Wooden boardwalks connect the cabins and the lodge. It reminds me of tourist camps along the Zambezi in Africa. Clients come here on a tour boat from the town of Peace River.

The caretakers, Rob and Linda, greet us with their dog, Buddy, and ask if we're staying for supper. We all nod enthusiastically.

I comment on the special quality of the light here.

Rob explains: "The forest on this island has never been logged. These are old-growth black cottonwood, black poplar, white birch and white spruce. It probably looked like this when Mackenzie came by. Come to think of it, a lot of the forest around here probably looked like this ... not that scrubby stuff."

In the evening, Connie and I walk to the tip of the island to watch as the sun goes down, painting the river in shades of pink. The sun, a big red rubber ball, plunks into the water beyond the next bend, or so it seems to us. Behind us, a full moon rises above the river.

"I just never expected the Peace River to be so beautiful. I'm sure glad you're along to share all this with me," I say to Connie, as we snuggle together, sitting on the edge of a cut bank with our legs dangling in the air. The upward-spiralling trill of Swainson's thrushes rings from the tops of the tallest trees. They sound like veeries (my favourite bird call back east) in reverse – an ascending, instead of a descending, flute-like trill. "I think that sound must go straight to heaven," Connie muses. Sunset is about ten o'clock, reminding us that we are heading north.

We camp overnight and leave late the next morning, after a huge breakfast of pancakes and eggs served up by Rob and Linda.

Below Peace Island, bubbles break on the river's surface, produced by natural gas emitted from the riverbed. Mackenzie didn't mention these. Perhaps they are a recent phenomenon, or perhaps he was sleeping.

All this natural pollution does not seem to affect the fish. I try a cast where the relatively clear waters of the Cadorette River enter the Peace. A metre-long pike immediately latches on (I'm still using the $7 telescopic rod with the broken tip). The pike tries a few rushes, but the water is only about half a metre deep. I play the tired fish in to shore and carefully release it. It is very pale and silvery – a result of the murky waters. I wonder how it can find fish to catch. Feeling sorry for these deprived pike, I decide to leave them in peace.

The weather continues very HOT! We do not expect such hot weather this far north. Connie and I stop for a swim in the clear waters of the Notikewin River. I set up our camera on my little tripod, balanced on a pack in the canoe, to take a photo using the self-timer. After the shutter clicks, just as we are both swimming away, we hear an ominous splash. I look at the canoe, and, sure enough, the camera is gone. Luckily, it has fallen into the clear waters of the Notikewin, or we never would have found it. We dry it out as best as we can, under the hot Peace River sun, and hope for the best. A few hours later, the camera is working, but the lens has condensation that refuses to dissipate. At least I have a telephoto lens that works, along with the backup "point-and-shoot" camera.

The Peace is getting bigger, the valley continues to broaden, and the prairies have given way completely to forests of birch, aspen, and spruce. It seems to take forever to paddle around these big, sweeping curves, which are kilometres long.

"So, Max, what are some of our favourite things?" asks Connie, bored with paddling around yet another endless bend that looks exactly the same as the last one – and the next.

"Umm, I think a good ball hockey game is right at the top of my list," I say.

"Oh, really," Connie replies. "I thought they might have been expendable."

Ooops! Wrong answer, I think to myself. I hope that she doesn't ask any really hard questions – like, if I had only one day left to live, would I prefer to play ball hockey, paddle, or spend it with her?

"I also enjoy watching landscape pass in front of me at the speed of walking or paddling," I add.

Connie lets me off the hook. "I won't ask you any X-rated questions, 'cause all this is on video," she says, pointing the camera at me.

"I also like pie and ice cream. I could sure use some now." And music. Some of my favourite times have been at Rasputin's (a folk music club in Ottawa). "How many songs do you know, Connie?" I ask, trying to change the subject.

"Not enough to sing us to Fort Chipewyan," she answers.

"I'll teach you the three 'bums' song," I reply brightly. "You know, the one that goes: 'Just bummin' around the railway ... ' "

And we paddle off, both singing loudly to the river, the trees, the sky: "Just two good bums, jolly good chums, living like royal Turks ... "

We stop at the deserted Native village of Carcajou (French for "wolverine") for a look. It had been a beautiful community. Several sturdy log homes still stand, surrounded by weeds and white picket fences, the paint now flaking and faded. A 23-foot flat-bottomed wooden river scow lies half-hidden in the long grass that was once a lawn. Locust trees and honeysuckles grow wild around the homes and form living fences around old pastures. The largest building had once been a hardware store, we conclude from the invoices that we find blown on the floor from a once-neat pile on a desk. The most recent invoice is dated 1968. There is an income tax return from 1970, completely filled out. We think about the work and dreams that had gone into this little community. As we leave, Connie picks up a 1973 copy of *Chatelaine* magazine, in perfect condition, and she takes it to read in the canoe.

We know that we are in the boreal forest now. First, we see the spruce. The forests are becoming completely dominated by spruce. Next, the bears. We see two black bears swimming across the river today. Then, the black flies – swarms of them. Finally, there are the clouds – the first that we have seen since Hudson's Hope. It starts to rain, and keeps on raining, as if someone has just turned on a tap. We're camping on a muddy island (the gravel islands and banks are long gone) in the river, just downstream of the Clayhurst Ferry. A paved road winds up the muddy bank from each side of the river.

By morning, the canoes are half-filled with water (we had washed them out, thinking that, on the positive side, the rain would give us several days' supply of nice, clean drinking water), and our "island" is semi-liquid. Our muddy campsite is becoming more like water than land, as the rain continues to fall in sheets. We might just get washed away.

But the tents, pitched among high grasses, are holding solid, and the river isn't rising too quickly. There seems to be no cause for alarm, but it clearly is not a day to travel. By noon, Connie is restless and looking at the provincial road map.

"Max, why don't we hitchhike into La Crete. Its only about 30 kilometres, and the ferry is running. I bet we'd get a ride right away," she says.

Connie and I paddle upstream to the ferry, while Brenda and Eric stay behind, to move camp in case the river floods. We get to the dock just as the ferry arrives with a full load of cars, pickups and RVs. We pull *Teal* well up from the water and hide her in the woods. Then we jog over to the road, dressed in our best rain gear, and stick out our thumbs. The vehicles are just coming off the ferry. A big, baby-blue Cadillac pulls over right away. The driver introduces himself as Peter Rempel, and his daughter, Nicole. They live in La Crete, which, Peter says, is about a thirty-minute drive away.

The ride to La Crete is a revelation – mile after mile of rich farm fields of wheat, oats, and peas. From the river, we had no conception that just beyond the trees lay this extensive northern agricultural land. (We begin to wonder about the water that we have been drinking from springs and small streams in the area.) In the distance, the grey outline of the Buffalo Hills rises above the prairie.

Peter tells us that much of this land was natural prairie before the settlers came. Mackenzie wrote about farming at the trading post: *"In the summer of 1788, a small spot was cleared at the Old Establishment* [at the mouth of the Boyer River, downstream from present-day Fort Vermilion] *and was sown with turnips, carrots and parsnips. The first grew to a large size, and the others thrived very well. There is not the least doubt that the soil would be very productive, if a proper attention was given to its preparation."* According to Peter, "This is the most northerly wheat-growing area in the world. In 1893, Peace River wheat won first prize at the Chicago Exposition." Most people today in La Crete, he informs us, are Mennonites, whose progenitors recognized the rich agricultural potential early in the twentieth century.

Peter drops us off at the newest restaurant in La Crete, where we revel in a greasy supper and write postcards. We then move on to the other local restaurant for dessert. By 11 p.m., we think about heading back to our muddy camp. We toy with the idea of renting a hotel room for the night, but that seems too decadent, and Brenda and Eric might worry that we got mugged.

Connie warms up her thumb, and we stand by the side of Highway 697, the road to the ferry crossing. Every car that passes stops and asks where we are going. But no one is heading to the landing. Two teenaged fellows in a "muscle" car go by several times. The first time they just slow down to look us over. The second time they stop and ask where we are going. The third time they wave. The fourth time they stop and offer to drive us to the ferry if we pay the gas.

"How about $10?" I say.

They have a brief discussion and then say: "We've got to do something first, and then we'll be back."

And off they roar, tires throwing up gravel from the shoulder of the highway.

The hotel is looking like a better and better option. But a middle-aged woman with a kindly face who had stopped earlier comes by again and offers to drive us to the ferry. She was camping there when we arrived, she says, and recognized us as "the canoeists." Her name is Eva. Like most local residents, she is a Mennonite, and, like everyone else whom we have met here, she is kind, generous, polite and genuinely interested in us. Everyone here seems particularly peaceful and contented, even the two "hot-blooded" teenagers, who were very polite underneath their gruff James Dean exteriors. Eva tells us that it has rained over four inches, and more is on the way.

The next morning, the rain clouds are replaced by wind clouds. The wind howls out of the north, building up steep waves, piled up even steeper by the current of the Peace. We are ahead of Brenda and Eric, who are no doubt freezing and getting drenched by the spray with their small outboard going full tilt. We pull ashore at a sheltered cove to make tea and wait for them. Just as the water boils, they come around the bend, heads leaning forward into the wind. We wave them over, but they don't look up. We shout, but they can hear nothing above the sound of wind, water and the roar of the outboard. We run along the shore, hoping that they will see us, but the motor relentlessly pushes them around the next bend and out of sight.

It's 120 km (about 75 miles) to Fort Vermilion, and we've got all the food. Brenda and Eric have the maps.

There is a huge curve downriver from here known as "Hungry Bend." Apparently some river travellers ran out of food here. Unless Brenda and Eric realize that they have passed us, they will find the name most appropriate. We have not seen a sign of our friends and conclude that they are making the run all the way to Fort Vermilion. At 6:30 that evening, we pass a lovely campsite and decide to stop.

This section of the Peace seems interminable. Connie finds an Alberta road map, so we can vaguely keep track of where we are. The river winds around huge bends, at one section almost forming a circle. The current is slowing down, and we can't buy a wind for our seldom-used sail.

Conversation inevitably turns to food.

"What's left to munch on?" Connie asks.

"Umm, there's some sesame snaps and Eatmore bars still," I say, rummaging around in the grub bag. Eatmores are especially good for hot-weather trips, because they don't melt. I don't know why they don't melt. I put a package of sesame snaps and an Eatmore bar on my paddle blade and pass it up to the bow. It is at this moment that Connie gets her inspiration. Carefully separating two of the sesame snaps, she puts a piece of the Eatmore between them and takes a bite.

"Wow! This is AMAZING!" she moans ecstatically.

"Even better than the strawberry and Eatmore sandwiches back at Dunvegan?" I ask.

"Way better. This is perfection."

Connie makes a sesame-and-Eatmore sandwich and passes it to me on her paddle.

"Oh, you're right. This is AMAZING!" I exclaim.

And so we drift down the Peace, munching our special sandwiches slowly, meditatively, savouring every sensation that our taste buds can garner from this unlikely combination, making every mouthful last as long as possible.

A black bear swimming towards us snaps us out of our reveries.

"Hey, Connie," I say, "maybe we should try to videotape this one."

Connie picks up the camera, and I paddle hard to bring us alongside the bear. The poor fellow is worried now. Its eyes are open wide as it stares at us. We can hear it panting as it swims towards the opposite bank as fast as it can.

"Max, I think this is close enough," says Connie, who, with the camera zoomed in, has a viewfinder filled with the terrified bulging eye of a bear.

"Ah, don't worry, Connie, we're fine," I say.

Just then, the canoe runs aground on one of the sandbars that fill the Peace, and the bear's feet also touch bottom. Black bears are normally peaceful creatures that do not want to make trouble, but we haven't exactly been polite. Frantically, I push us back off the sandbar into the current. The bear shakes itself, regains its composure and calmly launches itself back into the river.

"You know, Max, I don't think it's a good idea harassing the bears like that. Just because we're biologists doesn't give us licence to harass animals. Besides, you never know when you'll run into a psycho bear."

"Yeah, I guess you're right," I say. I know that she is right, but I'm used to not having anyone around to tell me when I'm acting stupid.

We pick up an injured dragonfly, lying on the surface of the river. Its wings vibrate feebly, sending out ripples cross the mirror-like surface. We set it on a pack to dry out in the sun. It is incredibly beautiful, its long body banded in black and teal stripes. Sadly, it dies. I guess its time had run out.

Ahead, giant torsos cross the river. They are actually the concrete supports for the highway bridge just upstream of Fort Vermilion. Unfortunately, we cut behind an island, and, when we emerge at the downstream end, we realize that we have just paddled past the town. We head upstream and cross the main channel towards what looks like the centre of the community. The banks are steep and bushed in. We see no paths leading from the water's edge.

"Hey, Max, I smell French fries," says Connie.

We land where the smell is strongest and clamber up the bank over logs and through a thicket of wild roses. Connie's sense of smell never fails when it comes to French fries, and we emerge, a little scratched and dirty, at a road that parallels the river at the top of the bank. Across the road is a restaurant.

"Coke and fries," says Connie, her eyes gleaming in anticipation.

Inside the restaurant sit Brenda and Eric.

"We figured you two would find us here," Eric says.

Fort Vermilion has a rich history. In 1787, trader Charles Boyer built the Boyer Post, *"the Old Establishment"* as Mackenzie calls it), a few miles downstream from the present-day community of Fort Vermilion. In 1792, it was replaced by what Mackenzie marked on his map as *"the New Establishment,"* several miles upstream. It was known variously as Fort du Tremble, Old Aspin House, Finlay's Post and Lafleur's Post until 1828, when the HBC built a trading post here, and it took its current name. The oldest building in town is the Old Bay House, built in 1905 as the HBC factor's house and now a provincial historic site. There are many hand-hewn dovetailed log homes in Fort Vermilion, including the restaurant where we are eating our French fries.

When Mackenzie landed here in October 1792, on his way to set up his advance post at Fort Fork, he received quite a welcome at the New Establishment, still under construction. *"At six o'clock in the morning of the*

Vermilion Chutes, the only portage on the 1,300-kilometre length of the Peace River from Hudson's Hope to Fort Chipewyan. When Mackenzie passed this way, he described the falls as being about twice as high as they are today. Two centuries of erosion have made a difference.

20th [of October], we landed before the house amidst the rejoicing and firing of the people, who were animated with the prospect of again indulging themselves in the luxury of rum, of which they had been deprived since the beginning of May, as it is a practice in the North-west neither to sell or give any rum to the natives during the summer." Already about three hundred Natives looked to the post to trade furs for supplies. Mackenzie stayed here three nights, until *"the thickness of ice in the morning was sufficient notice for me to proceed."*

The HBC post grew a vegetable garden, but Roman Catholic missionaries sowed the first grain grown here in 1871. Wayne, manager of the local motel, where we have booked a room for the night, knows a lot about the town. He tells us that in 1876, wheat from here won a gold medal at the World's Fair in Philadelphia during the U.S. Centennial celebrations. A flood of settlers soon followed. But dreams of northern cities and transcontinental railways never materialized. Today, Fort Vermilion remains a peaceful, vibrant community of about 1,000 people, rich in the heritage of the fur trade, farming, its most recent wave of settlers (the Mennonites), and its First Nations roots.

Brenda and Eric are running out of time. They had hoped to travel all the way to Fort Chipewyan with us. Sadly, they have to leave us here – the last road access to the Peace. Connie and I continue on, but we feel a big loss. No longer do we look ahead to watch for Brenda waving us over, Eric shouting: "Coffee's on!"

We paddle downstream through an unchanging landscape of flat boreal forest. We stop early to camp at the Caribou River, where Wayne has told us there are fossils to be found. But we see no sign of them. Perhaps the water is too high from all the rain. The Caribou River runs into the Peace in a series of standing waves, like chocolate cake batter, or a thick chocolate milkshake – the kind that I remember from when I was just a kid.

In the middle of the batter swims a beaver, leaving a wake of chocolate ripples. By the shore, I see clouds of mud slightly more opaque than the muddy water. I sit by the shore and watch the swirls. Finally I make out the outline of a fish about 20 cm (8 inches) long, resting in such shallow water that its back slightly protrudes above the surface.

Without Brenda and Eric, we are both depressed that evening. The Peace looks very big, and we feel very small.

One day downriver is Vermilion Chutes, the only portage on the Peace. Mackenzie described the falls when he landed here on 17 October 1792: *"The river at this point is about four hundred yards broad, and the fall about twenty feet high."* Erosion has reduced the falls to about 3 metres (around ten feet), which we still have to portage. We carefully pick our way down the rapids – a series of low limestone ledges – above the main drop. Just below the main drop is a convenient ledge about one metre above the water. We lower *Teal* and our packs down to the water. A strong eddy pulls *Teal* towards the falls, so I hold her by the bow and stern lines until Connie is settled in, and then I jump in. It all goes surprisingly smoothly.

Vermilion Chutes is a truly beautiful site. The chocolate-cake batter that passes for water on the Peace churns over the falls, stretching in a frothy brown line across the entire river, broken only by a few small islets of brown limestone. The banks of the river are made of low limestone cliffs. We find a nice rock beach to pull out our canoe, and we set our tent up on top of the limestone cliffs, with a great view upstream of the falls. Big prairie storm clouds are blowing in from upriver – the kind that look as if the hand of God is about to reach through to pluck up us mere mortals. We add extra rocks to the guy ropes holding down our tent, sit back with our hot chocolate – a little less opaque than the river water – and get ready to enjoy the show.

When steamboats ran the Peace, a 14-km (about eight miles) road ran from the head of the rapids to the community of Little Red River, where all freight and passengers were transported. With a strong tail wind at last, we sail into Little Red River. Two outboard motorboats and two canoes are pulled up on shore – the first water craft that we have seen on the river since the ferry in La Crete.

There is a large clearing here, and several old log buildings. The field is pink with fireweed in full bloom. A trail leads from the landing to an area where the grass and weeds have been cut. In the middle stands a small shrine made of wooden planks, built in the shape of a pyramid about 2.7 m (8 feet) tall, with a cross on top, painted white. Beside the shrine stands a frame for a teepee. Inside, behind a window, sit sacred objects. Bison horns represent traditional Native beliefs. Catholic symbols abound: a picture of Jesus, perhaps cut out from a book, glued on to a plastic juice bottle; porce-

A large clearing filled with fireweed on the banks of the Peace River marks the site of Little Red River, an abandoned Native community. A lovely shrine has been built here by local Native people.

lain statues of Jesus and Mary; a cross made of two twigs tied together with twine; candles with full-colour, life-like images of Jesus on them; a wicker basket of cheap silk flowers; a plastic glass with a picture of the archangel Gabriel glued on it; a white silk robe embroidered in silver; a silver cross on a chain; and a gold-coloured metal chalice filled with stones. The sacred objects, blending two spiritual traditions, are arranged on a woven blanket that looks as if it came from a tourist shop in Arizona. The dominant colour is red. We stand in awe, transfixed by the spirituality of this simple shrine.

A white canvas tent is set up in the meadow at the edge of the forest. Smoke comes from a stovepipe extending through the roof. We walk over to visit. As we approach the tent, we call out "Hello!," but no one answers. We can see several people in the tent sleeping under their blankets. A young man is awake, but he makes no acknowledgment of our presence. We don't feel welcomed, but perhaps they are just shy. Or maybe this is a site where we are out of place. We wave goodbye and walk back to *Teal*.

The wind is still blowing strong from the west. We hoist sail and "haul ass," managing to sail even around the bends in the river. In the late afternoon, a thunderstorm blows in and sucks up all the wind. We paddle the last few hours, intent on reaching the community of Garden River, where Connie is certain that she can find a Coke. On the way, we cross the boundary of Wood Buffalo National Park, at the site of an old trading post known as Fifth Meridian, which marks the western boundary of the park. We celebrate by eating our last chocolate bar.

Wood Buffalo is one of the largest national parks in the world. The rest of our trip to Fort Chipewyan – about 300 km (about 180 miles) – will be through the park. To quote from a brochure for park tourists: "Canada's biggest national park is home to the world's largest bison herd and the only nesting site of the endangered whooping crane. This vast wilderness of bogs, forests, meandering streams, huge silty rivers and great tracts of

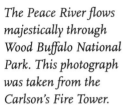

The Peace River flows majestically through Wood Buffalo National Park. This photograph was taken from the Carlson's Fire Tower.

spongy muskeg has changed little since the days of the fur traders. Cree and Chipewyan residents still hunt, fish and trap here for their livelihood." I have an admission to make – I wrote that piece over a decade ago, as part of a brochure describing all of Canada's national parks, but this is the first time that I have actually seen, smelled, and got myself dirty in the park.

The park was established in 1922 to protect the last remaining herds of wood bison – a larger relative of the better-known plains bison. Only a few hundred wood bison remained when the Canadian government began to protect them in the 1890s. Soon after the park was formed in 1922, the government shipped in about 6,600 plains bison from southern Alberta. The two species interbred, but some pure wood bison may still exist in the park.

The plains bison, as well as introducing new genes, also brought bovine tuberculosis and brucellosis. Ranchers who graze their cattle in summer in the rich meadows near the park worry about the spread of the diseases. Park officials have rounded up and inoculated the animals and shot any suspected of carrying either microbe. Some people think that all the bison should be killed as a preventive measure. Since the bison in the park are hybrids, they claim, they are not true wood bison, which diminishes their value. I'm sure that the bison don't care. They just want to be left alone. We just hope that we get to see one.

This is just one of many controversies in the park. Managing a wilderness as big as New Brunswick is not simple, as we are to find out, and the park is much more than a home for bison.

Soon the sight of a row of houses on a bluff overlooking the river welcomes us to Garden River. There is no road connecting this community to the "outside," but there is a small confectionery set up in a trailer. A family from Fort Vermilion – the Roses – runs the store. Karl, the father, suggests that we camp on the bluff overlooking the river. The Roses are very friendly and very good junk-food salespeople. We walk out of the store laden with pop, potato chips, chocolate bars, and – best of all, as we find out later – big jugs of Sunny-D.

Karl says that the local people are often very shy, and many don't speak English. We pitch our tent in the meadow overlooking the river. A Native woman in a house close by motions us to fill our water containers at the faucet on her house. She says not a word to us, as we fill our plastic bottles – mostly empty Cokes – but gives us a friendly smile. Connie and I stroll around town that evening and sit on the steps of the pretty log church to watch the sun set, drinking our Sunny-D.

The wind is back in our faces again, and the current is much slower. The banks are low, the beaches are wide, and the river is full of sandy islands. The sun and wind are relentless. Although we are almost in the Northwest Territories, it is so hot and dry that we feel as if we are paddling through a desert. There is no shade on the shore or on the sandy islands in the river. Our supply of drink is quickly depleted. The river seems monotonous, the scenery repeating itself over and over as if we are paddling on a treadmill. The river cuts through clay banks with stands of large white spruce, almost a metre in diameter – by far the largest trees that we have seen since the Rocky Mountains, except for the big cottonwoods on Peace Island.

Seeing these big trees, we understand why logging produced such controversy here in the park. This was the only national park in Canada that allowed commercial logging – part of the agreement to create the park. These riverside forests of white spruce are rare ecosystems in Canada, and park managers were concerned about the ecological damage caused by logging. Recently, all such activity has been stopped, and the companies involved have received compensation.

Hordes of dragonflies hover and swoop over the river. Black bears frequently swim across it. We share an island where we camp with a bear for the evening, before it decides to swim across the rest of the river. Although we complain about the heat and the monotony, the region works its magic – the long sandy beaches, the abundant firewood, the sunny weather, the lack of mosquitoes, and the beautiful sunsets lull us into a sense of oneness with this old river. We like the Peace.

But we also like hot showers, and we can feel the pull of Fort Chipewyan moving *Teal* forward. There is a beautiful meadow at the Jackfish River warden's station, overlooking the river. One of the two cabins in the meadow is made of logs and was once cosy, but now the roof is falling in. Buffalo rangers – wardens who patrolled the park on snowshoes and with dog teams – used to stay here. Pope and Taylor – the Americans who paddled from New York to Nome during the Great Depression – spent much of

As the Peace River swings north, the prairies have been left behind, to be replaced by the land of black spruce, black flies and black bears. We saw black bears swimming across the river daily.

their winter layover in Fort Smith, Northwest Territories, working with the park's buffalo rangers. Most of the work involved shooting bull bison to thin the herd. I wonder if they ever stayed in this cabin?

We camp outside the cabin, amid a lot of stale bison droppings. That night we hear strange sounds, unlike anything that either of us has ever heard – a deep, eerie wailing from somewhere in the spruce. We don't know what kind of animal is there, but I may find out at breakfast. Connie is still snug in her sleeping bag, and I'm boiling up hard bread soaked overnight in water to make a traditional Newfoundland treat called "brewis." Hard bread ("hard tack") is still baked commercially in Newfoundland and exported to grocery stores across the north, where it is popular trail food. Kept dry, it lasts forever.

The brewis is cooking up nicely when I hear a large animal crashing through the woods, heading our way. I hope that it is a wood bison, but a big black bear emerges from the trees and heads straight for the breakfast fire.

"Hey!" I yell. "We're just having brewis."

The bear turns and scoots back into the woods. Obviously, it has had brewis before.

The current picks up again as we head for Boyer Rapids. Here the river flows through white and light-brown gypsum cliffs, capped by dark forests of spruce. The cliffs have eroded into spires that remind us of castles from childhood fairy tales. Bald eagles and peregrine falcons soar above them. Colonies of cliff swallows have glued their mud nests to the sheer rock faces. High above us, a tiny black cross etched on the blue sky is another large bird of prey – perhaps a golden eagle. It reminds us that soon we will be flying home, high up in that blue sky.

But first we have to change the date of our return air tickets, and we haven't seen a telephone booth in a long time. We are, of course, much later than we anticipated. Just downstream of the Boyer Rapids and the wonderful gypsum cliffs is the community of Peace Point. We hope to refill our empty Sunny-D containers there. At a break in the gypsum cliffs, we see a landing area, with an outboard motorboat pulled up on the shore. On the top of the cliffs – only about 10 m (about 33 feet) high here – a steel tower looks like an overgrown Mechano set, painted red and white, with a flashing light on top. Beside it, a new log bungalow sits in a meadow dotted with wildflowers.

We land and walk over to the bungalow. No one is around. Connie waits at the front while I walk around the building. To my amazement, I see one of those blue metal signs with the symbol of a telephone, and, sure 'nuff, a pay telephone booth is around the back.

"Connie," I shout to her, "do you have a quarter?"

Then I collapse, laughing uncontrollably, because the situation seems so ridiculous.

We hear a dog barking not too far away and walk in that direction, look-ing for the community. About a half-kilometre from the river is a group of six neat log homes. A man outside the nearest one is chopping wood. He waves us over.

"I'm Charlie Simpson," he introduces himself. "Let's have some tea."

He leads us inside, where his wife, Bev, and their twelve-year-old son Richard, are having lunch.

"We're fixing up the cabin here for the winter. We live in Fort Chipewyan, but we like to come here on weekends to trap. Come 'ere, I'll show you something."

Beaming proudly, he spreads out two lynx pelts. They are beautiful. I know that Connie is having a hard time reconciling trapping with her own ethics. So am I. Especially since we are in a national park, where we are used to thinking that all wildlife is protected. Wood Buffalo, however, is different. Charlie explains to us that after the park was created in 1922, people in the area who harvested natural resources for subsistence could continue to do so. Special regulations ensure sustainable use. For Charlie, being out on the land is an important part of his cultural heritage, and it is what makes him feel most alive.

"My father, Archie, trapped here all his life," Charlie continues, a dreamy look in his eyes. "He made his rounds with a dog team. He would set more than a hundred traps and checked them every three days. What a lot of work that was."

We both murmur agreement.

Charlie goes on, eager to tell his story: "I use a skidoo, so it goes a lot faster. I really like it in the spring, when everything thaws out and you can hear water running everywhere in the bush, over the beaver dams, everywhere is the sound of water. I like to sit at the edge and wait for the beaver to come down to the river. When they see you, they hit the water with their tail. I like that, and the sound of the ducks, and the birds singing in the woods."

We are a captive audience, but we enjoy listening.

"You know, sometimes you get nothing, sometimes there's lots. Last winter was good for lynx because there were lots of rabbits. Trapping was my dad's life, and it's my life too. When I'm out on the trap line, I feel good," he concludes.

It sounds like a good life to us, too, and an enlightened way to run a national park this big. Charlie fills up all our water containers with clear, cold water from a tap on his cabin.

We camp on the bluff overlooking the river and watch the sun set – a big red rubber ball in a smoky purple sky – as we munch away on the usual beans and rice, mixed with rehydrated salsa, all rolled up in tortillas. We can see why Peace Point is considered a sacred place. From here, we can look miles up and down the river. According to Mackenzie, this was the spot where the Cree and the Beaver peoples settled a long-standing dispute. Both the point and the river derive their name from this historic agreement.

Below Peace Point, the river loops drunkenly, in huge lazy curves that seem to take forever to paddle around. There is no valley now. We have entered the vast Peace/Athabasca delta. This is one of North America's most impressive wildlife areas. Huge flocks of geese, swans, ducks, and other water birds funnel through here each spring and autumn on their migrations. Bison also depend on the rich sedge meadows of the delta for their food.

In the 1990s, people began to notice that the delta was drying up. Many blamed the W.A.C. Bennett Dam, more than 1,300 km (about 800 miles) upstream. Charlie Simpson told us about this and also that he was concerned about the effluent put into the river by pulp mills. He said that the water is muddier now, and often oily slicks appear on the surface.

The traditional way of life in Fort Chipewyan is at stake, as well as the wildlife that depends on the rich vegetation and aquatic life. The annual cycles of flooding, according to Cree elders, have been changed by the dam and the regulation of the Peace River flows. Global climate change is responsible for the drying out of the delta, some scientists argue. There have been attempts to integrate the traditional knowledge of the Cree, Métis and Chipewyan people of the area with scientific research. There are still many questions to answer, but the Bennett Dam appears to be largely responsible for the drying up of the delta. Despite innovative efforts, such as creation of artificial ice dams to recreate the spring floods, the delta is drying up. The population of bison has fallen, from over 11,000 animals to just over 2,500 – because of disease, change of habitat following the drying of the delta, or a combination of both. It is one more challenge for the national park.

The sun is relentless, and soon we are wading to cool off, the mud squishing up between our toes like chocolate icing. You can tell that we're a little "bushed" because everything reminds us of dessert.

"You could sell this stuff. The mud, I mean," says Connie. "My feet have never been so clean, and my skin feels great."

The cool mud feels so good that we plunk ourselves into the murky water. It washes over us, feeling cool and refreshing, leaving our skin feeling cleansed, rather than dirty. It is good, clean mud.

A picnic table and a metal fire pit mark the site of Sweetgrass Landing, once the site of the biggest logging operation in Wood Buffalo. An old road leads from here to the Sweetgrass Bison Management Station, where the animals were once corralled and inoculated in some of the wildest roundups ever. We intend to hike into the station overnight, hoping to see bison. There are bison droppings everywhere, and we wonder too about bison-sized depressions in the forest.

We hike along a ditch with a trickle of water in it – the Claire River, whence Mackenzie left Fort Chipewyan on 12 October 1792 on his way to the Peace. *"We accordingly steered West for one of the branches that communicates with the Peace River, called the Pine River* [the Claire], *at the entrance of which we waited for the other canoes, in order to take some supplies from them."*

Mackenzie took a direct route west to the Peace from Lake Athabasca, cutting through the delta: *"It is evident, that all the land between it* [the Peace River] *and the Lake of the hills* [Lake Athabasca], *as far as the Elk river* [the Athabasca], *is formed by the quantity of earth and mud, which is carried down by the streams of those two great rivers. In this space there are several lakes. The lake, Clear Water, which is the deepest, Lake Vassieu, and the Athabasca Lake* [now Lake Claire – not present-day Lake Athabasca], *which is the largest of the three, and whose denomination in the Knistineaux* [Cree] *language implies, a flat low, swampy country, subject to inundations. The last two lakes are now so shallow, that, from the cause just mentioned, there is every reason to expect, that in a few years, they will have exchanged their character and become extensive forests. The country is so level, that, at some seasons, it is entirely overflowed."*

Perhaps Mackenzie's predictions about the lakes drying up are coming true, but not in the way that he envisioned. It is hard to imagine paddling down the Claire River today.

Once we're on the Claire, away from the Peace, the mosquitoes descend in force. We lose the trail that we're following and decide instead to head to Fort Chipewyan – with dreams of chocolate cake, to go with all that chocolate icing oozing up between our toes.

Back on the Peace, we soon see the Carlson's Fire Tower, situated on a high sandy bluff above the river. We land and climb up to the tower, the sand falling away from under our feet with each step. This is the highest elevation that we've seen for days. An open forest of jack pine grows on the sandy soil. There is a well-maintained park cabin beside the tower, with a picnic table outside. The cabin is open, and we are out of tea. How could I have not brought enough tea? Sure enough, there is a tea canister in the kitchen. We "borrow" enough tea bags to see us through to Fort Chipewyan, along with a packet of hot chocolate for a special treat.

There is the expected "No climbing" sign by the tower, so up we go, on a rickety metal ladder. I open the trap door leading to the room at the top, and we both clamber through. The view is amazing. A sea of boreal forest flows from horizon to horizon, split by the mighty Peace – a broad ribbon lying in great, swooping loops on the land, shining silver in the sun. A view to last a lifetime.

When we're back on the river, the lazy current sweeps us past more swimming bears and through endless meanders. We stop for a break at a trapper's cabin on Moose Island. The winter road from Fort Smith to Fort Chipewyan crosses the Peace River here. A yellow, diamond-shaped road sign by the river tells us that Fort Chipewyan is only 50 km (30 miles) away, by road. The sign seems very out of place, like the telephone booth at Peace Point.

We are enjoying a cup of pilfered park warden tea when a motorboat pulls up. An elderly man is piloting; an old woman sits in front, with two little dogs. One of the animals is white and fluffy, with black patches, called – you guessed it – "Spot." The other is a tiny puppy, wrapped in a blanket. We walk down to the shore to help pull up the boat.

The husband and wife both step out. She looks around and says, wistfully: "There used to be a nice community here, and a big garden. But no more. Now everyone has moved to town. I grew up here, you know."

They don't stay long to chat. They are in a hurry to get to Fort Chipewyan. We are too.

We are looking for the mouth of the Quatre Fourches – locally pronounced "Catfish" – (four forks) channel of the Slave River. We have to go UP the Quatre Fourches. Soon we find its mouth and bid goodbye to the Peace.

For more than 1,300 km (820 miles), we have ridden on its waters and watched them change from crystalline to opaque. We feel as if we are leaving an old friend.

The current in the Quatre Fourches is swift and relentless, and progress is slow. After a few miles of creeping up the bank, which is thick with willow, aspen and alder, we see an outcrop of pink granite, a harbinger of the Canadian Shield. After a thousand miles of limestone, sandstone, shale and mud, the first sight of granite is like the first robin of spring! Children of the Canadian Shield that we are, we stop and hug the rock, lie on it, roll on it, dance on it. We revel in its solidity. We jog back to *Teal*, excited about the prospect of camping on rock.

But the willow forest closes back in, and we end up camping on a soggy patch of scouring rush, a carpet of nearly fluorescent green sandwiched between the water and the willows. But it is a beautiful campsite. A stand of tall, golden marsh grass waves in the breeze in front of our tent. Through the willows, an open forest of spruce and poplar grows on top of the low banks. Beyond the banks, the land falls away into the flatness of the delta. If a dam were built here, like that on the North Saskatchewan at Grand Rapids, future canoeists would get lost trying to find the submerged river channels, just as I did on Cedar Lake, back in Manitoba.

As we are chowing down on Kraft Dinner, Charlie Simpson roars by in his motorboat. He has a passenger, Frank Voyageur.

"I thought I might find you two here," he says. "You're making very good time."

They stop for tea, of which we now have much stock. Charlie gives us a bunch of fresh grapes and a bowl of cherries. The juicy, fresh fruit tastes so good.

The next morning – the last of our trip – we paddle around an endless succession of bends that all look identical. We have about 40 km (about 25 miles) to go to the channel leading to Lake Athabasca. We feel as if we're on a treadmill again, and after six hours of hard paddling (the call of Coke and goodies in Fort Chipewyan is very strong!), we stop to eat lunch on a fallen log – the only dry, solid thing that we can find to sit on. Our feet are submerged once again in mud up to our calves. We eat fast, pack up and continue on the river again. We are tired and grumpy (at least I am), but no more than five minutes after lunch, we see the Quatre Fourches – the spot where four channels meet. Here is where we turn left, taking the shortest channel to Lake Athabasca.

There is an unpainted plywood cabin by the river, and a tall thin man outside, telling his dogs to stop barking. We stop to be polite, as he waves us over.

"I'm Joe Wandering Spirit," he introduces himself. Wow. What a great name. "Connie" and "Max" seem to pale beside it. He shows us a plastic tub filled with big pike, walleye, whitefish and suckers, which he has caught in nets set near his cabin.

"Dog food," he says.

The storms of the morning have passed, and a strong west wind blows us down the channel leading to Fort Chipewyan. We hoist our sail and relax. Connie reads aloud from the final chapter of the Louis L'Amour novel that has been keeping us company along with Mackenzie. Just as we get to the lake, the son of the story's hero is taking revenge on the three bad guys who did in his Pa. Out in Lake Athabasca, we can see the town, white buildings, a big white church, with the blue waters of the lake spreading horizon to horizon, broken only by small, rocky, spruce-covered islands. Behind the town rise the spruce-covered hills, with pink granite outcroppings, of the Canadian Shield.

Falling farther behind us are the flat expanses of the delta, the mud of the prairies, the Rocky Mountains, the Pacific Ocean. I've come a long way.

Fort Chipewyan is a fitting place to end my travels for this year. Mackenzie himself returned here for the winter after his trip to the Pacific. Fort Chipewyan was the regional headquarters for the fur trade for almost two centuries. It is the oldest community in Alberta, yet there is still no all-weather road to it. Access is by air, by winter road, or, of course, by canoe.

We sail into harbour in style, landing at the town dock. As we slide *Teal* into the town, we are swarmed by children, leaping into the water and swimming around us. One of them yells out our names. He is Richard Simpson, son of trapper Charlie, whom we met in Peace Point. We feel as if we have come home.

Arriving in style at Fort Chipewyan on the shores of Lake Athabasca. Fort Chipewyan, the oldest European settlement in Alberta, is still not connected by road. The rivers remain the highways here.

Part III

Fort McMurray to Cumberland House, August–September 1999

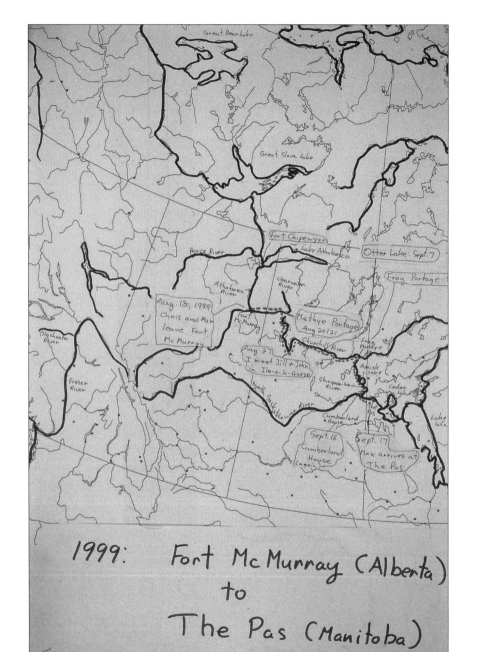

Great Bear Lake

Great Slave Lake

Fort Chipewyan

Lake Athabasca

Otter Lake: Sept. 7

Peace River

Frog Portage:

Clearwater River

Athabasca River

Aug. 13, 1999
Chris and Max
leave Fort
McMurray

Fort McMurray

Methye Portage
Aug 20/21

Churchill River

Frog Portage

Blackwater River

Aug 27
I meet Jill + John
in Ile-a-la-Crosse

Amisk Lake

Fraser River

Sturgeon-Weir River

Cedar Lake

North Saskatchewan River

Cumberland House

The Pas

Lake Win

Sept. 16
Cumberland
House
(again)

Sept. 17
Max arrives at
The Pas

1999: Fort McMurray (Alberta)
to
The Pas (Manitoba)

17

Getting Ready:
The Last Leg

IT IS 12 AUGUST 1999. I'm in a big silver jet again, high above the prairies. A month from now I'll be paddling back this way.

"Our cruising altitude will be 28,000 feet," the captain announces, just after the big jet has levelled out. "That's 10,000 feet lower than usual, to avoid strong headwinds," he explains.

Lucky me. I have a window seat, and the view will be great. Underneath me passes the La Vase Portage to Lake Nipissing, which I struggled over in the spring two years ago. Here comes Sudbury, a plume of white smoke trailing to the southwest, directly towards the white crystalline La Cloche Mountains. To the south in the blue mistiness lies Georgian Bay, with its lovely granite islands, breaking the surface of the water like the smooth, luscious curve of a woman's thigh. North of the coast of Lake Superior, I see the 10-km (6-mile) wide channel between the mainland and the Goulais Peninsula, where I had my scariest crossing. Here comes Pancake Bay, a whole day of travel compressed to a few seconds now, where I met Karen and paddled with her to Wawa. Then the jet heads out over the blue expanse of Lake Superior, where no paddler dares go, and into the clouds. That's where I'm going now. That's where we all go, into a future that we cannot see.

After Mackenzie and I reached Fort Chipewyan, we pass very different winters. While Mackenzie broods and struggles to write up his journals, I am preoccupied with matters very far removed from canoeing. While I have been deliberately not planning my future, it is clearly time to change this attitude. Now, for the first time, I'm planning for a future that includes more than me. Connie and I are having a baby!

In the spring of 1999, instead of being concerned with the logistics of another long canoe expedition, as has been the case for many years, I am shopping for diapers, strollers, baby gates, infant car seats, "Never Leave Baby Unattended" Swingomatics, and other items about which I have no previous knowledge. My little house on the shore of the Ottawa River no longer fits our growing family, and we are scrambling to find another. The house that we are lucky enough to buy – a beautiful log home close to my beloved Ottawa River – fills up with receiving blankets (I shudder to think what they will receive), cribs, sleepers and rattles. Most of these items I don't know how to use, or even what they are. I learn about snap technology, now used to fasten tiny T-shirts around little baby bottoms, instead of holding spray covers on canoes. Talk runs high over the merits of disposable diapers verses non-disposables and the benefits of breastfeeding (benefits to the baby, that is).

"Can you get life jackets for infants?" I ask, and I get blank stares in return.

Connie thrives in her, um, condition. She blossoms with health, vitality and beauty. I struggle with heartburn and pre-natal courses.

Baby Isaac Thelon (named after my favourite river) Downes Finkelstein arrives ahead of schedule, on 25 May, but, lucky for me, not in a canoe. It is not long, however, before he is subjected to his first canoe trip, secure in his infant car seat nestled in the bow in front of Connie. I solve the infant life-jacket issue with a rope and an empty plastic Coke bottle.

"Max, I think you should finish your trip," Connie says to me, as we are swinging in a hammock in our yard, baby Isaac on her lap, under the dappled shade of an old birch tree.

"Connie," I say, "it would be too difficult with baby Isaac. We would go so slowly, we'd never get anywhere. And the Methye Portage would take days to do."

"No, you don't get it." She shakes her head and sighs. "I mean you should go yourself. Just don't dilly-dally."

"But I'll miss Baby Zak. He'll forget his daddy. I'll be so deep in diaper-changing debt that I'll never catch up," I protest.

Left: Oh, how life has changed.

Below: Leaving Baby Isaac and Connie is not going to be easy.

"You really want to finish this. I know that." Connie is adamant. "You'll regret it if you don't go. I know that."

I know that Connie knows what is right for me. Brenda and Eric already have their little 2-hp motor oiled and ready to go. They agree to join me for the run up the Clearwater, over the Methye Portage, to Ile-a-la-Crosse, at the headwaters of the Churchill River. *Teal* is out west, and I have an empty bow seat. Chris Taggart agrees to join me for the run from Fort McMurray to Ile-a-la-Crosse.

"Gosh, Chris, that's great, but you've already done this part of the route," I say to him.

"Max, I'd like to actually see this part of the route. The last time I did it, I was so tired, I don't remember it at all."

Two hockey and canoeing buddies, Jill Jensen and John Pedlar, are keen to paddle the Churchill. Jill, you might recall, appeared briefly in the chapter on the Ottawa River. She had met me on the Muskrat River, 'way back near the beginning of the trip, for a one-day paddle to Pembroke. Jill and John will meet me in Ile-a-la-Crosse and paddle to Otter Lake. John will drive out with *Loon*. The last portion of the trip I will do alone in my beloved *Loon*. The logistics are set. We have a plan.

I get on the telephone to book my flights.

"And when will you return?" asks the voice on the other end of the line.

"Well, I'll be returning from The Pas, Manitoba." I look at the map of Canada pinned to my wall at the office and do some quick mental math – two weeks to Ile-a-la-Crosse, ten days to Otter Lake. Jill flies back on 8 September. Then 500 km or so to Cumberland House and a quick 150 km down the North Saskatchewan – that would be another ten days.

"September 18th," I blurt out. Connie said not to dilly-dally.

We have a plan.

18

Up the Clearwater:
The Link to the North

This river, which waters and reflects such enchanting scenery, runs, including its windings, upwards of eighty miles, when it discharges itself into the Elk river, commonly called by the white people, the Athabasca River.

— ALEXANDER MACKENZIE

ANOTHER MOTEL IN ANOTHER NORTHERN TOWN. I saunter up to the registration desk, thumbs hooked in my belt.

"I'm looking for someone," I say, just like in a western movie, to the pale, thin lad behind the counter. He's wearing round, wire-rimmed glasses.

I describe Brenda and Eric and then Chris.

"No, sir," he stammers. "They haven't checked in yet."

We had all agreed to meet at the Peter Pond Motel. Peter Pond is a big name in Fort McMurray. Peter Pond, fur trader, explorer, and all-round nasty guy, was the first white man, as far as we know, to see this country, back in '78. That's 1778. As well as the motel, there's a shopping centre and a main street named after him.

I head over to the shopping centre to pick up some last-minute items – a T-shirt (with nothing written on it for a change), some fishing line, a bag of gingersnap cookies. I am at the fishing-gear aisle in Zellers, when someone taps me on the shoulder. It is Eric. Brenda is standing behind him, smiling. Once again, I meet the intrepid videographers at one of the edges of Canada. I always meet these two near to where the roads end, and often beyond.

Peter Pond and Alexander Mackenzie travelled here in the late eighteenth century, but it took almost another 100 years for the Hudson's Bay Company to build a trading post here, in 1870. It named the post Fort McMurray, after its chief factor of this region, William McMurray.

Furs may have attracted the first white men to this area, but is was the promise of oil – "black gold" – that kept drawing them here. Alexander Mackenzie was the first to document the oil in this area: *"At about twenty-four miles from the Fork* [of the Clearwater and the Athabasca], *are some bituminous fountains, into which a pole of twenty feet long may be inserted without the least resistance."* There are no pools of oil today along the river, as Mackenzie described. But his words seem always to be deadly accurate.

Before Mackenzie and Peter Pond, of course, the local people were well aware of the oil and even used it to seal the seams on their canoes.

The first serious attempt to sell the stuff occurred in 1922, when the McMurray Asphaltum and Oil Company opened. Many firms tried and failed to extract the oil from the sands commercially. In 1967, the first huge oil-extraction plant, the Great Canadian Oil Company (now Suncor Energy), started up. Syncrude Canada Ltd opened in 1978. The money and the tax breaks flowed in, making Fort McMurray the wealthiest city in Canada, and the oil flowed out.

These operations are truly on a planetary scale. As with the W.A.C. Bennett Dam, you have to see it to understand what human beings are capable of when there is big money to be made. There is big money to be made, as the Athabasca Oil Sands contain more oil that all the known reserves of the Middle East. Huge mechanical diggers shovel the gooey black sand into the biggest trucks in the world. Each shovelful holds 100 tonnes of sand. Each truck holds 400 tonnes. The tires are higher than I can reach. With equipment like this, Mackenzie probably would have changed the courses of great rivers, reworking the map of Canada to his liking.

Chris wanders in the next morning, looking dazed and bewildered after a long bus trip from the east. He is becoming an expert in long-distance travel by bus:

"The secret is to have a few drinks before you get on so you smell like booze, and then no one will sit beside you," he says.

By noon, we're ready to go.

The Clearwater River rises at Broach Lake in northwestern Saskatchewan and flows for almost 300 km (187 miles) to its confluence with the muddy Athabasca. The Canadian Heritage Rivers System designated the 187-km (117-mile) section in Saskatchewan as a Canadian Heritage River in 1986,

Left: The crew on the Clearwater, from the left: Max and Chris Taggart with the videographers Brenda Beck and Eric Harris.

Right: The rest of the crew, Sir Alex, Christopher and Mackenzie, ready to go, all together for the first time on a river.

because of the fur trade on the 7.5-km (12-mile) Methye Portage (also known as Portage La Loche), which links the Hudson Bay and Arctic watersheds. The Alberta section has been proposed to the CHRS, and we will meet many people along the river who are helping to develop a management plan for it. There are several potential conflicts, mostly involving recreational use. Jet-boating and jet-skiing are popular in oil-rich Fort McMurray and do not mix well with wilderness paddling. Like oil and water.

We will be canoeing the lower section of the river only, to the historic Methye Portage. This is the part that Mackenzie travelled and that all the fur traders knew.

Heading upstream from Fort McMurray, we find the current swift, but manageable. It's nothing like the Fraser. The Clearwater does not over-power you. There are many sandbars, and Eric has to pay close attention, with the little 2-hp running full bore.

In several places the river cuts through dull black slopes of bitumen. The bitumen looks and smells just like the black asphalt used to repair roads. It looks solid, but we can see that it slowly flows, like a glacier, down the steep slopes into the river. In places it has formed black standing waves. Some of the tops of the waves are broken off to reveal fresh, shiny black bitumen inside. There is an oily slick where the bitumen meets the water. I make a tiny fire and toss on some hunks of bitumen to see how well they burn, but they merely melt, leaving tarry black goop on my hands and feet. Hunks of black bitumen, like big bear droppings, lie on the sandy riverbed.

We stop for the night, camping in the yard of Tom Weiber. Tom is on the town council and a member of the Clearwater Heritage Committee. He and his wife live in a lovely wooden house, accessible only by boat or snow-mobile.

The current picks up above Tom's house, but we still make steady progress, fuelled by luscious blueberries and raspberries growing all along the river. Already, although we are only 30 km (18 miles) from Fort McMurray, we feel deep in the wilderness. Wolf and moose tracks are common along the riverbanks. We surprise a big black bear munching on some riverside shrubbery as we come around a sharp bend. With the sound of the rushing water covering our paddle strokes, we manage to get right beside it before it sees us, "woofs" in surprise, and scrambles up a steep bank. I'm always amazed at how fast bears can run through dense vegetation, as if it weren't there at all.

Despite the feeling of wilderness, we are still within range of jet-boats. With its sandbars and shallow water, the Clearwater is made for jet-boats and jet-skis. They zoom up and down, skimming over the sandbars. Everyone is friendly and courteous and not in too much of a hurry to stop for a chat. I hate to say it, but they have as much right to be here as we do.

The Clearwater is a gem of a river to travel up. The current is swift, and the river shallow. But the riverbed is smooth rock, and the water warm. Tracking the canoe up is a treat, a refreshing stroll compared to the Fraser. Shallow rocky rapids alternate with long sandy sections. Along the shores of the river are large grassy meadows dotted with wildflowers interspersed among forests of jack pine, spruce, and poplar. The campsites are beauti-ful, open, sandy beaches, with the river winding through its broad, U-shaped valley like a silver ribbon. We are really enjoying our ascent.

The entire Clearwater, the Alberta portion having been nominated in September 1996, is a Canadian Heritage River, and it is easy to see why. It is significant to the fur trade, but it is also one of the best wilderness canoeing rivers that we've paddled (but we both agree that next time we would like to paddle down it).

Mackenzie mentions in his journals a number of *"mineral springs, whose margins are covered with sulphureous incrustations."* We find several springs bubbling out of the ground just a few yards from the river's edge. When we smelled the sulfur from the river, thoughts of hot springs danced in our heads. But these ones are icy cold, as if they have emerged from the middle of a glacier. The smell of sulphur dioxide, the familiar odour of rotten eggs, hangs heavy in the air. The pools where the springs emerge are miniature fairy-landscapes, where bright magenta algae cover the bottom and purple strings wave in the current. Where the sulphur-laden water tumbles over rocks, it leaves a residue of creamy yellow goop.

I wake up in the middle of the night. According to my "buy two films and get a free watch" digital watch, its 2:50 a.m.. The sky is filled with light. Northern light. Aurora borealis. Metaphors fail me. The lights dance across the sky and then dance back. They dance up to a point near the North Star and dance back down. Their primary colour is a bright, light shade of green. They shimmer like curtains waving in a breeze, then condense into criss-crossing beams, and then transform into spires and points. Always moving, always changing.

According to scientific explanation, the northern lights are triggered by a solar wind carrying photons and electrons that release energy from nitrogen and oxygen atoms in the earth's magnetic field. The released energy travels along magnetic lines of force, and when it reaches northern and southern polar regions, it produces the coloured lights that we see. All this happens in the ionosphere, some 60 to 500 km (approximately 37 to 312 miles) above us. This scientific explanation makes no sense at all to me. I guess it's just plain magic.

To add to the skyworks, we are in the midst of the Pleiades meteor shower. Shooting stars streak across the sky. It is hard to sleep. I don't want to miss anything. Fish leap in the river just outside the tent. A moose plods through the shallow water. Ah, the peace of a northern night.

There are skyworks even during the day. One afternoon, we see a tiny silver dot in the sky. Through Eric's 10x binoculars resting on a tripod, we can see a silver globe with six columns extending downwards and a small white box suspended a short distance beneath it. During the entire afternoon, as we make our way upriver, we watch the object, which we conclude is a weather balloon. We are heading east, the wind is from the west, yet the balloon appears almost stationary. Basic trigonometry tells us that the balloon must be very big and very high. We continue to watch it after we set up camp. It slowly drifts east, which seems odd, as the wind blows steadily from the west. Hours after the sun has set, it is still illuminated by the sun's rays, glowing like a tiny moon in the evening sky. If we had not seen it during the day, we would think that we were witnessing a supernova or some other galactic phenomenon.

I find out after I get home that this is a NASA balloon launched at Lynn Lake, Manitoba. Its altitude is approximately 11 km (35,000 feet!). It has a volume of 28,000 cubic feet (3,100 cubic metres) and carries a payload of 2,272 kg (5,000 pounds). That's one big balloon – as big as a two-storey house!

The river becomes steeper, and we have to track the canoe up shallow rapids. The river is even more beautiful here, and white dolomite cliffs covered with bright orange lichens frame the water. Near Pine Rapids, the cliffs are impressively high. Exploring inland, we find an "enchanted" forest. Pillars of limestone, like the ruins of an ancient city, stand among the trees. There are deep caves and huge boulders suspended between rock pillars. Some of the pillars have flat caps of limestone balanced on top. All this in a spacious jack pine forest.

Between the trees elfin meadows of pale green lichens look just like the "trees" for miniature model railways. Robert Hood, midshipman on the ill-fated Franklin expedition of 1819, wrote: "We passed a portage on which limestone rocks were singularly scattered through the woods, bearing the appearance of house and turrets overgrown with moss. The earth emitted a hollow sound. The river was divided by rocks into narrow channels, every object indicating that some convulsion had disturbed the general order of nature at this place."[1]

The area today looks exactly as Hood described it almost two centuries ago.

We track up all the portages except for Whitemud Falls. Often, Chris and I each handle one of the canoes, while Brenda and Eric videotape us. Sometimes Chris hauls both canoes.

Tracking a canoe can be fun. But it usually is not. Normally, the water is freezing, the shore blocked by alders, cliffs and other usual shoreline obstacles. If you are not sinking up to your hips in mud, then you are falling between big, slippery boulders. Usually, you are doing all these things at the same time. But not on the Clearwater. It is a perfect tracking river. Warm water; firm, flat "grippy" rocks; an open shoreline. Tracking heaven.

Tracking is tricky, much trickier than it looks. When tracking alone, which is usually a good idea, since you can't get mad at anyone else, I tie a 16-m (50-foot) piece of good-quality rope to each end of the canoe. It is best to make a bridle, as Bill Mason describes one in his book *Path of the Paddle*,[2] by looping a short piece of rope around the belly of the canoe at each seat and attaching the long rope to it. This directs the "pull" away from the bottom of the canoe, reducing the risk of an upset if the canoe gets sideways to the current, as it most assuredly will.

Chris shows me his "lazy man's" technique, tying the ends of the rope to the seats close to the gunwale on the side of the canoe away from the shore. Then he loops the rope under the canoe, so that the pull is from below the water line. This works well, but the rope may slip out from the bottom, and then the "pull" comes from the gunwale, and that's not good. But the technique works just fine unless the section to be tracked is long and difficult Always load the canoe extremely stern-heavy for tracking upstream.

The theory of tracking is simple. Pulling on the bow rope (and thereby lengthening the stern rope) makes the current push the canoe towards the shore. In contrast, pulling on the stern rope (and thereby lengthening the bow rope) makes the current push the canoe away from shore. By keeping the canoe on a slight angle away from shore, you let the current help you pull the canoe upstream.

The key is to find the perfect angle. Too little, and the canoe ends up stuck on the shore. Too much, and the bow will be grabbed by the water and the canoe will turn sideways and fill with water in about .5 nanoseconds. It will then be too heavy for you to hold and get swept downstream, to be wrapped around a big rock in another 2.5 nanoseconds. Sometimes before you even know it, you're in trouble. Really. Tracking is tricky. Use good rope. Never use reef knots. Never have a reef knot holding anything that you value. Use a bow line knot to attach the ropes.

Despite all these cautions, tracking is an essential part of the canoe traveller's repertoire of skills.

After five days and eighty miles, we cross the Saskatchewan border from Alberta. The river now meanders across the floor of a deep broad valley, over shifting sandbars and low islands. At an open, grassy flat on the south shore, in the belly of a meander, a lone metal chair – the kind that one sees at community centres and meeting halls – sits on the bank, looking very out of place. We land and clamber up the steep sandy bank to investigate. A well-defined trail heads south. This is the famed and feared 21-km (about 13-mile) Methye Portage – the longest portage on the entire fur trade route across Canada.

In 1778, Peter Pond crossed the Portage La Loche, or Methye Portage (loche or methye, known also as ling or lingcod, is a kind of fish common in the north), which links the eastwards-flowing waters of the Churchill to the Athabasca River watershed. This route opened up the rich fur country of the north to the fur merchants of Montreal.

There is little to indicate that this was once the major route to the north. A clearing by the river makes an ideal campsite, but no sign remains of the buildings that were once here. The route was used continuously from 1792 into the twentieth century. At first, Cree porters were hired to help transport the loads. After 1850, the trail was widened to allow packhorses and oxcarts.

*Above: Near the Alberta/
Saskatchewan border. The
Clearwater is a delight to paddle.
Left: Open jack pine forests with a
thick, spongy carpet of lichens and
moss, line much of the Clearwater.*

A 21-kilometre carry is a formidable undertaking. We definitely want to
do this in one pass. A two-carry portage would mean 60 km (about 36
miles) of walking! In addition to the normal gear for a canoe trip, we have
an outboard motor, gasoline and a lot of video equipment packed in waterproof Pelican cases.

Packing up for the portage, we all feel as if we are getting ready for the
Stanley Cup Finals or some other life-defining event. Perhaps portaging
the Methye is a life-defining event. Chris lights up a cigarette, as if it is his
last one ever. Brenda tapes all her toes with duct tape – "to prevent blisters," she says. Eric and I fidget with the packs and canoes. I load up my
pack with food. It must weigh 50 kg (110 pounds)! Brenda and Eric, who
are well past the age of most voyageurs (Eric is, as he says, "a senior citi-
zen"), have planned for this and rigged up an ingenious device. They have
taken a standard waterproof plastic barrel and turned it into a roller. They
will roll their aluminum canoe and outboard and all the loose gear over the
Methye. It works like a charm.

Chris and I start off portaging the old-fashioned way. The trail is not
used much today, but it is still wide enough for a voyageur canoe to pass.

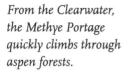

From the Clearwater, the Methye Portage quickly climbs through aspen forests.

As it begins to climb out of the valley, it cuts like a trench into the side of the hill – evidence of its once-much-heavier use. We feel close to the voyageurs as we lug our packs and the canoes up the trail. We take turns portaging the canoe up the big hill at the start of the portage.

The Methye Portage climbs steeply almost 270 m (800 feet) out of the valley of the Clearwater. There have been more emotional descriptions written about the view from the top of the valley than about any other portage in Canada. Mackenzie writes in his account: *"Within a mile of the termination of the portage, a very steep precipice rises upward of a thousand feet above the plains beneath it and commands a most extensive romantic and ravishing prospect ... From thence the eye looks down on the course of the little river, by some called the Swan River, and by others the Clear-water and Pelican River, beautifully meandering for upwards of thirty miles. The valley ... displaying a most delightful intermixture of wood and lawn ... some parts covered with stately forests, relieved by promontories of the finest verdure, where the elk and buffalo find pasture."*

Lieutenant John Henry Lefroy (1817-1890), a Royal Artillery surveyor who was here in 1844, observes: "It is celebrated for the view from the north end. It is a wide and regular valley, of great depth, stretching for a distance of thirty miles to the west. A portion of wood in the distance was burning, and there was an uncommon felicity in the manner in which the columns of smoke rose up against a dark mass of Pines which crossed the valley behind them. The Clearwater River winds through the midst, sometimes expanding into a placid little lake, then diminishing to a thread of light barely caught among the trees. Upon the whole I have seen few views more beautiful."[3]

When Shel Taylor and Geoff Pope came over this momentous portage in 1936 on their New York/Nome trip, they hired a local Native and his mare to haul their canoe and gear over on a *travois* – two long poles with a tarp stretched in between. There was still a small village at that time at each end of the portage.

In 1971, when Verlen Kruger and Clint Waddell portaged, the trail was becoming overgrown. They describe the view from the valley top: "the scene was breathtaking. That huge valley lay before us with its high and beautiful wooded ridges of hills. It was one of the grandest spots for scenery we had seen on the journey."[4]

For us, the view is not so breathtaking. Perhaps the trees have grown up and screened the view, or perhaps we are just too tired to appreciate it. Also, most descriptions of the view from the top of the valley are written by travellers heading north. No wonder they wax poetic, knowing that the portage is almost over and that the rest of the portage, and their entire journey, is downhill and downstream. I identify more with the description of Philip Turnor, a surveyor for the HBC in 1792, who was heading the other way. "We began to carry up a rather steep hill and came to a ridge about two yards wide at the top the sides of which are very steep and not less than a hundred yards to the bottom on either side and if a person was to make a slip to either side he would be shure of being at the bottom before he stopped."[5]

It takes us almost half a day to get to Rendezvous Lake – a small lake about 1.6 km (one mile) across, some 6.5 km (four miles) into the portage. Chris and I stumble straight in for a swim. Brenda and Eric, with Brenda pulling the Grumman on the barrel-roller like a packhorse, are not far behind.

Rendezvous Lake is beautiful, bordered by beaches of white sand and park-like meadows. It was here that fur trade brigades from the south and north would rendezvous to exchange furs for trade goods, just as at Grand Portage on Lake Superior. Members of the Fort Chipewyan brigade left in

Rendezvous Lake. On this little lake, furs and trade goods were exchanged, and passed over the divide separating waters flowing to the Arctic and waters flowing to Hudson Bay.

mid-May, as soon as Lake Athabasca was clear of ice, and headed up the Athabasca and Clearwater. They then carried their heavy 41-kg (90-pound) *pièces* up the steep hill to Rendezvous Lake. There they exchanged their loads with the La Loche brigade, which had travelled from Lake Winnipeg, leaving in early June, when the ice is out. Parties usually left their boats at the landings at each end of the portage.

Our dip in the lake is so refreshing that we decide to camp on the far side, where there is an extensive sandy beach. As we paddle across the lake, a helicopter swoops low over the surface, picks up water in a huge fabric bucket, and zooms off. When we have set up camp, the helicopter returns. It hovers over us and lands a short distance away. The co-pilot, a big fellow in orange overalls, shouts above the roar of the engine:

"Is it OK if we camp here? We're flying a crew in."

"Sure," I shout back. "We'll enjoy the company."

As he starts back to the chopper, he turns to me and says: "You know, it was the dangdest thing ... we're flying over this lake miles from any other, and we see two canoes on the water. Like you just came out of nowhere."

It is always amazing to watch helicopters take off and land. They are such remarkable machines. This one is bright yellow and black, like a monster dragonfly. It soon returns with half the crew. I notice that the pilot is a woman.

"Ya' don't see many women pilots," I say to the crew chief.

"Well, *she* used to be a guy," he answers. "But she or he," he shakes his head, "is the best pilot I've ever flown with."

The fire crew consists of ten Cree from La Loche, including a few women. They speak Cree to each other, but English, of course, to us. One asks if he could borrow a canoe, and I offer him a fishing rod as well. He paddles out to the middle of the lake with another member of the crew, and a few minutes later they return with a nice fat pike, which they boil up for supper.

Late that night, Chris and I stand on the shore of the lake, facing north. All around, the land is flat, the sky a big dome speckled with stars and streaks of northern lights. All water runs downhill from here, down to the Arctic Ocean, down to Hudson Bay. We feel on top of the world. Chris and I dance with our paddles. There is no greater high, as Chris says, than crossing a height of land.

From the lake, the trail runs straight and level for 14.4 km (about 9 miles). We leave in the morning. Eric says encouragingly: "All we have to do is get this pile of stuff to the lake at the other end of this little path. That takes six hours of hot, hard work." Brenda continues to be the "horse," hauling the

The entire crew pose at the bronze plaque marking the south end of the Methye Portage at Lac La Loche.

Grumman on the roller. Chris and I take turns dragging *Teal*. I reinforced the bottom of the canoe last night with fibreglass in preparation for this. Halfway along, the helicopter buzzes overhead. We give a "thumbs up," OK sign, and it zooms off. To be caught on the trail in a forest fire would not be pleasant, to say the least, and it is reassuring to know someone is watching out for us. The trail runs through open jack pine forest – the kind that burns every thirty or forty years. There is definitely smoke in the air.

The trail ends abruptly at a beaver pond on a swampy creek – the head-waters of the mighty Churchill River. We skid the canoes over several beaver dams and across a flooded log bridge that was once part of the trail before the beavers got to work. The creek twists and turns through a swamp of willow and alder but finally opens up to a straight, shallow channel clogged with aquatic weeds. A short distance downstream, where the creek runs into La Loche Lake, a stone cairn and bronze plaque mark this historic portage as a vital link in the fur trade. Someone has left a rusty bedspring at the base of the monument.

Tonight, 21 August, the sky really puts on a show for us. We can see the lights of the village of La Loche twinkling across the lake to the south. To the west, jagged white bolts of lightning sizzle and split the sky. To the north, the sky glows red from forest fires.

We paddle into La Loche the next morning and decide to spend a day there, have a restaurant meal and buy a few groceries. We set up camp near the town dock around noon. We have lots of visitors this afternoon. Kyle and Percy, both ten years old, are yo-yo experts. I show them the Cree dictionary in Mackenzie's journals. They recognize many of the words.

They tell us about a dance a few miles from town tonight, and we decide to head out there. We walk out to the highway and hitchhike. Soon an elderly Cree man named Solomon stops. He is on his way to the dance. He explains that it is a celebration of the old days, with Native music, dancing and gambling.

It is like a country fair, with gambling tents and a big community hall for dancing and music. There is a live band, with fiddles, guitars, and drums. Everyone, young and old, is dancing. Reels and jigs, line dances and square dances. Solomon grabs Brenda by the shoulder and whirls her away. We are amazed by his energy. Brenda is swept away by the whirling dancers and lost to sight. Like a paddler in a "souse-hole," she surfaces occasionally before disappearing again. She recirculates several times and finally eddies out by us, panting.

"Whew," she exclaims, "that was tougher than the Methye!"

We imagine that the trip down the little La Loche River, the headwaters of the mighty Churchill, will be easy. This messy little river has hardly enough water to float the canoes. We wonder what it was like when Mackenzie and all the other fur traders came this way. Mackenzie writes that the river *"in the fall of the year, is very shallow, and navigated with difficulty even by half-laden canoes. Its water is not sufficient to form strong rapids, through from its rocky bottom, the canoes are frequently in considerable danger."*

This little river has every obstacle you can think of, except a waterfall. First there are the rock piles; we have to lift and walk the canoes through. Then there are the meanders. The windings seem never-ending, and as the river is only about a foot deep, our progress is painfully slow. We keep getting stuck in the mud. Then we come to the fallen-tree section. Where the little river unwinds onto a soggy plain, the forest along it has been burned recently. We can still smell the charred wood. In many places, large spruce trees have fallen across the river, and we have to cut our way through or drag the canoes over them. Finally, there is the beaver-dam section. At the first dam we rejoice, as the dam has backed up the water for us. I am ashamed to admit that we broke the first dam, hoping to ride the crest of the floodwaters down the river. But our plan is foiled, as there is another dam a few hundred yards downstream, and another, and another, until we lose count. Finally, we break through, 55 km (33 miles) and almost three days later, into the clogged-weed section, where the water weeds are so thick that they ball up on the bows of the canoes, and we can barely paddle through them.

But we also find a lot of beauty along this little river. One night we camp on an unburned knoll overlooking the river and the vast, burned forest. I feel as if we are in the Everglades of Florida. It is not fire, but the setting sun, that sets the sky ablaze in a sheet of colour that changes constantly, from the red of molten iron to the soft purple of the inside of clamshells. The sharp-pointed, burned spruce forest is like a signature, the signature of the boreal forest, against the sky. An osprey circles lazily.

We soon forget the frustratingly slow and hard-gained progress of the day once we light the campfire. As the sky darkens, the silver light of the almost-full moon shines on the little river. The splashing of a moose wading in the stream, and the crackling of the flames, are the only sounds. Our little expedition is at peace.

A day later, windbound on the shore of Peter Pond Lake, we feel autumn in the air. Literally. Flocks of Canada geese fly overhead, heading south. Loons raft up on the water. The leaves of the poplar and birch are turning yellow. I hope that Jill and John remember to bring my rubber boots. Running-shoe season is coming to an end.

Peter Pond Lake is an ocean today. Big combers come rolling in up the beach. Whitecaps speckle the lake like a loon's back. We are camping on a sand dune just west of the town of Dillon, where Solomon, who whirled Brenda off her feet at the dance, comes from. He told us that night that after god made the earth he rested in Dillon. Watching the moon rise over the meadows, while the sun sets over the lake, we can believe that.

It's 25 August, and we have to meet Jill and John on the 27th in Ile-a-la-Crosse. Brenda and Eric have a plane to catch, and Chris has to head back east to work. We've got to get a move on. We get up at dawn, but the wind has already woken. We launch in the surf and get blown to Dillon. But it is not a day to travel. The flags are snappin', and the Canadian flag over the post office is half ripped away. We wander up the road to the town to buy a soft drink. Several people drive by in pickup trucks. One of them hollers at us out the window. We had met him at the dance in La Loche.

"It's gonna be a three-day blow," he yells above the sound of the wind and the motor. "I'll drive you to Buffalo Narrows if you'll fill my tank." So it goes on long canoe trips. It is only a long, one-day paddle from there to Ile-a-la-Crosse.

In Buffalo Narrows, we stay with friends whom Chris met two years ago – Ray and Marie Laprise. They run a restaurant (the town's best) and put on a big steak dinner for us. In Ile-a-la-Crosse, on the 27th, we cruise the main street, and, sure enough, Jill and John drive by, with my beloved *Loon* tied on top of their car. The next phase of my journey is about to begin.

19

Down the Mighty Churchill,
River of the Lonely Land

*The abundance of the finest fish in the world, the richness of
its surrounding banks and forests, in moose and fallow deer,
with the vast numbers of the smaller tribes of animals, and the
numerous flocks of wild fowl that frequent it in the spring and
fall, make it a most desirable spot.*

— ALEXANDER MACKENZIE

THE CHURCHILL. ITS NAME HAS long been part of my river mythol-
ogy. This is the famous and beautiful river of remote northern
Saskatchewan, stretching across the province like a string of pearls at the
edge of the Canadian Shield. It flows through a land of rock, water, spruce,
and birch, a land that looks just as it did when Mackenzie and the other fur
traders paddled its shimmering lakes, ran its rapids, and sweated over its
portages. Ghosts of those days still stalk the portages, it is said, and phan-
tom brigades paddle across the lakes in the pre-dawn mists. This is a river
to dream about.

The Cree name for the Churchill is "Missinipe," Big River.[1] The
Churchill is a big river. An important river. It was a key link in the fur trade
route to the west and north. It is Canada's fifth-longest river. But more significant than its overall length is the distance that it flows unimpeded by
dams. No dams mar the Churchill until Island Falls Dam at Sandy Bay.
Below this point, the mighty Churchill is harnessed, its course diverted,
its power channelled through turbines to generate electricity for the
south, for us. From Ile-a-la-Crosse to Frog Portage – a distance of almost
500 km (about 300 miles) – it has been nominated as a Canadian Heritage

River for its significance as the main route to the northwest and because it still appears much as it did in the days of Mackenzie.

In this country, the passing of the fur trader still seems very recent. Trading posts have been replaced by "Northern" stores, which are owned by the Hudson's Bay Company, the oldest surviving firm in North America, founded in 1670. The country is still largely untouched by roads.

Jill and John will leave me at the town of Missinipe, on Otter Lake, one of the few places where there is road access, 386 km (about 232 miles) from Ile-a-la-Crosse. We anticipate meeting many Native people living along the river, as the river is still the main pathway to fishing, hunting, berry-picking, trapping and friends and neighbours. The people here still depend on it for food and wealth – netting whitefish and walleye from its pristine waters in spring, gathering wild rice, cranberries, and blueberries in summer, hunting moose in the autumn, and trapping in winter – moving with the seasons. The river is their front yard and backyard.

Jill's research indicates that all the historic portages are still in use, although sections of railway track and wooden skidways have replaced the traditional footpaths on some to allow the passage of outboard motorboats up and down the river past the rapids. The Churchill, unlike many of the historic rivers of Canada, is still the main highway here, connecting people and communities upstream and down, connecting the past to the future.

The Churchill follows the edge of the Canadian Shield, alternately passing through rugged country, in a maze of rocky channels, and dipping down into the prairies, where it flows through rich wetlands. Coursing as it does on the edge of prairie and boreal forest, it derives richness from both environments.

It is really more lake than river – a series of shimmering, island-studded, rock-girded gems connected by waterfalls and rapids. Primeau, Nisowiak, Drinking, Trade, Keg, Otter, Shagwenaw, Dipper, Sandfly, Pinehouse, Knee, Sandy, Black Bear Island, Trout, Stack, Lake of the Dead, and Devil – we will pass through them all, in rain or in sunshine, in calm or in stormy weather. There is a story in each name. Heck! There is a story along each inch of the Churchill. The Churchill certainly earns its Native name, Missinipe – Big River.

Ile-a-la-Crosse has been here since before Mackenzie's time. Thomas Frobisher built the first post here in 1776,[2] probably where we will camp tonight, on the long, sandy peninsula across the bay from the present site. From his location, one can look northeast, up the long arm of the lake that

There are 56 sets of rapids on the Heritage River section of the Churchill River. This is one of them. Most of the rapids are runnable in open canoes.

we will follow, and northwest, up the Aubichon Arm, towards Buffalo Narrows.

Mackenzie was clearly enthused by the beauty and rich resources of this area: *"This lake and fort take their names from the game of the cross* [probably lacrosse, introduced to the area by Iroquois voyageurs] *which forms a principle amusement among the natives. The situation of this lake, the abundance of the finest fish in the world to be found in its waters, the richness of its surrounding banks and forests, in moose and fallow deer* [caribou?]*, with the vast numbers of the smaller tribes of animal, whose skins are precious, and the numerous flacks of wildfowl that frequent it in the spring and fall make it a most desirable spot for the constant residence of some and the occasional rendezvous of others of the inhabitants of the country, particularly the Kniesteneaux* [Cree]*."*

We can hardly wait to get going. We spread our gear on a plastic tarp on the marsh grass back of the town dock. I have mailed a box of food and gear to John at his home in Sault Ste. Marie, and, of course, I can't remember what was in it. Jill and John have each brought some food. More important, Jill has brought a fat envelope from Connie. I carefully, reverently, seal this in a zip-lock bag and look forward to opening it tonight, alone in my tent. We repack the food into bags for breakfasts, lunches, suppers, snacks, and drinks and then walk over to the Northern store to buy extra peanut butter, cookies, and potato chips. The northeast arm of Ile-a-la-Cross Lake is about 60 km (about 36 miles) long, so, with no portages for a day or two, we can indulge our cravings for junk food.

Satisfied that we have everything that we need, and more, we launch in the late afternoon. Jill and I paddle *Teal*, and John is in my beloved *Loon*. The wind is still brisk, and white-capped waves roll in from the Aubichon Arm. We don't go far, just a couple of kilometres, to a long sandy point.

This is no doubt where Thomas Frobisher built the first post, with a view up both major arms of the lake.

The moonrise is incredible, a big silver balloon rising up over the far shore of the lake.

"They aren't kidding about that slogan on the licence plates here: Saskatchewan – Land of Living Skies," says Jill.

"Humph!" I retort. "You ain't seen nuttin' yet."

This is a great campsite, backed by meadows, with stands of spruce cutting the wind. Elements of the scene repeat themselves from hundreds of other campsites across the country: gulls and terns circle over the lake; sandpipers run along the waterline, probing the sand for goodies. We puzzle over the white bones of a strange skeleton spread out on the sand. The skull is flat, like a pike, with a very long upper jaw and two long, thin, bow-shaped lower jawbones.

"It's a pelican!" We three biologists have epiphanies at the same moment. The skull is beautiful. Elliptical holes lighten its weight without sacrificing strength. The skull speaks to the perfection of form and function that can be attained only after thousands of trials. Just like the design of a good canoe.

That night, I open the envelope from Connie. Inside is a card from her brothers and sisters and parents and nephews. Her sister Anne has sent a fancy cigar. Her mother has sent a package of jelly dinosaurs. Her brother included a note that said: "Wanted to send some 'grass,' but didn't have any." I'm sure that he means sweetgrass. There is a letter from Connie, with photographs of Isaac. I feel very much a part of this family, a feeling that is new to me, and I'm not sure what to do with these feelings. A bit of a dilemma for the "lone canoeist." A nice dilemma.

The next morning we head up the lake, with a slight tailwind. The wind picks up, and we stop to cut poles and rig up a big tarp between the two canoes.

"Now we're cooking," says Jill. John, in little *Loon*, is gripping his paddle tightly, his expression not one of total comfort, while Jill and I munch potato chips in *Teal*. We count the headlands and enjoy the rush of wind in our faces and water passing under the hulls.

The southwest wind continues to increase, and it is getting difficult for Jill to pass potato chips back to me on her paddle without their blowing off. We are verging on being out of control, something that always seems to happen to me when I sail. We untie the lines and let the canoes separate and the sail flop in the water. There's a nice sandy beach just ahead, and it's time to camp.

The wind continues to strengthen, but we set up our tents and build a fire in the shelter of the woods. The lake is a sea of whitecaps. After dark, as we're sitting around the campfire, sipping hot chocolate with a little hootch added, we hear the slapping of a motorboat pounding on the waves. The sound gets louder, and we head down to the beach. A wooden boat, with a sharply upturned bow and painted blue with white trim, is just coasting in. This is a boat clearly designed for travel on the big waters of Lake Ile-a-la-Crosse. It carries four people, huddled in blankets for warmth – a Cree couple and their two teenaged children.

"Hey, we saw your campfire and just wanted to check that everything is OK," the father shouts, as we pull the boat up the beach.

"C'mon up to the fire, we're just having some hot chocolate," I invite them.

Soon we're all cosy around the fire, and the father offers us each a beer. Jackpot!

"We live in Patuanak, at the head of the lake. We were just visiting some friends in Ile-a-la-Crosse. You're the first canoeists we've seen this summer," he says. "Not too many come by here."

There are no roads into Patuanak, and travel when the water isn't frozen is still by boat. When I remind them of the Lakehead University expeditions in the big voyageur canoes, they all remember them and nod enthusiastically.

"I remember when Gordon Lightfoot paddled this way. That was almost twenty years ago," the father says.

The visit ends abruptly: "Well, we've got to get home."

They quickly pack up and head down to their boat. They are just checking up to see what is happening on their lake and river. We are camping, so to speak, in their backyard. It was a nice visit.

The stars are blazing in an Arctic-clear sky, and the wind continues to increase. It's that damn southwest wind that follows me everywhere. We are close to the end of the lake, and I hope that we can sneak along the shore tomorrow. Patuanak, and the Churchill River, are just around the corner.

That night it feels good to crawl into a sleeping bag, to lie awake listening to the waves slapping on the shore. But I am a little anxious. Jill has a plane to catch in ten days, and we don't have a lot of time to be windbound.

Morning brings sun and more wind. The lake is speckled with whitecaps, but a slight bend in the shoreline offers us a little protection from the main force of the waves. We think that we can safely paddle with the wind behind us, as long as we can launch without swamping. The paddler in the front always gets the worst of this. I get wet only up to my knees from wading in the water, but Jill is soaked from the neck down by a big wave that breaks over the bow as we launch.

"Pretty dry?" I ask Jill, when we are beyond the breakers.

"Max, I needed to wash my hair anyway," she retorts.

We're on our way, surfing down the waves, enjoying the ride. I have this habit of doing a mental inventory, usually too late, and as the wind blows us past the next point, I ask:

"Jill, did you pick up the bag of maps?" I remember that we had the zip-lock bag of maps for the trip out this morning, checking the route to Patuanak.

"Nope," she says.

We paddle over to John and shout the same question. "Nope," he replies.

We land in a sheltered little cove, and, sure enough, there are no maps in either canoe. We have travelled about five kilometres (just over three miles). We all look back at the sea of whitecaps, and Jill and John look at me.

"Ok, I'll take *Loon* back and find the G-D maps," I sigh. Only *Loon* could make headway into that wind and those breaking waves.

While I paddle back, cursing the wind, I'm actually enjoying being back in *Loon* again, feeling her roll with the waves. It takes me two tries to find the beach where we camped, and, sure enough, the bag of maps is there. I also find two old paddles washed up on shore. Elated at recovering the maps, I launch Loon into the surf and really enjoy the ride back. It took almost an hour and a half to paddle back into the wind, but only about twenty minutes to return, surfing down the fronts of the big combers. I'm having a blast!

Jill and John have soup and bannock ready when I land, and then we set off. Just as we pull away from shore, a big black bear walks out of the bush, nosing around our lunch site.

"I thought I felt someone watching us," says Jill.

The wind blows us to the end of the lake. The long rollers pick up *Teal*, and she hesitates for a moment as the white froth of the breaking wave hisses beneath us. Then she smoothly glides down into the black trough. It is exhilarating. John is having fun in *Loon*, too, getting used to the feel of her rolling under his hips. I'm a little jealous, I must admit.

We find the exit of the Churchill River and the current sweeps us down easy rapids into Shagwenaw Lake, past flocks of white pelicans, which look at us with stern disapproval as we drift past into Patuanak. Pulling the canoes up on shore, we see several brightly painted wooden boats just like

the one belonging to the family that visited us last night. In fact, we recognize its distinctive pattern of dark blue and white among the turquoise,
red and green boats. All have the same unique upturned hull, but each has
a distinctive paint job. Their owners clearly take pride in them.

A wooden church, its slender spire splitting the azure sky, and the
wooden clapboard house beside it, both freshly painted white with blue
trim, stand on a grassy point by the river and seem to welcome us. So does
the Northern store, where we stock up on more junk food. I noticed on the
morning before we launched that one rudder cable on *Loon* was frayed and
held by only three thin strands of wire. I used duct tape to reinforce the
cable, but we purchase some extra snare wire in case the tape doesn't hold.
(Of course, my temporary repair job will last until I lend *Loon* to a friend
the following summer, and he graciously replaces the cable as a token of
his appreciation.)

Loaded down with bags of potato chips and Coke (Connie would have
been pleased), we relax under the shade of a tree on the lawn outside the
church. Across the lake, thick grey smoke billows thousands of feet into
the air. The base of the smoke column glows red. Forest fires are scary and
beautiful at the same time.

We head out into the wind, which is still strong, but Shagwenaw Lake is
too small and broken up to build scary waves. Soon we find the outlet of
the river once again. The shores are low and swampy, and the forest on
both sides has recently burned. We look in vain for a piece of the Canadian
Shield to camp on. Jill and John, like me, are children of the Shield, and we
love the solid feel of worn granite under us. We finally give up looking for
a rocky site and camp on a grassy flat – well, not very flat. There are
rounded river stones underneath the grass.

The first serious rapid on the Churchill is Drum Rapid, rated as Class III
in the guide that Jill has printed out from the Canoe Saskatchewan web
site. We can hear the pounding roar of water dropping over rocks well
before we see the white peaks dancing at the top of the rapid. The current
picks up speed. John has run only a few rapids in his entire canoeing
career and has never paddled solo before.

We eddy into shore before the real rapids begin. Jill and I can see a safe
route to the calm water below the rapids. We explain our strategy to John.
Backferry across here, before those big rocks.[3] Stick to the side, avoiding
the main flow. Look for the valleys and smooth spots, and avoid the cliffs
and mountains. John nods knowingly.

"John," I say, "Jill and I will go first. Just watch where we go."

We launch into the current, backferrying slowly towards the far shore through 60-cm (2-foot) standing waves to avoid a line of boulders downstream. We are trying to make this look easy. The river bunches together, like a cat getting ready to pounce, as it squeezes between the rock shore on one side and a big pile of boulders on the other. We eddy out below the boulders and paddle to shore.

I'm ready to walk back upstream and run *Loon* down, thinking that this might be too much for John's first rapid, when we see John already in the river, heading downstream. He follows our route, bouncing through standing waves with a big grin. *Loon* hurtles down the chute near the boulder pile. John's wooden double-blade whirls like a helicopter blade. He hurtles by us, manages to turn *Loon* into the quiet water, looks back at us, and shrugs.

"Was that OK?" he grins.

Clearly, John is not going to have any trouble adapting to paddling *Loon* in rapids.

The river sweeps us along through several less-intimidating rapids. The Churchill is a lively river. Fish swirl in the shallows. Ducks rise from each quiet reedy bay that we pass. Pelicans watch us go by at each set of rapids. Despite their huge bills, they are incredibly graceful, seeming to float in the air with no effort, like a good canoe on water. Serenity in motion.

At Dipper Rapids, Jill and I hop from eddy to eddy, working our way down the rapid "step by step." Although Jill's guide rates it as Class IV, I always like to have a look. Often there's a way to sneak down.

"Gosh, Jill, I think we can slither down this. Way over on the right."

"Max, it says there's a railway around this rapid. I think that might be easier, and more fun," Jill says.

We paddle back up the river, to an obvious landing site. Sure enough, there is a section of railway track and a wooden cart on steel wheels. We load both canoes on the cart and push it along. When it picks up speed, we all hop on for the ride. Heading down to the bottom of the portage, the cart begins to accelerate, and we jump off, grabbing the ropes that we fortunately tied on, anticipating something like this. With all the fooling around, the portage takes us about two hours. But rarely have we had so much fun on a portage.

We decide to camp here, so that we can play on the railway car some more. We cook up a scrumptious supper of fresh pickerel, topped off by blueberry–Saskatoon berry crisp with custard sauce. Life is tough on the trail.

The river loops back into the prairies at Dipper Lake, winding through rich sedge marshes. The abundance of water birds amazes us. Mallards

Trying to catch a walleye for supper – but this time without success.

and black ducks whistle overhead. Cormorants, grebes and loons float on the water, appearing and disappearing as they bob in the waves. Canada geese guarding tiny islands of grass hunch up as we paddle by, as if trying to make themselves invisible. The omnipresent sandpipers run on skinny little legs along the muddy line between the sedges and the water. Marsh hawks patrol the wetlands, while, higher in the sky, golden eagles and bald eagles soar. Highest of all, tiny cross-shaped silhouettes way up in the leaden sky, sandhill cranes drift on the wind.

The weather has turned grey and wet, and a wickedly icy wind stabs at us from the north. We work through the convolutions of Primeau Lake, named for one of the voyageurs who accompanied Thomas Frobisher in 1776 in the first party of white men to come this far into this region. We round a point like any other and see a group of white canvas tents and big orange tarps set up across the lake. Grey smoke from a campfire rises from between the tents before it is whirled away by the wind. We figure that it's a fishing camp, probably from the community of Elak Dase, not far downriver. We are all cold, and the thought of huddling around a campfire is enticing.

"C'mon, let's invite ourselves for lunch," I suggest.

Jill is reluctant.

"Maybe they don't want guests for lunch," she says.

Jill and I argue back and forth, while John wisely awaited our decision. In the end we decide to eat on our own. We huddle under a big spruce tree and get a smoky fire going. Soup and bannock with melted cheese are on the menu today (and tomorrow and the next day and so on). I am cold and wet, and I look forlornly at the camp down the lake, with the big bonfire and huge orange tarps.

Crooked Rapids, at the end of Primeau Lake, would be interesting on a fine day. But the wind is so strong that it almost blows us upriver. The rain is falling in sheets. We run the rapids in silence and efficiency, then look in vain for a campsite. The forest on both sides of the river has burned recently. The clearings are mucky and depressing.

Finally, just before the next set of rapids, we see an outcropping of Shield rock. It's not ideal. But it will have to do. John and I apply our combined engineering skills to set up a tarp, while Jill cooks up a quick hot meal of good old macaroni and cheese on the camp stove. The supper is ready long before the shelter is, as we struggle with tripods of crooked jack pines and tangled ropes. But soon we are all reasonably cosy and warm, with the sound of the rain smacking on the tarp and the edges snapping in the wind, flinging raindrops occasionally in our faces or our dinners.

Next day, the water is still low in the river, despite all the rain yesterday, and we run all the rapids without difficulty to Knee Lake. The weather is still brisk, and rain squalls blow through regularly, but the sun also peeks through the clouds at times, and all in all, it's a good day to travel. At the eastern end of Knee Lake is the Cree community of Elak Dase – a cluster of a dozen homes and a church. The church is very well-maintained, as are some of the homes, but no one is around. There are two wood-and-canvas freighter canoes pulled up on shore. Perhaps everyone is at the camp that we saw yesterday.

When Sig Olson and Eric Morse paddled this way in the late 1950s, they met Father Moraud, an old man who had been in this country for over forty years, travelling by canoe and snowshoe to isolated missions. He made a great impression on them, standing in the bow of a freighter canoe: "We would never forget his bearing, the white flowing beard, the jaunty way he wore his cap, the immaculate cassock over stained dungarees. His was the spirit of all the priests who had ever gone into the bush,"[4] Sig Olson wrote in his account of the trip, entitled *The Lonely Land.*

We are surprised to find that the door of the church is locked. We peer in through the windows but can't see much in the gloom. The church is clean, and the hymn books lie neatly on the pews. I wonder if they are still written in Cree, as they were when Father Moraud was the priest here.

Beyond Knee Lake, the Churchill dips back into the flat lands. Its banks disappear into vast marshes, where the delicate leaves of willow vibrate in the breeze and vibrant green sedges sway in the wind. Gull and terns soar over the marshlands. Yellowlegs, snipes, and sandpipers poke their long, thin beaks into the muck and raise their strident alarm cries as we pass. The usual mallards, teal, black ducks, and LBDS (little brown ducks) stick their rumps in the air as they forage for goodies among the rich aquatic vegetation. We are overwhelmed by the abundance of life here, but we also need a nice dry campsite.

We luck out, spotting a little knob of Canadian Shield in the flat wetlands. It is the best of all campsites – really. I can reach out the door of my tent and grab handfuls of the biggest plumpest blueberries that any of us has ever seen. They look like grapes, they are so big and round and juicy. For dessert tonight we feast on blueberry crisp with custard sauce, just the perfect end to a meal of baked pike, fresh bannock, and rice. We are already looking forward to the blueberry pancakes for breakfast.

Jill muses that we are the last of the "Blueberry Tribe." "This little-known culture," she says, "lived on blueberries. Their clothes were sewn from the dried skins of blueberries, and their skin and teeth were stained blue. They were feared warriors, who catapulted buckets of blueberries at their enemies."

We sit around the campfire, relaxing, our bellies full of good food and our minds filled with the sights and sounds of the river. Life has rarely seemed so full. The conversation takes a philosophical twist, as we discuss everything that we feel is wrong with society.

"You know," says John, the philosopher of our group, "I don't like the trend I see in our society towards the individual. Everybody is focused on himself or herself. It used to be people asked what they could do for their country, their community, their god. Now, they just ask what their country, their community, and their God can do for them."

"You're onto something, John," says Jill. "That's why so many social programs are in trouble, even though our society is wealthier than ever before."

I add, "And that's why everyone is paddling kayaks, too." They both look at me, puzzled.

"I'm not kidding. I really think it's a tangible result of the trend towards focusing on the individual. More kayaks," I continue.

"I think we need to develop a new economy," says John, "one based on the commerce of beauty, the value of beauty. Life without beauty is not worth anything. Look at how happy we are here, surrounded by all this beauty. Look at how fulfilled we feel."

"That's why getting out here, out in the wilderness, is so important. We do take a lot of the wilderness back with us to the city," I say. "In our memories. They form one of the foundations for our lives. Trips like this define us, they say who we are."

"I don't think we can change society's values," John says, "but we can stay true to our own values. If we all do that, then it will make a difference."

John is a wildlife biologist, but he is considering a major career change, to become either a minister or a chef. No matter which choice he makes, he will bring goodness into people's lives. Jill and I are pushing him towards cooking. Then he can test recipes on us.[5]

The fire has burned down to coals glowing orange. Jill stirs them with a stick, and we huddle closer to the fire, warming our hands on the burst of heat that she has just released. John is breathing deeply. He has already fallen asleep. It has been a good day.

All this philosophy has taken me from the Churchill back to the bigger world, and I'm thinking of Connie and Isaac, and missing them a lot.

Through the Haultain Marshes, the river breaks up into several meandering channels. Mackenzie called this section *"Grass River."* The richness of the marshes continues to astound us. Pelicans soar as if suspended on strings from the sky. Gulls and terns wheel and turn. At every bend is a bald eagle. Golden eagles at every second bend. Sandhill cranes. Great blue herons. Marsh hawks and others that we can't identify. The whistling of wings as flocks of ducks pass overhead is almost continuous.

We decide to take a small, easterly channel, hoping to cut off a big meander. It is pleasant, for a little while, to be paddling on a small channel. We have to pull over only one beaver dam, and we are back in the main channel, but we have saved over 8 km (5 miles) of paddling.

We run Snake Rapids, accompanied by a family of otters for much of the run. Halfway down, we pass through a swarm of flies.

"Jill, I can't see anything! I've got a ka-zillion bugs in my eye," I shout, a little panicky.

"I can't see either," Jill shouts back. "I've got bugs in my eye, too."

The unanticipated hazards of running rapids. Lucky for us, the rapids are easy.

The sides of the river here are piled high with huge boulders. We look in vain for a place to camp as the current sweeps us into Pinehouse Lake. As we enter the lake, we see an aluminum motorboat near shore, and we paddle over to ask about a good campsite.

"You can camp at the lodge," the fellow says. "Follow me."

We shrug and follow his boat a short distance to a dock on the shore. Several cabins and a main lodge building nestle in the pines not far from the water. There is an open forest of jack pine; Don, the fellow in the boat, says that we can set up our tents there. It is nothing like the accommodations of the previous night, but it looks fairly private, and we are ready to stop.

Don works for the lodge, as a guide and general handyman. He is shy and reserved and doesn't say much. But as we are setting up camp, he comes over with a load of dry firewood. He stands shuffling from one foot to the other, looking a little uncomfortable.

"Would you like some pike fillets for supper?" he quietly asks.

We nod enthusiastically, and in minutes he comes back with a huge platter piled high with fillets.

"These are great," says Jill. "I really like pike, except for the bones."

"No bones in these," he says. "I'll show you how, if you'd like." He was becoming less shy by the minute. "Why don't you come over to my cabin for coffee after?"

After our meal, we head over to Don's cabin. He offers us coffee and pickled pike. Don pickles the pike himself. "How many pecks of pickled pike can Don pickle?" Jill asks him. The pickled pike is a real treat.

Don also helps us fix the rudder on *Loon*. The aluminum rudder had broken earlier in the day. It just snapped, for no apparent reason, into one big piece and one little piece. Luckily, we didn't lose the big piece. It was held to the little piece by (what else?) duct tape. Earlier that day, John had been having difficulty pulling up the rudder. This is done by pulling on a string attached to the rudder by a piece of bungee cord. Our bungee is losing its elasticity, and it has never really worked very well.

"I can't get my rudder up, Max," John said to me earlier that day, on Sandy Lake.

"Can't get it up," I say, snickering. "Gee, John, I didn't know you had problems with that. I usually try fiddling with it." Jill cracks up, and snickers turn to guffaws until we are all laughing out of control.

At the lodge, Don takes the bigger piece of the rudder and fabricates a new rudder with it, trimming it into the shape of the old rudder with a hacksaw and drilling holes to attach it. We also tape some scrap pieces of metal tubing on top of *Loon*'s hull to keep the string that raises and lowers the rudder in proper alignment.

Back on the water the next morning, John tests out his new rudder.

"How's it work now, John?" Jill inquires.

"No problems, Jill, except it's a little short," says John, and we all collapse again, laughing uncontrollably.

Heading northeast on Pinehouse Lake, we observe a high, sandy bank of open spruce forest on the northwest side of the lake, looking very out of place in this land of rock. Mackenzie also noted this area: *"It is to be remarked here that for about three or four miles on the North-West side of this lake, there is a high bank of clay and sand, clothed with cypress trees, a circumstance which is not observable on any lakes hitherto mentioned, as they are*

bounded, particularly on the north, by gray and black rocks. It may also be con-
sidered as a most extraordinary circumstance that Chipewyans go North-West
from hence to the barren grounds which are their own country, without the assis-
tance of canoes; as it is well known that in every other part which has been
described, from Cumberland House, a traveller could not go at right angles with
any of the waters, without meeting others in every eight to ten miles."

Sandfly Lake is the most beautiful lake by far of any through which we
have paddled. It looks like Georgian Bay, with its sprinkling of tiny rocky
islands, except that the white pines are replaced by scraggly jack pines. We
have to camp here, on one of these islands, where the smooth rock is
encrusted with rusty orange lichens and the moss lies thick between the
pines, making the most comfortable mattress conceivable. We pick a site
where we can sit on the rock and watch the sun set.

Sandfly Lake does not disappoint us. The sunset is as good as they get,
painting the lichen-encrusted rock with a warm glow that reflects in our
faces. It is a night for skyworks. After the sunset has done its work with its
palette of purple, pink and mauve, the northern lights, not to be outdone,
put on an amazing show for us. Metaphors fail me once again. You just
have to see them for yourself.

At the end of Sandfly Lake, the Churchill is sucked over Needle Rapids,
so called, notes Mackenzie, *"for the sharpness of its stones."* How long would
a pair of moccasins last a hard-working voyageur, we wonder? We all wear
moccasins around camp at night but would not think of wearing them to
portage over rocks. If I'm wearing mine in town, I avoid walking on pave-
ment as much as possible, for fear of wearing holes in them. Perhaps by
this point in their trip the voyageurs' moccasins had worn out – David
Thompson notes in his journals that the voyageurs carried their loads over
the sharp rocks on the *Portage des épingles*, usually walking in bare feet!

We don't have to worry about the sharp rocks today. Poles laid over the
rocks make a skidway for dragging the big aluminum boats around the
rapid. We enjoy such conveniences and happily slide our canoes across the
portage. For us, the poles and the railway track at Dipper Rapids are not
intrusions on a wilderness experience, but show that the river is still very
much a part of the fabric of people's lives in this country. This is so different from the situation along most of the route, where so much has been
lost and forgotten, where rivers are merely obstructions that need to be
dammed or bridged.

We are now heading into the maze of channels and islands called Black
Bear Island Lake. Mackenzie notes that it *"is improperly called a lake, as it*

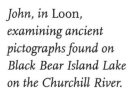

John, in Loon, *examining ancient pictographs found on Black Bear Island Lake on the Churchill River.*

contains frequent impediments amongst its islands, from rapids. There is a very dangerous one about the centre of it, which is named the rapid qui ne parle point, or that never speaks, from its silent whirlpool-motion. In some of the whirlpools the suction is so powerful that they are carefully avoided."

The water level is low, and we slip down the Silent Rapids without being sucked down into the icy black depths. Whew! A short distance below is the site of the oldest known pictograph in Canada. This is one of the few such sites that Mackenzie mentions in his journal: *"At some distance from the silent rapid, is a narrow strait, where the Indians have painted red figures on the face of a rock, and where it is their custom formerly to make an offering of some of the articles which they had with them, in their way to and from Churchill."*

We easily find the pictographs, on a sheer face of smooth grey rock. The rock has dark grey lichens growing on it, and the pictographs are faded and difficult to see at first. Then the figure of a caribou materializes among the lichens, then several human figures with uplifted arms, and finally other shapes, squiggles and jagged lines, whose meanings we can only guess.

Black Bear Island Lake is the "pikiest" lake that I have ever seen. Its quiet bays are lined with rushes, fringed with lily pads and rocky drop-offs into deep, black water. There must be some lunkers in here, but all we catch are skinny little "hammer-handles," as my father, Abe, called pike weighing less than one kilogram. They are everywhere, and almost every cast gets a strike. We finally decide to camp on a small rocky island beside one of the rapids in the "lake," hoping to catch a pickerel for supper there.

"Paddling through Black Bear Island Lake, with its maze of rocky spruce-studded islands and twisting channels, is a little like life," John says, as we are sitting, once again, stuffed with bannock and blueberries – but no pickerel – around a blazing little campfire.

"There's all these choices to make. But in the end, they all lead to the same place."

We have seen a couple of motorboats today. Not travellers, but fishing guides with their clients. One of the guides, a young Native man, said to us: "It's a good day to travel." He was right. It was cool, a little overcast, and the wind was light. He offered his remark just as someone in Ottawa might say, "Nice day, isn't it." It made us realize that travelling is still a way of life for the Cree who live on the river. This is such a contrast to most of the people whom I have met on the water during my journey, or just about anywhere.

"You know, I just don't get it," I say to the fire. "Motorboats are completely at home here now. They belong here as much as the birchbark voyageur canoes that carried Mackenzie belonged here. It's just the most practical way to get around. With those skidways and sections of railway, you can go all the way up and down the river in an aluminum boat. It makes perfect sense."

I'm rambling, I know: "But almost everywhere else, people are using these huge hulking fibreglass boats and giant outboards, and they can't afford to run them for more than a couple of hours, and half the gas goes back into the water anyway. And they can't actually go anywhere in them. With a canoe, we have complete freedom. We can go anywhere."

"We made a big mistake as a species when we gave up being hunter-gatherers. I think a high-tech hunter-gatherer society would be cool," I mumble, drifting away into sleep. My half-closed eyes discern the silhouette of a twisted jack pine and a sky laced with stars. The hot chocolate laced with scotch has done its work. There's no northern lights tonight, but who needs 'em, I think.

At the outlet of Black Bear Island Lake, the Churchill tumbles over Birch Rapids. The rapids are unrunnable, but it is easy to line the canoes down. So far, we haven't done one portage in the traditional way – carrying the canoes and packs. Would Mackenzie be envious of our luxury, or would he be contemptuous of the indolence of our ways?

We actually have to carry our canoes and packs on the little-used portage trail around Trout Lake Falls. The day is cold and rainy, with a stiff northeast wind. We stop to cook Kraft Dinner on the rocks below the falls and to try to catch a pike. Sig Olson, on his trip down the Churchill with Eric Morse and the rest of their party, reported that three of their group cast their lines in here, and on the first cast all three hooked and eventually landed three pike that weighed in total over 27 kg (60 pounds)! We try, but we catch only marginal keepers – 1 1/2 to 2 1/2 kg (3 to 5 pounds) – and

Most of the rapids have log skidways for portaging motorboats. The river is still the main highway in northern Saskatchewan.

no one feels like cleaning fish in the cold and wet weather. So we let them go, hoping that they will grow up to be like the lunkers that Sig Olson wrote about.

The river courses on, flowing through deep, rocky gorges and dropping gently over smooth ledges, finally dumping us into Dead Lake. Mackenzie wrote: *"On the left side is a point covered with human bones, the relics of the small pox, which circumstance gave the Portage and the lake its melancholy denomination."*

The wind tries its best to prevent us from progressing any farther today. But Jill has a plane to catch. Olson and his party also faced a gale on Dead Lake and had to decide whether to play safe and remain windbound or chance the 9.4-km crossing (about six miles). For both expeditions, the crossing wasn't/isn't dangerous – that's what canoe are made for. We are not sure which point Mackenzie was referring to, but the bones must be buried beneath a thick layer of moss by now or have been washed into the depths of the lake.

We camp at the eastern end of Dead Lake. This is our last camp together on the river. Tomorrow, we will be in Missinipe, and Jill and John will leave me to paddle the rest of the way to The Pas – some 500 km (some 300 miles) – on my own in *Loon*. We are sad and happy. Happy that the trip has gone so smoothly, happy with the company that we have kept, and sad that our little tribe is breaking up.

Our last day on the river, and the weather continues to be cold, wet and windy. As we approach Otter Rapids, we see a bridge over the river, the highway leading south to Saskatoon. A pickup truck stops on the bridge, the driver stopping, we think, to watch us run the rapids. These are what paddlers call big-volume rapids, with a train of big haystack waves down the centre and a big sousehole on the right. We decide to disappoint the spectator by sneaking down the left side. We dodge around rocks, stopping in each eddy to survey our route and discuss the next fancy moves, always staying out of the main current.

We watch John come down in *Loon*, following our route. My heart rises in my throat as I see him being swept towards a big rock, but at the last second he points the bow to the right and slides down smoothly into the quiet pool below. I ask John about his technique when he reaches the bottom of the rapids.

"Oh, I just paddle 'til I see a rock in front of me, and then I go left or right. I don't really plan ahead," John shrugs.

It always feels a little strange paddling into a town after a period without seeing many people. It is early in the afternoon, and we hike over to Rick Dridigier's Horizons Unlimited outfitting shop. I met Rick several years ago in Ottawa at an outdoor adventure show. He invites us to have showers, and I decide to stay in one of his cabins for the night to dry out. Cleaned up and warm from our showers, the three of us head over to the finest restaurant in town for supper – which, for the first time since Ile-a-la-Crosse, we don't have to cook ourselves.

It's 7 September. Jill has to catch her flight in Saskatoon the next day, and I will head on to The Pas, where my flight is booked for the 18th, giving me nine days to go some 300 miles. A bit of a push, but if the weather gods are kind, not at all out of the question in my beloved *Loon*.

20

Sturgeon-Weir:
The Road Home

It is necessary to cross the Portage de Traite, or, as it is called by the Indians, Athiquisipichigan Ouinigam, or the Portage of the Stretched Frog-Skin, to the Missinipi [Churchill]. The waters already described [the Sturgeon-Weir] discharge themselves into Lake Winipic. These which we are now entering are called the Missinipi, or great Churchill River.

— ALEXANDER MACKENZIE

TONIGHT, SNUG IN RICK DRIDIGIER'S CABIN in the town of Missinipe (Otter Lake), I re-read the letter from Connie while rain drums on the roof. I am thinking about heading home. This isn't just a canoe trip now, it's the only way to get back home.

It is raining in the morning, and I'm off to a slow start, lingering over coffee, thinking about going, but deciding instead to pour another cup of coffee. The rain lets up at noon, and I finally decide to leave.

Otter Lake is beautiful, with spruce and birch-covered islands, jutting granite bluffs, clear water – all the beauty of the Shield. Otter Lake ends abruptly at two sets of very lovely waterfalls. The river then blends gently into the next lake – Mountain. By evening, the rain squalls have passed, and it is a peaceful, calm night. I camp on an exposed point at the south end of Mountain Lake, just upstream of the village of Stanley Mission. I want to camp alone tonight, away from people. Here, I can look out of the tent up the length of the lake, framed by sheer rock cliffs. There is an unobstructed view of the northern sky in case it lights up later. I enjoy being a solo paddler again, and it feels great to be back in *Loon*.

*Robertson Falls, just downstream from Otter Lake, Saskatchewan, on the
Churchill River.*

My route is simple. Paddle down the Churchill to Frog Portage, over the
portage into the Sturgeon-Weir River, and follow the Sturgeon-Weir south
to Cumberland House, on the North Saskatchewan. From Cumberland
House, I will head downstream to The Pas, where I can catch a flight back
home to Ottawa.

It is still early in the morning when I paddle into Stanley Mission. I am
at Amachêwêspinuwin, as it is known in Cree, "the cliffs where hunters
shoot up their arrows."[1] Once known as Church Point, the name was soon
changed to Stanley Mission.[2] I'm looking forward to seeing the church here,
the oldest building in Saskatchewan, put up in 1851. It stands alone on a
grassy hill on the north side of the river, across from Stanley Mission. The
church is painted white, and its spire shines like a knight's lance pointing
heavenward. It is an impressive structure, named after Stanley Park in
England, home of the wife of its builder and first missionary, Robert Hunt.
No one is at the church, but the door is unlocked, and I go inside.

The interior is immaculate. Every surface is clean and polished. I stare
in awe at the 37 gothic, arched stained-glass windows, made of 1,000
pieces. The morning sun shines through them, creating rainbow patterns
on the wall. The stained glass travelled in 1860 from England to Montreal
by ship and from Montreal by canoe, along the same route that I am
taking. I sit in the church, enjoying the quiet, the sunlight shining through
the stained glass tinting the walls and the interior a peaceful shade of rose.

The church at Stanley Mission, erected in 1851, is the oldest building in Saskatchewan. The spectacular stained glass windows were brought from England to Montreal, then by canoe over the same route I am travelling.

After a meditative respite, I wander through the graveyard beside the church, reading the inscriptions on the stones and wooden crosses, feeling saddened as always by the number of children who died before they really had a chance to live.

I run Stanley Rapids, just downstream of the church, and find it more exciting than I had anticipated. The Churchill is a big river now, and getting pushy. So am I. I'm starting to hurry. I push on to Nistowiak Lake, where I make a short detour up the Rapid River to Nistowiak Falls. I can hear the thunder of the falls from where the pellucid waters of the river rush into the lake. This river drains vast Lac la Ronge. There is a fishing lodge here, where once was only a portage trail. In between the days of the fur trade and the fishing lodge, there was a uranium mine here, but no one would ever guess that now.

A sign outside the lodge with an arrow directs me towards the trail leading to the falls. The thunder grows louder, and I begin to run up the trail. I am not disappointed. I clamber down to a shelf of flat rock where the translucent green water smoothly pours over a lip of rock and falls 16 m (50 feet), exploding into foaming, surging mounds of white. It is one of those sights so beautiful, like the northern lights, that words can only begin to describe it.

On my hike back to Nistowiak Lake, a great grey owl stares at me with giant yellow eyes from a spruce tree. I try fishing where the river runs into the lake but catch only skinny little hammer-handles. Perhaps this should be called "the river of little stick pike."

I paddle through Drinking Lake and Keg Lake, portaging Keg Falls (obviously booze was a valuable trade item), and finish up the day somewhere beyond the edge of the map. I pitch my tent on a bed of sphagnum moss, nestled between spruce trees. It's a very cosy camp, almost cave-like in the shady, damp forest. No one would ever see me, I think, as if there actually were anyone to look for me. Tomorrow I will leave the Churchill at a widening of the river called Trade Lake and turn south, heading over Frog Portage and down the Sturgeon-Weir towards home.

It has taken me twelve camps to get here from Ile-a-la-Crosse. Governor George Simpson paddled from here to Ile-a-la-Crosse in five days, heading upstream, with an elite crew of paddlers in a specially designed express canoe.

Frog Portage is only 300 m (1,000 feet) long – amazingly short distance for such a significant portage. Joseph Frobisher was the first European to walk across Frog Portage, in 1775.[3] In Mackenzie's time it was known as *Portage de Traite* (the trading portage). According to Mackenzie, "*Mr. Joseph Frobisher, one of the gentlemen engaged in the trade, met the Indians from that quarter* [the north and west] *on their way to Fort Churchill* [at the mouth of the Churchill River on Hudson Bay] ... *it was indeed with some difficulty that he could induce them to trade with him, but he at length procured as many furs as his canoes could carry. In consequence of this transaction, the Portage received and has since retained its present appellation. He denominated these waters the English River.*"

For more than half a century, since 1719, the Cree had been taking long trips each spring to Hudson Bay to trade with the Hudson's Bay Company. Now they had another option – one that no doubt involved a lot of rum. Thus began the intense competition between the HBC and the traders out of Montreal, which helped shape Canada. Once again, standing on the same trail that Frobisher did, I am smacked in the face with the reality that the fur trade routes indeed form the roots of Canada.

According to Mackenzie, Frog Portage, or "Portage of the Stretched Frog-Skin," is the name that the Cree gave it "*when they first came to this*

This historic plaque marks the famous Frog Portage, connecting the Churchill River to the Sturgeon-Weir. Note the bullet holes in the plaque.

country, and either destroyed or drove back the natives, whom they held in great
contempt, on many accounts, but particularly for their ignorance in hunting the
beaver, as well as in preparing, stretching, and drying the skins of those animals.
And as a sign of their derision, they stretched the skin of a frog, and hung it up
at the Portage."

Today, a section of railway track crosses the 300-m (1,000-foot) portage.
A heavy wooden cart on steel wheels takes motorboats across the portage.
I load up *Loon* and my pack and haul the cart up the slope from the
Churchill. This is hard work – much harder than portaging. The cart must
weigh hundreds of pounds. As I finally attain the crest of the portage, I
hop on for the ride downhill. The cart begins to pick up speed, and I have
visions of its flying off the end of the track, scattering me and *Loon* and all
my gear into the muddy headwaters of the Sturgeon-Weir. I jump off, grab
a rope, and try to slow it down. I fall, bounce along on my behind for a few
yards, and finally regain my footing. The cart hits the wooden boards at
the end of the track with a loud thump. I'm at the Sturgeon-Weir. At least
I'm not in it.

Mackenzie knew the Sturgeon-Weir as the *"Rivière Maligne,"* or the *"Bad*
River," "as it is a continual rapid for about thirty miles, the poles in use [upstream]
nearly the whole way." But for me, it is the road home.

The Sturgeon-Weir end of Frog Portage consists of a wild rice swamp –
black water with light-green shoots of wild rice rising above it – and a
pretty little channel just wide enough for a canoe winding through it. The
waterway looks a little confusing, and on my 1:250,000 topographical map,
someone's notes scribbled in black magic marker obscure many details
(an unknown park planner made a field trip to this area many years ago to
survey its potential as a national park). But my plan looks simple enough.
Just head downstream.

The swamp pops me out onto Lindstrom Lake. At the end of the lake is
a beaver dam, with water flowing south, towards the North Saskatchewan.
Good! Another narrows soon follows, partially dammed by beavers, but
this time the water is flowing towards me. I push on into the next lake, but
now the pattern of land and water does not look right at all. I should be in
Wood Lake, a big lake stretching away to the south. Instead, I'm on a lake
full of islands. And how could the current be coming into the lake? If I'm
going upstream, I would paddle into Manawan Lake, a big lake stretching
northeast. I paddle back over the partially submerged dam and set up
camp on a small island. I will look for the outlet tomorrow. Things always
look clearer in the morning.

It is pitch dark. I am cooking chili over a campfire, when I hear the sound of an outboard. The motor slows at the narrows where the beaver dam is and then speeds up again, heading northwest, towards Frog Portage. An hour later, another motorboat goes by. Then another. Well, this certainly is curious. Where is everybody going, and, more significant to me, where are they coming from? The local people are so at home on these waters that they travel in the dark, and I get lost in the daylight. What a klutz!

I hear another motorboat approaching. What the heck?, I think. I might as well embarrass myself. I build up the fire. I hear the motor slow down as the boat approaches the beaver dam and then speed up again. Now the driver should be able to see the fire. I signal with my flashlight – three flashes, then a pause, then three more flashes. Hey! The motor slows down and then stops. Now I can hear two male voices, but cannot distinguish the words, and a lot of banging on aluminum. What the heck are they doing?

I wait. And wait some more. The fire burns down, and I almost give up and go to bed, but then I hear the motor start, and the boat cautiously approaches my camp. "Hello," I say loudly, as the blacker silhouette of the boat and two men materializes on the black night water and sky.

"Hello yourself," one answers back.

"Want some tea?" I ask.

"Sure!" one replies.

They land and come over, as I pour tea into a mug and a bowl for them.

"Hey, I know this sounds dumb, but do you know the name of this lake?" I ask, kind of shyly, holding out my map, flashlight in my hand.

"This is Linstrom," one of them says, pointing with his finger to the black smudges on the map. "That's Pixley after the beaver dam."

Pixley is downstream on the way to Wood Lake, according to the map. I'm confused. I thought that I was already past Pixley.

"So?" I ask. "How come the water on the dam is flowing into this lake from Pixley? I thought it should flow the other way."

"It goes both ways," the other laughs. "The lakes slosh back and forth. You know, when we saw your fire, we almost didn't come over. We thought you might be a camp of moose hunters. But you were too quiet."

"We're out setting nets. We come from Wood Lake. You'll pass by there tomorrow."

They finish their tea and leave. I'm still a little confused. If I'm only here (and I definitely am here), how did it take me two hours to paddle two and a half kilometres (1 1/2 miles) on Linstrom Lake? Maybe it was the Maymaygwashi – those little men who live in stone, who have long arms with six fingers on each hand, whom I saw images of back on the

Churchill and on Lac La Croix in Quetico. Maybe they had something to do with this.

I head out the next day, passing through swampy Pixley Lake and into the big water of Wood Lake. At the head of Wood Lake lies a community of the same name, where the men whom I met last night live. It consists of a few scattered cabins on the narrow channel leading to the lake. It is a beautiful location. Beds of bright green lily pads line the shores, and smooth rock outcroppings frame the lake.

On Wood Lake, I pass a motorboat with two men pulling up their nets. I paddle over to see what they have caught. One of the men is very elderly, the other a teenager. The old man introduces himself: "I'm Eli Custer," he says, in a strong voice. "This is my grandson."

I comment that it is a nice way to spend a day.

"Yep. I'm eighty-four years old, and I still trap and fish. I got a cabin in the bush and a home in Pelican Narrows, beside my daughter. I figger I got just about everything a man could want," he says. A lot of us could learn a lot from Eli, I think.

I nod in agreement and paddle off. Eli's got eleven more nets to check, and I'm heading to Pelican Narrows. I must pick up the pace a bit, or I'll miss my flight home from The Pas.

At Medicine Rapids, the fishermen have dynamited a channel and, even with the water being low, I run *Loon* through the shallow channel. I pass Eli and his son, dragging their heavy boat across on a log skidway. He smiles and nods to me. A few minutes later they zoom by me on their way to Pelican Narrows. An hour or so later, I land at the float-plane dock in the community, which is on a hill overlooking the lake. I'm anxious to find a telephone and call Connie, because – well, just because.

A white fellow comes down to the dock. I ask him if there's a pay phone in town, and he shows me one right on the dock. Bingo! His name is Bruce Letkeman, and he works here and in the Philippines. He invites me to stay with him overnight and takes me to the finest restaurant in town – the only restaurant, of course – but we have a sumptuous meal of fresh white-fish and homemade blueberry pie with ice cream. Deee-licious.

I get an early start in the morning. Bruce has talked to some of the pilots, and they told him that I would never make it to The Pas by the 17th. It's September 12th today.

"They tell me its about 300 kilometres," he says.

"That's only about 60 kilometres a day, and I'll do 120 on the North Saskatchewan in a day, so I should be OK. Tight, but OK," I say.

He shakes his head incredulously and waves me off.

A strong north wind pushes me down the 20-km (12-mile) length of Mirond Lake. Thick grey clouds hang heavy in the sky. It looks like it should be pouring, but no rain falls. At the end of Mirond Lake, the Sturgeon-Weir pours in a deep-green torrent through a rock-walled channel. I paddle on, running through some smooth standing waves, and then see the river ahead tumble over big rocks. I stop to investigate. It is a runnable rapid, but a little bit too much "on the edge" for my liking.

I decide to line *Loon* down the side, hopping from boulder to boulder. I am cold, and I'm getting pooped. I tie one line around the stern and another to the bow. Somehow, I mess up my standard bow line knot, shrug, and tie a reef knot instead. I think to myself that this is a rinky-dink bit of lining, and it doesn't really matter. At the bottom of the rapid is a one-metre drop, with a pile of boulders about one *Loon*-length in front. I need to let the canoe come over the drop quickly, pointing straight downstream, and then shorten the bow line and pull hard, while keeping tension on the stern line, to make a hard right turn to miss the boulder pile. Lining downstream is tricky. When you're going with the current, events happen very quickly, especially when you are hopping from boulder to slippery boulder. When I give a good hard tug on the bow line at the critical moment, the reef knot lets go.

I watch helplessly for a moment, the bow line hanging limp in my hand, as *Loon* ploughs into the boulders. Then I leap into the water, half swim and half wade out to *Loon*, and lift her half out of the pounding water. Luckily, the spray cover has kept out most of the water. I reattach the bow line, muscle the canoe off the rocks, and pull her to shore.

Below the next rapids (which I portage), the Sturgeon-Weir flows slowly through a series of long, narrow lakes. It is mid-September, and the leaves of the birch trees are turning bright yellow. The yellow of the leaves, the white trunks, the dark-green spruce, and the dark-green water make me shudder at the beauty of it all. I am lucky to be here. There is a small rapid at the bridge where the Hanson Lake Road crosses the Sturgeon-Weir. I take a hard stroke with my trusty double-blade to avoid a series of boulders, and KER-SNAP! (really, it does make a sound just like that), the paddle shaft breaks. *Loon*, wise old bird that she is, somehow picks her way through the boulder garden without a scratch. I pick up the broken end, floating in the pool below the rapids, and limp to shore, paddling with the single blade.

This is serious. The double-blade is my "rock" paddle, and the Sturgeon-Weir is full of rocky rapids. There is a fishing resort – Pawistic

Heading downstream, there are only a few portages on the Sturgeon-Weir. Scoop Falls is the beautiful set of rapids on the river.

Lodge – at the bridge, and I walk over to its main building. Charlie Willet and his wife, Gail, take matters into their own hands.

"Well, can you make do with a slightly shorter paddle?" Charlie asks.

"Sure," I say.

Charlie drills and reams and drills and reams some more, cleaning out the plastic sleeve where the two parts of the paddle fit together. Then he pounds the broken end into the sleeve, and *voila* – a new, take-apart, double-bladed paddle, slightly shorter, and with an oddly angled offset. I thank Charlie and Gail for their help.

"Ah, this river is pretty good to us," Charlie says. "I don't mind doing something in return."

The river runs as a straight green line between forests of dark green and yellow. I jog the short portage around Scoop Falls. A few miles downstream, at Spruce Rapids, there are several fishermen in aluminum boats above the rapid.

"What's the rapid like?" I ask one of the fishermen.

"Bad rapid," he answers. "Don't try it."

I paddle to the brink and take a look. Not so bad, I think to myself. The bottom half is full of Volkswagen-sized boulders, but there is plenty of space between them. I give a hard sweep with my new and improved double-blade and hear an ominous CRACK! The paddle is still in one piece, but my confidence in it is shattered. I make it through the rapids in one piece, but I have to do something about my paddling arsenal.

A few miles below Spruce Rapids, I see a neat log cabin beside the river and a big man in orange overalls by the dock. He waves me over.

"Hi," he says, with a big smile on his broad, dark face. "You look like you've come a long ways. Come on in for coffee."

He motions me to sit at the table. There are several people in the cabin.

"I'm Jimmy Custer, and this is my wife, Shanelle, and my kids, Walter

Another photo of Jimmy Custer, once the world champion "flour-packer," at his cabin on the Sturgeon-Weir, with his son Walter (centre) and his friend Devon.

and Maryanne." He motions towards the others. "That's my friends John and Elaine and their son, Devon."

Jimmy asks about my trip and seems very interested, especially about the rest of the way down the Sturgeon-Weir. Then he tells me a little bit about himself.

"I hold the world record for flour-packing, 930 pounds."

"That's a contest to see who can carry the most flour, isn't it?" I ask.

"Yep, have to carry it 30 yards. I've seen men's legs break, the bone coming right out," Jimmy says. "There's a photo of me at the Trapper's Festival in The Pas in a *National Geographic* ... um, August 1987."

Jimmy and his family and guests are just heading out to go fishing.

"Make yourself at home," he says. "We'll be back by dark."

I reinforce my paddle with fibreglass and bring it inside to cure beside the wood stove.

They all come back as night is settling, with as nice a catch of pickerel as I have ever seen. In minutes, fillets are frying, and the whisky is flowing. The cabin gets too warm, and everyone takes a walk outside. It is a cold clear night. There will be a frost for sure. The northern lights are shimmering. Walter, who is about twelve, says: "The lights are so beautiful tonight." His voice is filled with awe.

It is a good show, to be sure, but not the best that I have seen.

"Walter, you must see northern lights like this just about every night. Why are you so excited about these?"

"I don't know," he says, thoughtfully, searching for his words. "I just never get used to them."

What a good way to be, I think.

We stay up way past midnight. Jimmy is up early in the morning, and I have several cups of strong coffee to wake up. Jimmy puts a huge pile of bacon and a hunk of moose meat in the frying pan.

"That should get you across Amisk Lake," he says.

The traverse across huge Amisk Lake is uneventful, and I have great fun picking my way down the numerous rapids heading to Namew Lake. The riverbed is made of smooth limestone. I camp just above the junction of the Goose River. It is a lovely campsite, on a big, flat hunk of limestone above the river, just below a rapid. Tonight, I see Orion for the first time in the southern sky – a sure harbinger of winter. The northern lights sparkle and flicker. Autumn is definitely in the air. It is cold, real cold, for the first time. I hear the whistle of wings as flocks of geese and ducks fly overhead, silhouetted against the northern lights. Barred owls call to each other from tall spruce trees. In the morning, I see lots of sandhill cranes heading south, flying thousands of feet up in the sky.

The Sturgeon-Weir sweeps me back onto the prairies at Namew Lake – a big prairie lake – at the community of Sturgeon Landing. Although it is still early in the day, I can see whitecaps on the lake. I pull into a dock at a fishing camp to get a weather forecast. It's not good.

"The wind is s'posed to pick up later in the day," the owner informs me. "I'm telling my clients not to go out on the lake today, but to fish up the river instead."

I look at the big, beamy, 6.5-m (20-foot) aluminum boats with 30-hp outboards at the dock. Serious boats.

"Well," I say, "then I better get a move on."

Several fishermen stare at me as I head out into the whitecaps.

"Thanks for the great big prairie welcome!" I shout to the wind. The wind hits me in the face hard, blowing 30 to 40 km (21 to 28 miles) per hour from the southwest, which, of course, is exactly the direction in which I am heading. Those winds, those winds, those damn southwest winds.

Namew, as I mentioned above, is a prairie lake, and on a prairie lake there are no hiding places. The shorelines are long and straight. There are no coves or headlands. No islands. A long point extends almost halfway across this lake, so you may as well just paddle down the middle, heading to the point. The water is shallow near shore, so there's no relief there. In fact, the entire lake is shallow, so the waves are steep and choppy. I pray that I don't hit bottom in a trough.

It is a painfully slow, wet, bumpy ride down the length of Namew Lake. But I finally get there.

I camp at Whitey Narrows, just before Cumberland Lake, on a lovely little knoll in the wetlands. I don't know what cued me to stop and look around for a campsite here, but many people have camped here before me.

Now I am paddling on the same thin line that I paddled two summers ago, along the south shore of Cumberland Lake. I see the dam at the outlet of the Tearing River, where I waved goodbye to Chris and Todd. The first time that I paddled here, looking for Cumberland House, I missed the outlet channel twice. This time, I keep a sharp eye on the map and find the channel of the Bigstone River leading to this community.

I land at the boat launch in town, walk to the same hotel for a second break-fast, and telephone Connie. Using my tiny 15-cm (6-inch) tripod and trusty self-timer, I take the required video footage and photographs of me stand-ing beside the stone cairn with the bronze plaque proclaiming this a site of national historic significance. I took the same images in 1997. I wonder if I look the same. There's been a lot of water under the hull since then.

My arrival at Cumberland House is very anticlimactic. There's no point in hanging around, and I still have 133 km (80 miles) to go to The Pas. It's 16 September. As I'm leaving, a group of young men come down to the landing, getting ready to head out on a hunting trip upriver. One of them looks at me and says:

"Wasn't that you here in that same canoe about two years ago?"

"Yeah, that was me," I admit. I tell him what I've been up to.

Cumberland House—again! September 16, 1999. The long trek is almost over.

My final campsite on my cross-continental odyssey, on the North Saskatchewan just downstream from Cumberland House.

He whistles through his teeth: "That's one long canoe trip." The familiar faraway look comes into his eyes. "Gee, I'd like to do something like that some day."

"Hey!" I say, bringing him back to earth. "What side is best for running the Bigstone Rapids?"

"This side," he says. "Stay close to shore, and you'll be OK."

I must say, I do a very neat run down the Bigstone Rapids, nimbly eddying in and out, taking not a single drop of water on the spray cover. I set up camp on a mud bar just below the junction of the Tearing River, the last camp on my cross-Canada tour.

In the morning, I set off, with a slight east wind in my face. I pack for a day in the canoe. I have my lunch and snacks ready, and plenty of water. I pee in the bailer. I tell *Loon* that there is no stopping until she reaches The Pas. It is a long slog down the muddy ol' North Saskatchewan. I recall each spot where I camped with Chris and Todd in 1997, each lunch stop. I tick them off – that's the second campsite, the second lunch spot. Of course, heading upstream in '97 took more than twice as long as heading down in '99.

I drift as I eat lunch. Afterwards a coyote plays hide and seek with me, waiting at each point and then running along the shore and hiding at the next point. Finally, it loses interest. I see beaver, mink, otters, Canada geese, pelicans, bald eagles, horned larks, yellowlegs, sandpipers, and a ka-zillion ducks. The North Saskatchewan runs through one of the greatest wetlands in the world. The scenery may be boring, but the wildlife is amazing. I would love to get away from the river and onto the wetlands – some other time perhaps.

Big prairie thunderstorms roll in in the afternoon. I put away my carbon-fibre paddle, which is a great conductor of electricity, I've been told, and use my wooden double-blade. The thunderstorms herald a cold front, and, when they are past, the temperature quickly drops. The moose knew that this was coming. I heard a cow moose calling last night, for the first time this trip. The rut is beginning.

At 6:30 that evening, cold and wet now, I paddle under the highway bridge over the river at The Pas. I pull into the dock near the Kinsmen Camp Site. There's no one to greet me, but there is a pickup truck with a man in it in the parking lot. He stares at me, mildly curious, I think, as I set up the video camera on my little 15-cm (6-inch) tripod, paddle back out into the river, and land again.

Then I hoof it over to the campsite, where Clem Jones, who takes care of the place, shows me the showers. A hot shower. That's what I need first. Clem takes me to the Miss The Pas restaurant for supper, where I had eaten two years earlier. The long trip is over.

21

Reflections

NOW THAT I HAVE PADDLED ACROSS THE CONTINENT, so what? What this experience has indelibly etched on my consciousness is that the route of this first cross-continent explorer is the most significant water trail in North America. Alexander Mackenzie's route embodies a wellspring of Canadian heritage and history. To a large extent, the route defines Canada and what being Canadian means. And most of us know little about Mackenzie the explorer and the route that he followed. But this experience affected me in ways that I did not expect. Let me try to explain.

I have sung my way across the waters. I have laughed and danced, and I have wept. I have known many pleasures, and many hardships. I have found that the greatest pleasures are the simplest and that they are inextricably linked to the greatest hardships. I will never, ever, forget how good it feels to drop my pack at the end of a portage, sit down, and lean my back against it, so that the pack supports me, instead of me supporting the pack.

The land and the water have sung and danced, laughed and wept, with me. Sig Olson, in his wonderful book *The Singing Wilderness*, writes of how the land north and west of Lake Superior sang most strongly to him. He heard – as I did, and do – the singing in the whisper of wings passing in the night, in the call of a loon on a misty lake, in the thunder of rapids (and of my heart beating in my chest when running them), in the drumming of rain on the tent, in the crackle of a campfire.

This is true, but I think that there is more to it. In the wild places, in the ancient places, in the quiet places, the land really does sing. You can hear it, if you stop and listen. In an ancient forest, it sounds like music playing on a radio, far away. Sometimes the tune is almost recognizable. At times, it seems so real that I've actually walked towards the sound, certain that I will stumble upon a party of geologists in the bush, but of course, it always fades away, like a rainbow that you try to touch. In the Barrens, the sound is different – a kind of dull hum. It is not the blood coursing through my veins, but a sound that comes from all around. Perhaps it is the sound of the earth turning or of tectonic plates grinding together. Perhaps it is the universal "Om." Many places on this trip, the land sang loudly to me.

Those who have come before me – the untold thousands of Native travellers, fur traders, explorers, dreamers and schemers – they also sang to me. I feel that I have come to Mackenzie and the rest in a way that I couldn't have unless I followed their footsteps and paddle strokes.

I am a lucky guy. During the voyages, something happened deep inside me, a transformation of sorts. I think that this is something that happens to everyone who undertakes long journeys. Trite as it sounds, I can't help myself from believing that a long canoe trip is a metaphor of a lifetime. It begins with a notion, an idea, or maybe an accident of circumstance, or a temporary feeling. On the journey, or as we grow, we change, meet challenges, sometimes think of quitting. At the end of the journey, all that we have left are memories, stories, legacies. All of us are on journeys, whether geographical, metaphysical, emotional, or just plain old day-to-day, get-by, same-old, same-old living. In the end, all the journeys are spiritual, because, in the end, that's all we are.

I began my journey as a teenager, not in years, but in many other ways. Friends who liked me described me as a grown-up stuck in perpetual teenage-hood. I am not sure what friends who didn't like me said. I finished the journey an adult. I am not sure how this happened or why. But it did.

I know that after my tour of the fur trade route, I was a different person inside. I now knew clearly what I wanted and, equally important, what I did not want. This affected me in all ways, from little day-to-day decisions, like what flavour of ice cream I wanted to buy (before, I would always covet the flavour that someone else had chosen), to BIG decisions that, if we're lucky, we have the choice to make or not make. Decisions such as: "What do I want to do when I grow up?"

These gloves have just paddled over 7,000 kilometres (about 4,200 miles). This is what they looked like on the last day of the journey.

I also had glimmerings of understanding about that well-known epithet by Reinhold Niebuhr, which I purposely won't quote here, because I want to paraphrase it as I remember it. Let's see – it goes something like: "God grant me the serenity to accept the things I can't change, the courage to change the things I can, and the wisdom to know the difference." Once I clued in to this, the trip became a lot easier.

I also began to understand what my father once told me, a few years before he died.

"Look for your happiness where it might be found," he said. "Don't look for it where it isn't." My father, who considered every day a bonus, understood this well. After this trip, I started to understand what he meant.

Don't get me wrong. I don't mean to imply that I am in any way better than you are. I do not recommend long canoe trips for everyone for personal growth. There is no easy road to growing up. This is just what happened to me, and I'm by no means an enlightened person, but I am a little wiser than I was before the trip.

As Popeye says: "I yam what I yam, and that's all that I yam."

I am Max the voyageur-in-training, Max the dad, Max the son, Max the friend of rivers, Max the paddler, Max the husband of Connie, my one true love, and Max the teller of stories.

I hope that you enjoyed my story and Alexander Mackenzie's story, one that I think we all need to know a little better.

Appendix A

What To Take

Rather than be without, I was thorough. As the weather warmed up, I mailed home items that I didn't need anymore.

FIRST AID KIT
gauze pads
bandages – strips, knuckle, butterfly, triangular
tincture of benzine (very important for making bandages stick to skin; rubbed
    on hands or feet, it dries to form a tough coating and helps prevent blisters.)
latex gloves
oil of cloves (for toothaches)
safety pins (these have a ka-zillion uses)
moleskin
tensor bandage
toenail clippers
folding scissors
antibiotic cream
Vaseline (for preventing abrasion, fixing stove pumps, and so on)
Gravol and Pepto Bismal
Tylenol
antihistamine
antibiotic pills (broad range)
anti-diarrhoea pills (Lomatil)
anti-inflammatory pills (Ibuprofen) (I used these a lot late in the journey!)
rehydration salts

PERSONAL GEAR
sunglasses (I don't know how the voyageurs survived without these – I have not
    come across anything in my research that they used for protection from
    glare. One way to prevent sore eyes is to drink a lot. I often had to stop in the
    late afternoon in a shady place to rest my eyes.)
toothbrush
toothpaste
shampoo/biodegradable soap
small towel
hand cream (helps prevent cracks, especially in cold, wet conditions, which
    seem prevalent in Canada most of the time. Cracks in the skin on fingertips
    and heels can become annoying if they get infected.)
nail brush (keeping hands clean prevents unavoidable little cracks, cuts, and
    scrapes from getting infected)
sunscreen
chapstick
watch (indispensable navigation tool)

ear plugs (for sleeping in motels and campsites)

glasses

magnifying glass (for fun and to help read maps – my eyes aren't what they used
    to be)

wallet with a few cheques, credit card, government ID card, Bell phone card,
    bank card, driver's licence

USEFUL (AND MAYBE INDISPENSABLE) GEAR

sponge (for the canoe)

bailer

paddles (bent-shaft carbon fibre and double-blade)

mast and sail

life-jacket

two carabiners

insect repellent (a 14% DEET cream worked well enough and didn't dissolve gear)

bug jacket (don't leave home without one)

matches in waterproof containers and book matches to put in pockets

Thermos blanket (for use as a ground sheet, poncho, cover)

nylon or plastic tarp with grommets and 4.5-m (15-foot) lengths of rope
    (for quick shelter)

compass (the most important piece of survival gear)

note pad and pencils

maps (1:250,000)

a few extra plastic bags

a few extra garbage bags

folding saw

small hatchet

knife (I used a small folding clasp knife, in addition to the Swiss Army knife and
    Leatherman tool. I rarely cut anything harder than cheese.)

leather gloves (indispensable for playing with campfires)

flashlight or headlight (and spare batteries!)

candle lantern and spare candles

100 feet (about 40 m) of nylon rope (including two 25-foot lengths for lining)

shock cords and straps

tent, fly and vestibule

sleeping bag

Thermarest

waterproof pack (I used olive barrels in a canoe pack and then switched to a
    canoe pack with a waterproof liner, lent to me by Bill Ostrom – the most con-
    venient system.)

day-pack

whistle

water bottle

water filter (fits water bottle)

mini-binoculars (for birdwatching – and for finding your way)

REPAIR KIT
heavy needles
heavy waxed thread
a few needles and lengths of thread
Swiss Army knife, Leatherman
lots and lots of duct tape
50 feet (about 20 m) of parachute chord
snare wire
wet/dry sandpaper
coarse sandpaper or small metal file
sharpening stone
hacksaw blade cut in half (that's plenty)
fibreglass repair kit (Bring extra bottles of hardener. Once opened, a bottle of
    hardener always disappears, no matter how carefully sealed.)
extra rudder cable (for *Loon*)
a few nails, plastic nylon ties, elastics, long twist ties
5-minute epoxy (fast setting)
contact cement
mini-vice-grips (these make a great clamp)

EATING STUFF
yoghurt containers (great as bowls and to keep leftovers – will last all summer –
    but from a health viewpoint, you're probably better off buying real bowls)
two nesting pots
frying pan
two metal plates (as lids for pot and frying pan and great for fanning campfires)
utensils
insulated metal mug
wooden spoon
spatula
"scrubbie"
dish soap (Green camp soap is fine for all washing purposes.)
wipe rag
stove and fuel
fire irons (two 18-inch, or 45-cm, pieces of angle iron to hold pots on the fire)
leather work gloves (crucial camping equipment for city-soft hands)

FISHING GEAR
collapsible rod
reel
a few flies/lures
spare line
wire leaders (if big pike are lurking)
fillet knife
pliers

CAMERA GEAR
video camera in Pelican case
three batteries for the video camera
solar panel to recharge batteries
point-and-shoot camera and spare batteries
35-mm camera
two lenses (35-105; 200)
spare batteries
full-size tripod
mini-tripod (a very useful six-inch tripod – holds video camera and 35-mm cam-
    era, even with 200-mm lens attached)
lens paper/cleaning stuff
waterproof bag or case for cameras

CLOTHES (FOR EARLY SPRING)
rubber boots (for cold weather and water – ditched when weather warmed up)
beat-up running shoes
moccasins (for camp wear)
two pairs of heavy wool or polypro socks
two pairs of liner/cotton socks
one pair of light cotton work pants or "quick-dry" pants
one pair of light polypro long johns
one polypro turtleneck with zipper
one polypro long-sleeved light shirt
long shorts (light nylon)
two T-shirts
one long-sleeved cotton shirt
four pairs "gotchies" (underwear)
rain suit
sou'wester
baseball hat or sun hat
extra hat (invaluable – easily blown off and lost)
wool toque
light wool or fleece gloves (can be worn under leather gloves if it's really cold)
light canoeing gloves, made of neoprene with a fake leather palm (to prevent
    blisters from using double-blade paddle)
one large bandana; one small one
wool (or fleece) sweater
heavy polypro underwear top
light nylon windbreaker
light nylon wind pants
light neoprene paddling gloves
nylon glove liners worn in leather work gloves (for colder weather)

<u>FOOD</u>

Although this was to be a very long canoe trip, unlike on other such trips I was to have plenty of opportunities to resupply along the route.

I did a long solo trip in 1990 – the Clean Water Dream Trip (and that is another story) – and relied on buying food in small communities. I soon tired of Kraft Dinner and instant oatmeal, cookies and chocolate bars, which is about all that you can buy at the small grocery stores associated with tourist camps and water-side parks. You cannot even buy raisins or peanuts (except for the kind dipped in honey and salt). These stores, of course, do not cater to paddlers. Everyone travels in cars or big motorboats or houseboats. Everything in these stores either is junk food or comes in huge family-size quantities. Don't get me wrong – I'm a real fan of junk food. There's nothing like an ice-cold can of Coke and a bag of potato chips after weeks in the bush subsisting on dried food. But a steady diet of junk food takes away the thrill and enjoyment of junk food binges and brings on malnourishment, especially if you are working really hard every day and freezing your butt off.

You can't even buy a loaf of decent bread at these stores. You can buy only white bread – the kind that turns back into dough when you squeeze it. (Of course, everyone knows that this kind of bread with cheese slices makes the best grilled cheese sandwiches). You cannot buy anything for supper except Kraft Dinner or hot dogs. Chris Taggart, who paddled across Canada to Prince George in one season, lived on Kraft Dinner, grilled cheese sandwiches, and instant oatmeal. He lost 18 kg (40 pounds) by the end of his trip, and he was skinny to start with.

Since I am not fond of those cheesy noodles more than twice a week, I packed boxes with foods that I have dried myself or that would be hard to acquire in small communities, and mailed them ahead to friends who live along the route.

Here's a sample list of food for two weeks:

<u>SUPPERS</u>
noodles, parmesan cheese, and dried spaghetti sauce (enough for three meals –
    one big bottle)
dried kidney beans (enough for four chili dinners – 1.33 cups)
Fantastic Foods Chili Mix (one bag)
dried black beans (enough for three meals of beans and rice – one heaping cup)
Minute Rice (three cups – I bring extra to add to the soup at lunch.)
couscous and lentils (three meals – two cups)
three boxes of Kraft Dinner (1 1/2 boxes fills me up, plus extra for those extra-
    hungry nights or to have one for lunch)

To add to each meal
dried tomatoes
dried onions
dried peas
dried green beans (from the garden)

dried corn
bacon bits
spices: curry, salt, pepper, basil, oregano, garlic
cooking oil (one small bottle)

DESSERTS
tapioca and custard powder mixed with dried fruits and fruit leather

BREAKFAST
oatmeal with dried fruit (raisins, dates, apples, apricots) and milk powder: six cups
brown sugar
granola (to sprinkle on top)

LUNCHES
peanut butter (one pound, or 454 grams)
honey (one squeeze tube)
jam (one squeeze tube)
dried soup (one serving each day)
bannock mix (flour, baking powder, salt): eight cups – enough for eight hearty
    single-portion loaves
tortillas (one package of ten)
dried hummus
butter (one squeeze tub, approximately half a pound, or 227 grams)

DRINKS
tea
coffee
hot chocolate
hootch
milk powder (1.5 cups)

SNACKS
Gorp (two small Ziplock bags)
chocolate bars (one-half per day. Preferably Mars, Snickers, and Eatmore – Mars
    for cold weather, Eatmore for warm. These are the densest bars available.)
cookies (Ginger snaps are my favourite)

Appendix B

Making Bannock

Here is my standard recipe for bannock, not necessarily the best, but it is the one that I use. Take one cup of white flour, one teaspoonful of baking powder (Blue Ribbon is reported to be the best, but I have not made scientifically valid comparisons), and a pinch of salt. I usually mix this up at home. To this basic concoction, you can add almost anything, as long as the mix is at least one-half white flour. Too much other stuff, and it will not rise.

For basic bannock, I measure two cups of the mix (this amount makes a bannock that fits in my frying pan – an ample snack for two people) into a pot or bowl. Add about half a cup of water and mix with a strong wooden spoon until the water is absorbed. Keep adding water slowly, while mixing, until the dough is stiff. It's perfect if you can pick up all the loose flour in the bowl by rolling the ball of dough around. This also cleans out the mixing bowl. Now add a few more drops of water, so that the final dough ball is slightly wet and sticky. It should be wetter and stickier than bread dough. If the dough is too stiff and dry, it will not cook through.

Now gently flatten the dough ball into your well-greased frying pan, until it is about 4 cm (1 1/2 inches) thick. Cover the pan and bake the dough slowly over a low fire – I use a metal plate as a cover. I also use two 45-cm (18-inch) lengths of angle iron as a support for the pan; otherwise, your arm gets tired. Patience is the key. Cook the bannock slowly, until the bottom is golden brown. It should take about 15 minutes to do one side. Then flip it over and slowly cook the other side. For a perfect two-cup bannock, ideal cooking time is 35 to 40 minutes, but you can speed it up with more grease. It may seem a long time, but it's very relaxing to sit around in the evening by the fire and bake bannock. Very meditative.

Now the fun begins. Basic bannock is very satisfying, but specialty bannocks are to die for, depending on your food cravings. Here's a few of my memorable bannocks.

Many times I've used bannock as a crust for pizza. Add dried tomatoes and dried tomato paste, dried onions, green peppers, olives, and your favourite dried meat, and – presto! – better than take-out. For the ultimate grilled cheese, mix fried onions into the dough, split the cooked bannock down the centre, add cheese, and cook until the cheese melts. Yummm.

To satisfy that craving for pie, add sugar and butter and fresh berries to the mix, and then stew the cooked bannock in a sauce of your favourite fruit leather or – even better – in a sauce of more fresh-picked berries. Exquisite!

Once I wanted a cinnamon bun more than anything else in the world. Bannock to the rescue again. Mix brown sugar, butter, raisins, currants, and cinnamon into the dough and bake in a pan over a low fire. Then fry the cooked bannock in a mixture of butter and cinnamon and brown sugar. It was so good the first time, I've never attempted it again, for fear of being disappointed.

Appendix C

If You Go

1. From Lachine to Mattawa on the Ottawa River

From Lachine to Ottawa, the river is big and lazy. The only obstacle is the dam at Carrillon. Portage along the lock. I've camped at the lock station there.

In Ottawa, the easiest route around the Chaudière dam is the road on the south side of Victoria Island. However, the traditional portage route is on the Quebec side, just below where the Chaudière Bridge crosses the river.

Stay on the Ottawa side going up the Remic Rapids and Champlain Rapids. If the water is not too high, you can paddle up these rapids on the south side. The traditional portages were on the Quebec side. You can still see remains of the old portage trail around the Remic Rapids – steps cut into the limestone and polished smooth by the passage of thousands of moccasined feet – just downstream from Cartier Brébeuf Park.

The Deschênes Rapids can be portaged on either side easily. The traditional trail is on the Quebec side. I usually paddle up a small channel on the Ontario side to where it rejoins the man channels and then portage about 30 m (100 feet) into the basin of the Britannia Yacht Club. This is private property, and you should ask for permission at the clubhouse.

I've portaged the Chats Falls Dam on both the Ontario and Quebec sides. The Quebec side is more pleasant. There is a trail that runs along an old "canal." I don't know the story of this very large ditch. Was it ever used to bypass the rapids? Or was construction halted before the project was completed? The trail begins at a group of cottages and is hard to find without snooping around private property. It's best to ask around.

At Portage du Fort, you can take the Muskrat River route, by pulling out on the Ontario side at a small bay a few miles below the dam. The portage trails between lakes no longer exist, and the streams are blocked by fallen trees, barbed-wire fences, and other modern obstructions. The other option is to portage on the north side of the dam. It's a very short, easy portage.

The next obstacles are the Rocher-Fendu Rapids, a 20-km (12-mile) section that is now one of the world's best white-water rafting areas. This is a beautiful section of river. I chose on my 1997 trip to avoid it by portaging 21 km (13 miles) along roads to Muskrat Lake and following the Muskrat River, which enters the Ottawa at Pembroke, thus also bypassing the rapids at Allumette Island just below Pembroke.

If you choose to paddle up the Ottawa, the easiest channel – and the traditional route for voyageurs – is the small one that runs along the Quebec side, Chenal du Grande Calumet. A good trail bypasses the Calumet Dam near the town of Bryson. The take-out, if you're heading upstream, is on the left bank just below the dam. In voyageur days, this was the longest portage east of Grand Portage – 2 km (1 1/3 miles). I wonder if the trail that I took around the dam when I went this way on another long trip in the late early 1990s is part of the original trail?

The rapids below Pembroke on the south side of Allumette Island can be lined or portaged. The traditional upstream route is a small channel on the Ontario side south of Cotnam Island. I once followed this route, and it appeared to have been dynamited to form a small canal. It had very little water in it. It didn't appear to be any easier than lining up the Quebec side. Going downstream, the main channel on the Quebec side appears runnable. Mackenzie described it as merely a "*décharge*," where the canoe was unloaded and tracked up the fast water.

The north channel around Allumette Island is much shorter, cutting off 17.6 km (11 miles). I have not gone this way, but the Shepardsons found a good portage trail around the Culbute Rapids at the western end of the island, as well as the remains of an old wooden lock.

There are two ways to get around the dam at "Duh Swisha." Going upstream, follow the main channel to the town. A road leads around the dam, about 1 km (1/2 mile) in length. If you're heading downstream, and aren't nervous about dragging your canoe over the log boom just above the dam, there is a steep trail on the north side that leads to the tail-race just below the dam. You can put in there, but watch out for big eddies and whirlpools. It would be best to ask permission from someone if you decide to do this. This is the last obstacle before the dam on the Mattawa River, a few miles upstream of the town of Mattawa.

2. From the Mattawa to Georgian Bay

The Mattawa River route is very easy to follow. All the portages are well-marked. Contact Mattawa River Provincial Waterway Park in North Bay (P.O. Box 3070, North Bay, Ontario, P1B 8K7). This is not the case with the La Vase Portages. Contact the Friends of La Vase Portage in North Bay – through Paul Chivers, phone: (705) 476-1977 – for detailed maps and descriptions. Or look at Eric Morse's book, *Fur Trade Routes of Canada: Then and Now*, which provides a useful map.

The most direct route on Lake Nipissing is along the southern shore. Nipissing is big, is very shallow, and can get extremely choppy, I am told. The outlet of the French River is easy to find. The French is a popular canoe route, and all portages are well marked. The only confusing part is near the mouth. It is difficult to find the channel using 1:250,000 topographical maps. The Friends of the French publishes an excellent map. Contact French River Provincial Waterway Park, c/o Services, Permits and Regulations, Sudbury District Office, Ontario Ministry of Natural Resources, 3767 Hwy. 69 South, Suite 5, Sudbury, Ontario, P3G 1E7; phone: (705) 564-7823.

3. From Georgian Bay to Sault Ste. Marie

For the most part, you just follow the shore. Through the maze of islands between the outlet of the French and Killarney, just keep the big water on your left and the land on your right. It's worth stopping at Killarney for Mr. Perch's Fish and Chips. From Killarney, you can head west across Killarney Bay and take "the Indian Portage" over Badgeley Point into Frazer Bay. From the bay, you can head to Little Current on Manitoulin Island or cut through the narrow La Cloche Channel to the Bay of Islands. I took the latter route.

The name La Cloche comes from a rock that reportedly rings like a bell. Eric

Morse describes how to find this extraordinary hunk of basalt (an anomaly in this land of granite, gneiss and quartzite) in *Fur Trade Canoe Routes of Canada: Then and Now*.

I followed the American Channel of the St. Marys River to Sault Ste. Marie. This is the upstream channel for lake freighters, so watch out!

4. From Sault Ste. Marie to Grand Portage

The coast of Lake Superior is canoe-friendly. Just follow these easy rules, and you'll have a great trip:

SUPERIOR RULES
- If there's any wind blowing at all at any time, always assume that it will blow harder later. Not always true, but a good assumption.
- If it's late in the day and the wind is blowing, always assume that it will probably not go down at night if you decide to keep paddling. If you decide to camp, it will go down.
- If you get up in the dark to paddle to avoid the wind, it will blow hard in the early morning and die down at 10 a.m., just to spite you.
- Always travel on Lake Superior with a beautiful woman (or guy, as the case may be), because it is such a beautiful place, you should see it with someone you love. Also, you can count on being windbound, so you may as well be windbound with someone you love.

The route is simple. Follow the shore. There are a few tips for the canoe traveller to heed.
- Be wary of the wind. It can come from any direction, especially when cliffs crowd the shore. I usually stayed within 1.6 km (a mile) of shore.
- Watch out for the seiche. A seiche is a slow ebb and rise of water level, caused by water in the lake, the sloshing back and forth, like water in a bathtub. I have seen the water level rise 1 m (3 feet) in a few hours. Make sure that your canoe is securely tied up, and camp well above the water line. Mackenzie describes a particularly strong occurrence: "The water withdrew with great precipitation, leaving the ground dry that had never before been visible, the fall being equal to four perpendicular feet, and rushing back with great velocity above the common mark. There is frequently an irregular influx and deflux which does not exceed 10 inches, and is attributed to the wind."
- Before you go to sleep, or for a long hike, make sure to weigh down your canoe with rocks or tie it up very securely. This also holds for your tent. Never underestimate the power of the wind.
- Paddle, like the voyageurs did, early in the morning. The wind tends to come up after lunch.
- The fog can roll in anytime, and it comes in fast. Fortunately, it is usually calm when the fog comes in. But not always.
- Accept the wind. Be patient. There's no hurry. And where you are is probably as pretty as any place that you've ever been. The wind always goes down, in a few hours or a few days.

Keep the open side up, because the water in Lake Superior is Arctic-cold. If you've seen the movie *Titanic*, you know what this means.

5. From the Pigeon River to Kenora

This is straightforward canoe-tripping. Get some detailed maps (or placemats) and enjoy the country, especially the section through Quetico Provincial Park and the adjacent Boundary Waters Canoe Area.

Eric Morse recommends taking the Namikan River route from Lac la Croix to Namikan Lake. It is much more direct than the border route that I followed.

6. From Kenora to Grand Rapids

I'm tempted to say, "Don't," but that would be selling Lake Winnipeg short. As on Lake Superior, be patient, use a spray cover, and enjoy the beauty. It is an amazing lake.

7. From Bella Coola to Eliguk Lake, British Columbia

Take a copy of *In the Steps of Alexander Mackenzie Trail Guide* by J. Woodworth & H. Flygare, available through the Alexander Mackenzie Trail Association, P.O. Box 425, Station A, Kelowna, BC, V1Y 7P1.

8. From the Source of the Blackwater to the Fraser River

I know of no recent trip guides written for the Blackwater. However, the river is one of the best that I've ever paddled. The quality of the trip depends on water levels. At low levels, the upper river would be too low to paddle. At high water, the canyons of the lower river would be dangerous. Chris and I were lucky to have medium water levels for our trip in early June, during a year with less-than-average runoff. Check with Rick Brine of the Prince George Canoe Club; phone: (250) 964-7400. B.C. fishing regulations schedule the Blackwater as a "fly-fishing only" river.

9. From the Junction of the Blackwater and Fraser Rivers to Prince George

I recommend not paddling upstream, but a trip down the Fraser would be wonderful. Lowest water levels are usually in early spring and in autumn. Phone Rick Brine of the Prince George Canoe Club for advice at (250) 964-7400.

10. From Prince George to Hudson's Hope

Be aware that Williston Lake is a reservoir, and contact B.C. Hydro to find out when and what the draw-down will be. At the time I paddled, there was no draw-down and the reservoir was filled to the brim, but this is not always the case. The Crooked River/Pack River route is easy and uncomplicated. Note that the Pack River allows fly-fishing only.

11. From Hudson's Hope to Fort Chipewyan

Length of trip: Three weeks is fast to cover the Peace. Four weeks would allow for a mellower trip. The current is fast at the beginning, but it progressively slows down, and the predominant wind is from the east.

Drinking water: Finding clean drinking water can be a problem. It's a good idea to carry plenty of containers to fill up at communities along the way. Boil and filter river water before drinking it. But unless you pre-filter the water through a cloth, water filters cannot handle the sediment in the Peace's muddy waters.

Weather: Even though the Peace is quite far north, the weather can be blisteringly HOT! We experienced many days over 33 degrees Celsius and had to take precautions not to get dehydrated and overheated. Swimming is a great way to cool off, and the mud doesn't stick. Strong winds often blow upstream, creating steep breaking waves.

Dangers: Not many. Watch out for sweepers and "bobbers" (trees partially buried in the riverbed). The roots and branches can act as strainers in the fast current, and they can be very dangerous if you're not paying attention. The only portage is Vermilion Chutes. The Boyer Rapids can be easily navigated by staying on river left.

Bugs: Not as many as we expected on the river, but be prepared.

12. From Fort McMurray to Ile-a-la-Crosse

Several excellent guides are available for the Clearwater River. Contact the Canadian Heritage Rivers System in Ottawa (donald_gibson@pch.gc.ca), or visit its web site at www.chrs.ca. Hälle Flygare's book, *Sir Alexander Mackenzie Historic Waterways in Alberta*, is excellent.
    The Clearwater is without doubt one of the finest canoeing rivers in Canada.

13. From Ile-a-la-Crosse to Otter Lake, Saskatchewan

Read Sig Olson's book, *The Lonely Land*. There are many good river guides to the Churchill. We used the one from the Canoe Saskatchewan web site. Rick Dridigier, of Horizons Unlimited, knows the river and this country very well. The web site for the Churchill is http://www.lights.com/waterways/.

14. From Otter Lake to Cumberland House

The Sturgeon-Weir is a pleasant downstream run. If you're heading upstream, I agree with Mackenzie's assessment. But if you're not paddling birchbark, it wouldn't be too difficult, although it would still test your patience. The fishing is great for pickerel and pike. If I had more time on the North Saskatchewan, I would take some of the smaller rivers, such as the Carrot River, into the wetlands.

Appendix D

If You Want to Go Farther

There are many organizations working to improve the environmental health of our rivers and lakes, to preserve the cultural heritage along their banks, and to raise awareness of the importance of traditional water routes in the history of Canada and to our Canadian identity. I list those most closely associated with Alexander Mackenzie's route across Canada.

Alexander Mackenzie Voyageur Route Association
P.O. Box 425, Station A
Kelowna, BC, V1Y 7P1
Fax: (250) 868-8698
e-mail: Macvoyage@silk.net

Canadian River Management Society
633 Fortune Drive
Orleans, Ontario, K1C 2A4
Phone: (613) 824-0410
e-mail: greco.crms@webruler.com

Canadian Heritage Rivers System (CHRS)

The mission of the CHRS is two-fold: first, to develop a river conservation program that is nationally valued and internationally recognized and that reflects the significance of rivers in the identity and history of Canada, and, second, to ensure sustainable management and development of the natural, cultural and recreational values of rivers in the CHRS.

The CHRS has designated rivers in all ten provinces and all three territories. The program was born in 1984. By 2000, it included thirty-seven rivers, totalling over 9,000 km (some 5,400 miles) of river, from wilderness rivers in the Barren Lands to rural and urban rivers in southern Ontario. A board made up of representatives from each member jurisdiction, plus two federal members – one from Parks Canada and one from the Department of Indian and Northern Affairs – oversees the program. Private individuals may also sit on the board.

To be included in the system, rivers must have nationally significant and outstanding natural, cultural or recreational values. The managing jurisdiction – that is, the federal, provincial, or territorial government – must nominate the river to the CHRS board. Public interest groups are often instrumental in bringing a river to the attention of CHRS board members. Once a nomination is accepted, the managing jurisdiction must submit a management plan that details actions to be taken to ensure maintenance of the significant heritage values of the river, communication of the river's heritage values to the public, and sustainable realization of its recreational potential for the river to be designated to the CHRS.

The CHRS is not based on any federal or provincial legislation. The title

"Canadian Heritage River" means that the managing jurisdiction has made a commitment in writing to protect the river. Carrying out this commitment is a question of honour and integrity.

For more information, contact:

Don Gibson, National Manager, CHRS
c/o Parks Canada, National Parks, Protected Areas Branch
Ottawa, Ontario, K1A 0M5
Phone: (819) 994-2913
e-mail: donald_gibson@pch.gc.ca
web site: http://www.chrs.ca

Notes

Dedication Page

From Dr. Seuss, *One Fish, Two Fish, Three Fish, Blue Fish* (New York: Beginner Books, 1960) 62.

Chapter 1 – Mackenzie and Canada

1. The name Lachine (La Chine) is derived from the French word for China, and the first French explorers who came this way were looking for a route to the Orient. Built in 1671, nine miles above Montreal at the head of the Lachine Rapids, Lachine was, for many years, the most important fur trade centre (the eastern headquarters) for the French, followed by the North West Company and, after 1821, for the Hudson's Bay Company.
2. Mackenzie noted in a letter to his cousin Roderick that the Turnor party appeared not well-provisioned for their trip. Turnor noted in his journal that "At 7:00 p.m., M. Alex Mackensie [sic] the master of the Athapiscow Lake settlement ... arrived with one canoe ...." Philip Turner [Turnor], J.B. Tyrell, ed., *Journals of Samuel Hearne and Philip Turnor* (Westport, Conn: Champlain Society Publications, 1934) 467.
3. William Coombe was a successful ghost writer for several explorers of his time, including John Meares. It is likely that Mackenzie took Meares' book on exploring the Pacific coast of North America with him when he returned from England to fur country in 1792. Ironically, William Coombe finished Mackenzie's book (1799) while in debtor's prison. There he remained until his death in 1823. See Derek Hayes, *First Crossing* (Vancouver/Toronto: Douglas & McIntyre, 2001) 253-4.

Chapter 2 – Crossing Canada By Canoe: A Brief History

1. Sir William Logan's quote taken from a conference brochure, not sourced.
2. The W.B. Yeats quote was found on the Internet through "River Quotes."
3. Quote attributed to J.J. Astor, generally accepted as common to the fur trade, according to the author.
4. Rick Steber, *New York to Nome* (New York: Pocket Books, 1987) 55.
5. Two years of two different personalities confined to one canoe and one tent erupted. The fight was a draw. Tension released, they went on to complete their journey.
6. *Heritage Riverscapes*, Newsletter of the Canadian Heritage River System, Spring 1998, Parks Canada; also found on the CHRS web site at www.chrs.ca/riverstories.

Chapter 3 – Getting Ready

1. The web site is still extant and can be accessed at http://www.voyageur.carleton.ca.
2. The Barton paddles are made by Greg Barton, the first American ever to win an Olympic gold medal in paddling sports. He is the president of a Seattle-based

company that manufactures high-performance paddles.
3. Grey Owl paddles are made in Cambridge, Ontario.
4. Kevlar is a synthetic woven material, very strong, flexible and lightweight. Made by Dupont, it is also used for bulletproof vests. The Kevlar, when soaked in an epoxy resin, hardens to become rigid yet flexible, and waterproof.
5. H.M. Robinson, *The Great Fur Land, or Sketches of Life in the Hudson's Bay Territory* (New York: G.P. Putnam's Sons, 1879) 117.

Chapter 5 – Over to Georgian Bay

1. Robert Perkins is a well-known author of books and videos dealing with the Barrens. It is a toss-up as to whether his books are more about canoeing or his philosophy of life. Robert Perkins lives in Boston.

Chapter 7 – Superior: The Rugged Northern Shore

1. Gordon Lightfoot's song, "The Wreck of the Edmund Fitzgerald," is a tribute to this shipwreck and the men who lost their lives (Moose Music Ltd., 1976). The *Edmund Fitzgerald* went down on November 10, 1975.
2. "Wood Smoke and Oranges" by Ian Tamblyn can be found on his CD, *Through the Years*.
3. "White Squall" by Stan Rogers can be found on his CD, *From Fresh Water*, 1984.
4. Carl Shepardson, *A Family Canoe Trip* (Merrillville, Indiana: ICS Books Inc.) 100-101.
5. Source of facts on Lake Superior from "A Superior Legacy: A Proposal for a Marine Conservation Area, Background Information" (Parks Canada, 1996).
6. For more information on pictographs, see Grace Rajnovich, *Reading Rock Art: Interpreting the Indian Rock Paintings of the Canadian Shield* (Toronto: Natural Heritage Books, 1994, reprinted 2002).
7. Bill Ostrom and his wife, Ann, run Ostrom Outdoors, manufacturers of extraordinary high quality gear for paddlers at Nolalu, Ontario.

Chapter 8 – The Boundary Waters

1. Sig Olson (1899-1987) wrote about the Boundary Waters area in his book, *The Singing Wilderness* (New York: Knopf, 1956).
2. Alec Ross of Kingston, Ontario, paddled across Canada in three stages and wrote a delightful account of his journeys, *Coke Stop in Emo* (Toronto: Key Porter Books, 1995).

Chapter 9 – Winnipeg: River and Lake

1. Eric W. Morse, *Fur Trade Canoe Routes: Then and Now* (Crown copyrights reserved reprinted 1971; Second edition, Ministry of Supply and Services Canada, 1979) 83.
2. Scott canoes are made in New Liskeard, Ontario, by Mid-Canada Fibreglass.
3. Alexander Henry, Barry M. Gough, ed., *The Journal of Alexander Henry the*

Younger, 1799-1814 (Toronto: Champlain Society, 1988-1992) 332-335.
4. Carl Shepardson, *The Family Canoe Trip*, 169.
5. *Ibid*, 170.
6. Eric W. Morse, *Fur Trade Canoe Routes: Then and Now*, 90.

Chapter 10 – Grand Rapids to Cumberland House

1. A Lapstrake-built (or clinker-built) boat has horizontal external planks overlapping downwards. Viking longboats were built using this method.
2. Samuel Hearne (1745-1792), explorer and fur trader, joined the Hudson's Bay Company in 1766. He was chosen to look for a trade route across the Barrens. Around 1770-72, he managed to reach the Coppermine River, having walked from York Factory on Hudson Bay. He followed the river to the Arctic Ocean. Two years later he founded Cumberland House.
3. Eramus Solomon, a Cree from Cumberland House, often teamed up with Serge Corbin from Quebec. Together they won some of North America's most challenging marathon canoe races during the 1980s and '90s.

Chapter 11 – Getting Ready ... Again

1. There seems to be some discrepancy in the presentation of the name of this town. Should it be Hudson's Hope or Hudson Hope? In this publication we have chosen to go with the spelling Hudson's Hope as several longtime residents of the village wanted to restore the apostrophe in the name as it was, in their opinion, in the original spelling.

Chapter 12 – Bella Coola to Eliguk Lake: The Long Portage

1. George Mercer Dawson, born in 1849, was a geologist in the British North American Boundary Commission set up to establish the boundary between Canada and the U.S.A. As Director of the Geological Survey of Canada in 1895, Dawson examined and explored every aspect of Canada's unknown territories in much of British Columbia and the Yukon. For more information see Lois Winslow-Spragge, Bradley Lockner, ed., *No Ordinary Man: George Mercer Dawson 1849-1901* (Toronto: Natural Heritage, Books 1993).

Chapter 13 – Down the Blackwater: River of No Return

1. John Woodworth and Hälle Flygare, *In the Steps of Alexander Mackenzie* (Kelowna, B.C.: Alexander Mackenzie Voyageur Route Association, 1987) 31.
2. For more on this story of Pan Phillips and Rich Hobson see Richmond P. Hobson Jr., *Grass Between the Mountains* (Toronto: McCelland & Stewart, 1966) and Cliff Kopas, *Packhorses to the City* (Sidney, B.C.: Grays Publishing Ltd., 1976).
3. William Hillen, *Blackwater River: Toa-Thal-kas* (Toronto: McClelland & Stewart, 1971) pnk.
4. *Ibid*, pnk.
5. *Ibid*, pnk.

6. In 1869, John Wesley Powell, the one-armed Civil War hero, led a party of ten men in four boats on a journey that would cover almost 1,000 miles through uncharted canyons and change the West forever. Three months after their departure, only five of the original company plus Powell would emerge from the depths of the Grand Canyon at the mouth of the Virgin River.

Chapter 14 – Up the Fraser: A River of Liquid Mountains

1. For more information on Ralph Brine and his amazing trip, see *Ralph Hunter Brine, Canada's Forgotten Highway* (Prince George: privately published, 1995).

Chapter 15 – Over the Continental Divide: Paddling Across the Roof of Canada

1. Despite the author's best efforts, more information on Ben Ferrier has remained elusive. A reference, *Sports Review* (1961) containing an article "Down Mackenzie's Bad River" by Ben Ferrier could not be located. Any information would be appreciated by both the author and the publisher.
2. The Canada Sea-to-Sea Expeditions, 1989-1993 – Final Report, Dr. Jim Smithers, Expedition Leader, Lakehead University, 1994.
3. Reminiscent of a line from Joni Mitchell's memorable song, "Both Sides Now."
4. Article by Jan Gould in *The Western Producer*, 1965.
5. R.M. Patterson, *Findlay's River* (New York: William Morrow and Co., 1968) 43.
6. Information on Nicholas Ignatieff obtained through personal communication with his son, also named Nicholas Ignatieff, Toronto, March 2002.
7. Recent communication informs us that Rheannan Bach, of Hudson's Hope, is playing the role of Cinderella at the Disney World Theme Park in Florida.

Chapter 16 – Down the Mighty Peace: A Long and Winding Road

1. We are indebted to Daniel Harmon (1778-1845) for much of our information on the fur trade. Daniel Williams Harmon, *A journal of voyages and travels in the interior of North America, between the 47th and 58th degree of latitude, extending from Montreal nearly to the Pacific Ocean, a distance of about 5000 miles, resident of nearly nineteen years in different parts of that country* (Andover, Mass: Flagg and Gould, 1820).
2. Today, Peterborough is home to the Canadian Canoe Museum, which houses the greatest collection of canoes in the world.

Chapter 18 – Up the Clearwater: Link to the North

1. Robert Hood, C. Stuart Houston, ed., *To the Arctic by Canoe, 1819-1821, the journals and painting by Robert Hood, midmanship with Franklin* (Montreal: Arctic Institute of North America, 1974) 118.
2. Bill Mason, *Path of the Paddle* (Toronto: Key Porter Books, 1984). In my opinion, this is the best book on canoeing techniques.
3. John Henry Lefroy, George F.G. Stanley, ed., *In Search of the Magnetic North, a soldier-surveyor's letters from the north-west, 1843-1844* (Toronto: Macmillan, 1955) 65.

4. Verlen Kruger and Klayton Kelin, *One Incredible Journey* (Fowlerville, Michigan: Wilderness Adventure Books, 1987) 209.

5. Philip Turnor, the surveyor for the Hudson's Bay Company whom Mackenzie had met at Peter Pond Lake in 1791, and who seemed to influence his decision to return to England to learn surveying techniques, wrote, when heading across the portage from north to south: "We began to carry up a rather steep hill..." Philip Turner [Turnor], J.B. Tyrell, ed., *Journals of Samuel Hearne and Philip Turnor*, 467.

Chapter 19 – Down the Mighty Churchill, River of the Lonely Land

1. Missinipe is the modern spelling but Mackenzie spells it as Missinipi, which he says is the Cree (or Kristeneaux, as he calls them) name for the river.

2. Thomas Frobisher (1744-1788), born in Yorkshire, England, was a fur trader who built the first trading post at Ile-a-la-Cross in 1776. The post was operated until the mid-1970s.

3. "Backferry" is a technique used when running rapids. The canoe is positioned facing downstream at an angle to the current, while canoeists are paddling backwards. It is important to keep the canoe at an angle to allow the force of the current to move the canoe laterally to the desired destination. This has the effect of slowing the action, while control of the canoe is maintained.

4. Sigurd Olson, *The Lonely Land* (Toronto: McCelland & Stewart, 1961) 87.

5. To bring us up-to-date, John Pedlar chose the chef route and plans to open a place in small town Ontario where people can go for good food and good music.

Chapter 20 – Sturgeon-Weir: The Road Home

1. From http://www.stanleymission.org/history.htm.

2. Church Mission was renamed Stanley Mission after Stanley Park, England. The hometown of the wife of its builder and first missionary, Robert Hunt.

3. Not to be confused with his brother, Thomas Frobisher, Joseph Frobisher was the first white man to cross Frog Portage, 1774. He went on to become a senior partner in the North West Company and ultimately retired to Montreal where he built a mansion that he named Beaver Manor.

Credits for Visuals

All visuals, unless otherwise indicated, are courtesy of the author.

Front Cover:
1. Max Finkelstein on the Ottawa River near Quyon, Quebec. *Courtesy of J.D. Andrews.*
2. *Shooting the Rapids, 1879* by Frances Anne Hopkins, original image 91 x 152 cm. *NAC Negative C-2774, courtesy of Canadian Heritage Rivers System.*

Back cover:
Scenic photos by the author.
1. Sunset on Lake Superior.
2. Supper on the Blackwater.
3. Connie on the Peace River.
4. Background: Map from Mackenzie's book of his travels.

Spine:
At the Methye Portage, on the Clearwater River in Saskatchewan.

Original Illustrations
All black-and-white sketches are by Christina Sadler, a visual arts teacher for the Ottawa-Carleton District School Board. See pp. v, 26, 126,206.

Maps:
Map of America from Mackenzie's book of his travels: pp. xii-xiii, 27, 127, 207
Route maps courtesy of the author: pp. 28, 128, 208

Chapter 1: Mackenzie and Canada
1. Portrait of Alexander Mackenzie, p. 8. *Courtesy of Old Fort William, copy of NAC 1348.*

Chapter 8: The Boundary Waters
1. Starting out with enthusiasm at Grand Portage, p. 90. *Courtesy of Brenda Beck.*

Chapter 17: Getting Ready: The Last Leg
1. Oh, how life has changed! p. 211. *Courtesy of Connie Downes.*
2. Leaving Baby Isaac and Connie is not going to be easy. p. 211. *Courtesy of J. D. Andrews.*

About the Author
1. Max Finkelstein with his son, Isaac Thelon. *Courtesy of Connie Downes.*

Annotated Bibliography

This list is by no means inclusive. These are the books that added the most to my experiences on the Alexander Mackenzie Voyageur Route.

Accounts of Crossing North America by Water

Ralph Hunter Brine, *Canada's Forgotten Highway*. Prince George: privately published, 1995.
An account of a journey in 1967 by freighter canoe and outboard from the mouth of the Fraser to Montreal, with ample historical notes from journals of those who had gone before.

Barry M. Gough, editor, *The Journal of Alexander Henry the Younger, 1799-1814*, two volumes. Toronto: Champlain Society, 1988.
A fascinating account of life during the heyday of the fur trade. It is fundamental to understanding the history of the fur trade and Native people. Like a fantasy novel, Henry's journals take you into another world. Follow him as he travels from Lake Superior to the mouth of the Columbia River.

Derek Hayes, *First Crossing*. Vancouver/Toronto: Douglas & McIntyre, 2001.
A very thoroughly researched history of Mackenzie. The artwork and maps set this book apart from all others.

William Least Heat-Moon, *River-Horse*. Boston & New York: Houghton Mifflin Company, 1999.
A unique account of a trip across the United States in a boat powered by twin outboards, in combination with a canoe.

Verlen Kruger and Klayton Klein, *One Incredible Journey*. Fowlerville, Michigan: Wilderness Adventure Books, 1987.
An account of a one-season, 7,000-mile cross-continent trip in 1973 by Verlen Kruger, the king of long-distance paddlers, and Clint Waddel. An amazing read. The energy and determination of the paddlers leave you breathless. Their goal is to reach the Pacific before freeze-up. Will they make it? At the ripe age of forty-nine, Verlen is an inspiration for all of us middle-aged paddlers contemplating crossing continents.

W. Kaye Lamb, editor, *The Journals and Letters of Sir Alexander Mackenzie*. Extra series no. 41. London: Hakluyt Society, 1970.
An account by the first European to cross North America by canoe. A fascinating look at the history of Canada. If you are retracing the Alexander Mackenzie Voyageur Route and can take only one book with you, this is the one.

Gary and Joannie McGuffin, *Where Rivers Run*. Toronto: Stoddart, 1988.
The best-looking couple ever to paddle across a continent, Gary and Joannie make their honeymoon trip an inspirational story.

Eric Morse, *Fur Trade Canoe Routes: Then and Now*. Crown Copyrights reserved, 1969. Second edition, Minister of Supply and Services Canada, 1979.
A necessary companion to anyone paddling the fur trade route across Canada.

Alec Ross, *Coke Stop in Emo*. Toronto: Key Porter Books, 1995.
Coming of age in a canoe – Alec's amazing cross-Canada journey.

Carl Shepardson, *The Family Canoe Trip*. Merrillville, Indiana: ICS Books Inc., 1985 (out of print).
A journal of the Shepardsons' trip from their home in New Hampshire to Alaska over three summers. This is not just another transcontinental canoe trip – the Shepardsons take their two young children in a 20-foot canoe. This makes all the other cross-continent canoe trips look like cakewalks.

Rick Steber, *New York to Nome*. New York: Pocket Books, 1987.
A great story of two New Yorkers, Sheldon Taylor and Geoffrey Pope, canoeing across the continent during the height of the Great Depression.

Historical Works of Interest

Barbara Huck, *Exploring the Fur Trade Routes of North America*. Winnipeg: Heartland, 2000.
A great book for those who prefer to explore the fur trade routes by car.

Jean Morrison, *Superior Rendezvous-Place: Fort William in the Canadian Fur Trade*. Toronto: Natural Heritage Books, 2001.
Fort William on Lake Superior, for centuries a pivotal place in the fur trade, is like a whirlpool of Canada's history where events and personalities are sucked in, spun around and hung out again across the continent. In this fascinating book the stories hidden in this whirlpool are revealed in a way that is both entertaining and easy to understand.

Peter C. Newman, *Caesars of the Wilderness*, Volumes I and II. Toronto: Viking, 1987.
A rollicking history of the fur trade.

Grace Lee Nute, *The Voyageur*. St. Paul: Minnesota Historical Society, 1931.
The definitive work on the men who paddled the great fur trade canoes from Montreal to the Pacific and the far northwest.

Regional Books

Hälle Flygare, *Sir Alexander Mackenzie Historic Waterways in Alberta*. Canmore, Alberta: Recreation, Parks and Wildlife Foundation of Alberta, 1983.
A detailed guide to Alexander Mackenzie's travels in what is now Alberta on the Clearwater, Peace, Slave, and Athabasca rivers. An essential companion to paddlers travelling in Alberta.

Toni Harting, *French River: Canoeing the River of the Stick-Wavers*. Erin, Ontario: Boston Mills Press, 1996.
An in-depth look at one of Canada's most historically important rivers.

Richmond P. Hobson, Jr., *Grass Beyond the Mountains*. Toronto: McClelland & Stewart, 1966.
If you think that canoeing is tough, read this account of cowboys on the Blackwater River in British Columbia.

Cliff Kopas, *Packhorses to the Pacific*. Sidney, B.C.: Gray's Publishing Ltd, 1976.
An amazing journey by pack horse from Calgary to Bella Coola, following the routes of the explorers and fur traders. Entertaining reading for anyone hiking the Grease Trail or paddling the Blackwater River in British Columbia.

Grace Lee Nute, *The Voyageur's Highway*. St. Paul: Minnesota Historical Society, 1941.
A detailed historical account of the voyageur route between Lake Superior and Rainy Lake.

Sigurd Olson, *The Lonely Land*. Toronto: McClelland & Stewart, 1961.
A classic account by one of North America's greatest conservation writers of a canoe trip down the Churchill River. One member of his party was Eric Morse, author *of Fur Trade Canoe Routes: Then and Now*.

Raymond Murray Patterson, *The Dangerous River*. London: Allen and Unwin, 1954.
_____. *The Dangerous River*. Sidney, B.C.: Gray's Pub., 1966 (First Canadian edition).
_____. *Dangerous River*. Post Mills, Vermont: Chelsea Green Publishing, 1990.
This book ranks among the best river adventures ever told.

Grace Rajnovich, *Reading Rock Art: Interpreting the Indian Rock Paintings of the Canadian Shield*. Toronto: Natural Heritage Books, 1994 (reprinted 2002).
In this book the meanings of the ancient and mysterious rock paintings, found along Mackenzie's route as far west as Saskatchewan, are revealed. I recommend this work as a companion to Mackenzie's book should one choose to take this journey.

John Woodworth and Hälle Flygare, *In the Steps of Alexander Mackenzie*. Kelowna: Alexander Mackenzie Voyageur Route Association, 1987.
An essential trail guide companion for backpackers following Alexander Mackenzie's overland route from the Fraser to the Pacific on the Grease Trail. Don't leave home without it.

Fictional Books

Ainslie Manson, *A Dog Came, Too*, illustrated by Ann Blades, a Meadow Mouse Paperback. Toronto/Vancouver: Groundwood/Douglas & McIntyre, 1992.
A wonderful story of the dog that accompanied Mackenzie on his journey to the Pacific

Richard Pope, *Superior Illusions*, illustrated by Neil Broadfoot. Toronto: Natural Heritage Books, 1998.
Epic poetry and original artwork carry us along the fur trade route from Lachine to Lake Superior. A wonderful companion for anyone travelling this section of the route. Don't peek ahead at the ending.

Index

About the Author

Max Finkelstein works as a communications specialist with the Canadian Heritage Rivers System (CHRS), Canada's national program for river conservation. When he is not writing about, speaking about or otherwise promoting Canada's river heritage, he can usually be found paddling on a river. He has covered more than 20,000 km (over 12,000 miles) throughout Canada, Africa and Australia. His most recent undertaking was to retrace Alexander Mackenzie's historic crossing of North America. His next endeavour is to retrace the explorations of geologist A.P. Low from Labrador to James Bay.

Max lives in Ottawa on the shores of the Ottawa River with his wife, Connie. They are introducing their new son, Isaac Thelon, to a life of travelling on and learning about rivers.